CHRONOS
history

a contextual & chronological homeschool curriculum guide

Introduction

This is not a textbook.

It's also not a book in which I tell you which version of history to believe.

Chronos isn't a curriculum in the traditional sense: it's a guide developed over the past several years and created for the purpose of helping parents understand (1) different interpretations of the past, (2) the vast number of reputable sources in which to self-educate, and (3) how to think for themselves about human history. As a homeschooler, I believe the best teachers are well-informed parents, and Chronos is a tool for that purpose.

About Chronos

Chronos can be used in any way which is helpful.

It can simply be a list of websites and books, or it can be followed the way in which it was intended: 16-weeks per semester (32 weeks per academic year) and recycle the lessons every year from K-8th grade. It was originally written this way to develop a familiarity with human chronology so that later, when more official curriculum is introduced, students can easily insert more complex and detailed information about the past in the places they belong. Knowing chronology is extremely important in understating how people and events fit together.

This guide can also be a great refresher for high schoolers in between grades, as there are deeper lessons and questions for those levels. But really, *Chronos* is first and foremost a tool for parents and guardians to self-educate: historical illiteracy is a generations-deep problem in the United States, and this is a small but valiant effort to correct that problem. *Chronos* will be a success in your homeschool if you--the parent-- become knowledgeable in the subject matter so that you can answer your child's questions, or help them find the answer. Again, this is not a textbook which tells you what to think, but rather a guidebook helping you cover and review important elements of human history which everyone should know.

For this purpose, *Chronos* begins with world history, then narrows to Western Civilization after the Fall of Rome, and finally narrows to American history during the Age of Exploration. This narrowing is intentional, as *Chronos* seeks to answer the multi-generational historical illiteracy found specifically in the United States. (Note: World history is vitally important as well, and a separate curriculum should be used to address this subject. I've written a supplemental world history curriculum as a free download for middle schoolers here: *teacherspayteachers.com/Store/The-Homeschool-Historian*)

How does Chronos work?

Each lesson has a simple summary, lists of primary sources, websites, YouTube videos, fiction and non-fiction books, terms to know, and enrichment activities. It also has a "Making Connections" section which explains how the lesson connects to those before and after, as well as "Questions to Ask" which help ask honest questions about the subject. How you incorporate these lessons into your homeschool depends upon the age, ability, interest, and unique development of your child. For younger students (ages 5-8, for example) you may want to just read the summary for yourself and "translate" it for your child at their level. Then, choose a book or two and maybe an enrichment activity, reviewing the summary throughout the activity. That's it. History should be an invitation to explore the past, and especially for these ages, not about memorizing facts and dates they will probably forget. Instead, show them on a timeline "where they are" in each lesson, so they can visually grasp the passing of time. Eventually they will come to know that the Bronze Age is before the Iron Age, and the Late Middle Age is after the High Middle Age—but this isn't important in the early years. Grabbing your child's interest through interesting stories and experiences is the most important thing.

For upper elementary, you might want to incorporate *Questions to Ask, Terms to Know, Making Connections,* and begin to include primary sources in your lesson. How you decide to do this is up to you, but there are suggestions in the back of the book in the Resources section. Middle school can include more advanced Enrichment options and more mature video content if appropriate for your family. High schoolers can use this as a refresher or overview. Each YouTube source is organized by **elementary, middle, and high (school).**

Chronos is organized and written in Turabian format (the preferred format of historians). This is intentionally done so that parents and students are familiar with it should they look up scholarly sources online now or later in their academic journey.

Special Considerations for Christian Homeschoolers

There are certain considerations which require a special section, the first being that although I'm a Christian, *Chronos* does not exclude secular sources. This is intentional, because not all good historians are Christians and not all Christian historians are good. (**Note**: If you are a Christian, the Holy Spirit will guide you in discernment and wisdom as you review these sources and determine which ones you will use.) A difference of opinion is crucial in the study of history because, although it *wishes* to be a science, history is a pseudoscience: interpretation of the past depends upon the worldview of the person interpreting it. Being able to identify bias, decipher subjectivity from objectivity, fact from opinion, and the different historiographical schools, are absolutely essential in knowing how to think about the past. These skills prepare students to face conflicting views in the universities and the workplace. In the spirit of discernment, I recommend viewing and downloading *16 Types of Media Bias*[1] from All Sides: this is an incredible tool to help you decipher the types of bias you encounter every day and how to test what is true.

The book lists in *Chronos* include recommended ages for each item (as listed by each author), but the videos do not: some material is sensitive, some have stronger language than others, but all were hand-chosen by me due to the supremacy of the research and/or the way in which the research is presented. Not every family will appreciate or use certain videos (such as Crash Course History's channel, which is very well done but also liberal-leaning in some of their interpretations), and that is perfectly fine. **VERY IMPORTANT**: Please view ALL MATERIAL before showing it your child. What is deemed "safe" by one parent is not so by another.

In addition, Chronos doesn't cover every aspect of human history; there is no book or curriculum which can possible include everything. Instead, it serves as a chronological guide for both broad and basic historical events so that when new information is discovered (in subsequent classes or in self-study), the student knows enough about chronology to "file" the new information where it belongs. Think of Chronos as a skeleton, and the rest of your child's history education (which ideally will evolve during his entire lifetime) are the muscles, tissue, and other components.

Lastly, the links (including YouTube videos and web articles) may become broken or be deleted over time. My plan is to check all of the links each year and post the updates or changes in a free download (or you may purchase the completed, updated version each year). Follow my social media accounts to know when these changes will take place and how to access them.

Conclusion

I hope Chronos is a blessing to your family and helps give you confidence to present the very important subject of history to your children. Studying the past can help us understand our current world, identify its lingering effects in our culture, and prevent us from repeating its mistakes. I pray for wisdom and discernment for your family now, and in the future. Thank you for using this source in your homeschool.

---

[1] https://www.allsides.com/media-bias/how-to-spot-types-of-media-bias

Part 1: History

Basic Ancient to Contemporary Timeline

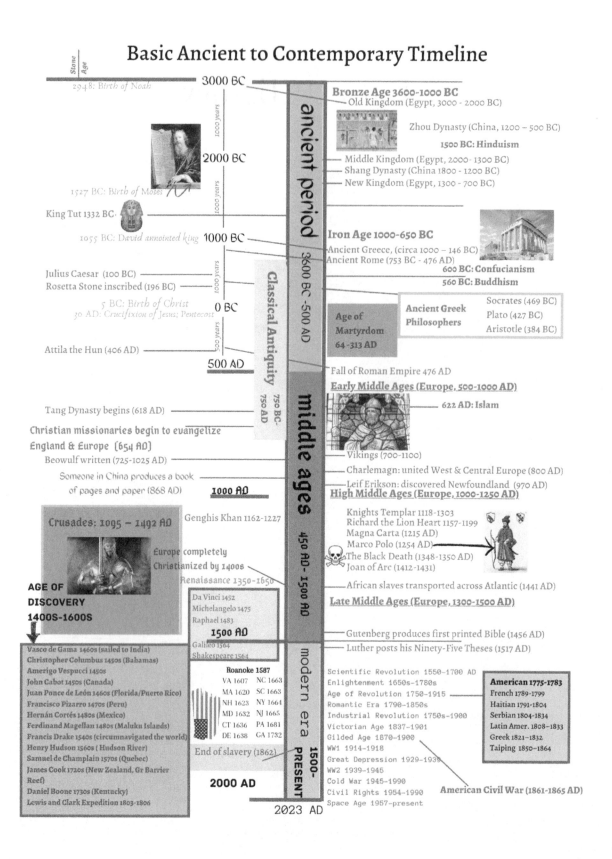

Stone Age

3000 BC

2948: Birth of Noah

1000 years

2000 BC

1527 BC: Birth of Moses

King Tut 1332 BC

1000 years

1055 BC: David annointed king 1000 BC

Julius Caesar (100 BC)
Rosetta Stone inscribed (196 BC)

1000 years

5 BC: Birth of Christ 0 BC
30 AD: Crucifixion of Jesus; Pentecost

Attila the Hun (406 AD)

500 years

500 AD

Tang Dynasty begins (618 AD)

Christian missionaries begin to evangelize
England & Europe (654 AD)
Beowulf written (725-1025 AD)

Someone in China produces a book
of pages and paper (868 AD) 1000 AD

Crusades: 1095 – 1492 AD Genghis Khan 1162-1227

Europe completely
Christianized by 1400s
Renaissance 1350-1650

**AGE OF
DISCOVERY
1400S-1600S**

Da Vinci 1452
Michelangelo 1475
Raphael 1483
1500 AD

Galileo 1564
Shakespeare 1564

Roanoke 1587

VA 1607	NC 1663
MA 1620	SC 1663
NH 1623	NY 1664
MD 1632	NJ 1665
CT 1636	PA 1681
DE 1638	GA 1732

End of slavery (1862)

2000 AD

Vasco de Gama 1460s (sailed to India)
Christopher Columbus 1450s (Bahamas)
Amerigo Vespucci 1450s
John Cabot 1450s (Canada)
Juan Ponce de León 1460s (Florida/Puerto Rico)
Francisco Pizarro 1470s (Peru)
Hernán Cortés 1480s (Mexico)
Ferdinand Magellan 1480s (Maluku Islands)
Francis Drake 1540s (circumnavigated the world)
Henry Hudson 1560s (Hudson River)
Samuel de Champlain 1570s (Quebec)
James Cook 1720s (New Zealand, Gr Barrier Reef)
Daniel Boone 1730s (Kentucky)
Lewis and Clark Expedition 1803-1806

ancient period 3600 BC -500 AD

Classical Antiquity 750 BC- 750 AD

middle ages 450 AD- 1500 AD

modern era 1500-PRESENT

Bronze Age 3600-1000 BC
Old Kingdom (Egypt, 3000 - 2000 BC)

Zhou Dynasty (China, 1200 – 500 BC)

1500 BC: Hinduism

Middle Kingdom (Egypt, 2000- 1300 BC)
Shang Dynasty (China 1800 - 1200 BC)
New Kingdom (Egypt, 1300 - 700 BC)

Iron Age 1000-650 BC
Ancient Greece, (circa 1000 – 146 BC)
Ancient Rome (753 BC - 476 AD)
600 BC: Confucianism
560 BC: Buddhism

Ancient Greek Philosophers	Socrates (469 BC)
	Plato (427 BC)
	Aristotle (384 BC)

Age of Martyrdom 64-313 AD

Fall of Roman Empire 476 AD
Early Middle Ages (Europe, 500-1000 AD)

622 AD: Islam

Vikings (700-1100)
Charlemagn: united West & Central Europe (800 AD)
Leif Erikson: discovered Newfoundland (970 AD)
High Middle Ages (Europe, 1000-1250 AD)

Knights Templar 1118-1303
Richard the Lion Heart 1157-1199
Magna Carta (1215 AD)
Marco Polo (1254 AD)
The Black Death (1348-1350 AD)
Joan of Arc (1412-1431)

African slaves transported across Atlantic (1441 AD)

Late Middle Ages (Europe, 1300-1500 AD)

Gutenberg produces first printed Bible (1456 AD)
Luther posts his Ninety-Five Theses (1517 AD)

Scientific Revolution 1550–1700 AD
Enlightenment 1650s–1780s
Age of Revolution 1750–1915
Romantic Era 1790–1850s
Industrial Revolution 1750s–1900
Victorian Age 1837–1901
Gilded Age 1870–1900
WW1 1914–1918
Great Depression 1929–1939
WW2 1939–1945
Cold War 1945–1990
Civil Rights 1954–1990
Space Age 1957–present

American 1775-1783
French 1789-1799
Haitian 1791-1804
Serbian 1804-1834
Latin Amer. 1808–1833
Greek 1821-1832
Taiping 1850-1864

American Civil War (1861-1865 AD)

2023 AD

Lesson 1: The Stone Age
(? – 3300 BC)

Lesson 1: The Stone Age (Creation to 3300 BC)

Introduction

The Stone Age is tricky subject because the dates included by secular scientists and historians in the Stone Age are far older than a large portion of homeschoolers recognize. As a result, rather than make a definitive claim regarding the age of the earth, I will be sharing resources from various perspectives. This will ensure parental autonomy and also give an opportunity to explore different views.

Secular sources generally propose that the Stone Age began 2.6 million years ago until the time in which archeologists discovered bronze (about 3300 BC). The emergence of stone tools marks the beginning of the period, which is classified into three eras: the Paleolithic, Mesolithic, and the Neolithic Periods. Various Christian interpretations of this period range from theistic evolution to young-earth Creationism (all of which are beyond the scope of this guide). For more information on the views of creationism, see this link:
https://www.blueletterbible.org/faq/creation.cfm

The most important element that we need to know about this period is that it encompasses the last ice age, as well as the transition from small tribes of hunter-gatherer nomads to larger groups who began to settle in one place and built permanent dwellings. Historians also believe the first Americans traveled from Asia across the Bering Strait (or possibly through water travel) during this period. The Bronze Age—the period which follows the Stone Age—developed at different times in different regions but is generally accepted as 3300 BC. **Note**: Biblical figures of the Stone Age period would include Adam and Eve, their children, Enoch, Methuselah, and any people or writers through 3300 BC.

Questions to Ask

1. What are the main views of creation today?
2. What was life like during the Stone Age?
3. Are religious beliefs and secular science compatible in terms of creation and evolution?

Primary Sources

- Eurodocs: History of Prehistoric and Ancient Europe:
  https://eudocs.lib.byu.edu/index.php/History_of_Prehistoric_and_Ancient_Europe
- Historical Association: The Stone Age to the Iron Age:
  https://www.history.org.uk/primary/categories/the-stone-age-to-the-iron-age

- Ancient History: Primary Sources (University of Washington):[2]
  https://guides.lib.uw.edu/research/ancient/primary

General Spines, Series, and Reference Books

(These are good for the entire Ancient Period)
DK Eyewitness Books: Ancient China (Cotterell)
DK Eyewitness Books: Ancient Civilizations (Fullman)
DK Eyewitness Books: Ancient Egypt (Hart)
Explore! Stone, Bronze, and Iron Ages (Newland)
Life in the Stone Age, Bronze Age and Iron Age (Ganeri)
Rand McNally's Historical Atlas of the World
Streams of Civilization series (Stanton)
The Usborne Internet-Linked Ancient World (Chandler)
Usborne Timelines of World History (Chisholm)
World History Encyclopedia: A Complete and Comprehensive Guide to the History
of the World (Ganeri)
Going to War in Ancient Times (Butterfield)
Everyday Life in the Ancient World (Tagholm)

Web resources

- Britannica:
  https://www.britannica.com/event/Stone-Age

- History Channel:
  https://www.history.com/news/prehistoric-ages-timeline

- World History Encyclopedia:
  https://www.worldhistory.org/Stone_Age/

---

[2] This source can be used throughout the ancient period.

YouTube videos

- The Stone Age (World History) (Tom Richey)

- The Agricultural Revolution: Crash Course World History #1

- What are the Different Views of Creation? (Church Split)

- Stories from the Stone Age - 1of15 (All Histories)

- The Dawn of Human History | Mankind: The Story of All of Us (S1, E1) (History)[3]

Fiction & Nonfiction Books

Title	Author	Age	Period
24 Hours in the Stone Age	Kling	9+	Stone Age
Life in the Stone Age, Bronze Age, and Iron Age	Raintree Perspectives		Ancient Period
Live Like a Hunter-Gatherer	Walmsey	7+	Stone Age
Stig of the Dump	Ardizzone	8+	Stone Age
Stone Age Boy	Kitamurra	4+	Stone Age
Stone Age to Celts	Discover & Learn	8+	Stone Age
The First Drawing	Gerstein	4+	Stone Age
The Genius of the Stone, Bronze, and Iron Ages	Howell	8+	Ancient Period
The Great Cave	Deary	7+	Stone Age
The History Detective Investigates: Stone Age to Iron Age		9+	Stone and Iron Ages
The Secrets of Stonehenge	Manning	7+	Stone Age
The Stolen Spear	Pirotta	8+	Stone Age
The Stone Age: Hunters, Gatherers, and Wooly Mammoths	Williams	5+	Stone Age

---

[3] The beginning of this episode briefly mentions the Big Bang.

The Way to Impossible Island	Kirtley	10+	Stone Age
The Whitestone Stories		9+	Stone Age
The Wild Way Home	Kirtley	10+	Stone Age
Wolf Brother	Paver	9+	Stone Age

Terms to Know

1. smelting: the extraction of metal from its ore by a process involving heating and melting.[4]

2. hunter-gatherers: a member of a nomadic people who live chiefly by hunting and fishing and harvesting wild food.

3. agriculture: the science or practice of farming, including cultivation of the soil for the growing of crops and the rearing of animals to provide food, wool, and other products.

4. animal domestication: the process of taming an animal and keeping it as a pet or on a farm.

5. Ice Age: a glacial episode during a past geological period.

6. artifacts: an object made by a human being, typically an item of cultural or historical interest.

7. flint: a hard gray rock consisting of nearly pure chert, occurring chiefly as nodules in chalk.

8. archaic: of an early period of art or culture, ancient

9. archeology: the study of human history and prehistory through the excavation of sites and the analysis of artifacts and other physical remains.

10. prehistory: the period of time before written records.

---

[4] All of the definitions listed in this book are from Oxford Languages unless otherwise noted.

11. <u>protohistory</u>: a branch of study concerned with the transition period between prehistory and the earliest recorded history.[5]

Enrichment Activities

General Enrichment Ideas:

- <u>Letters from the Past</u>: write a letter during each lesson from the perspective of a person living during that time period. Be sure to include the date, mention anything historically relevant, and try to understand the perspective of the person in which you're writing. Keep the letters in a folder or binder.
- <u>Book of Eras</u>: Create a timeline for each lesson, illustrating key people and events, and writing the dates chronologically. When the year is over, you have a whole history book you created yourself!
- <u>Book of Bios</u>: Focus specifically on the people you've learned about this year. Create a bio for one or more important people from each lesson and think of creative ways to document their lives and roles in the past. (Ex: create a social media "profile" for each person, or a text/conversation between two or more people.)
- <u>A Taste of History</u>: For each lesson or time period, research a recipe from that era and write it on a notecard. Save your recipes in a recipe box and cook your way through the past. Another idea is to keep a blog or YouTube channel documenting each recipe, how it was typically prepared (comparing/contrasting it to modern day methods), and any other historical tidbit you find interesting.
- <u>Travel Thru History</u>: For each lesson, create a travel brochure depicting important areas of interest in the area. (It can be funny or serious.)
- <u>Diorama</u>: Choose one (or more) period to illustrate with a diorama.
- <u>Fashion through the Ages</u>: Design a fashion magazine using what you've learned about each era's dress and style.

Specific to this lesson:

- Bake "Neolithic Bread" from Research Parent:
  https://researchparent.com/stone-age-bread-activity/

- Create cave art (like the Lascaux caves) as seen on ArtLessonsforKids:
  https://artlessonsforkids.me/2009/03/15/cave-art-comes-alive/

---

[5] Collins Dictionary

- Make a stone axe using natural materials (rocks, wood, etc.), or use clay to make it look like stone. You can also make a paper mache axe from Imagining History: https://www.imagininghistory.co.uk/post/stone-age-axe-craft

- Watch the documentary on YouTube, Secrets of the Stone Age (by DW, broken into two parts). Then, create an illustrated book, timeline, or comic strip showing the unfolding of the Stone Age.

- Learn about Stonehenge on the following website. https://www.english-heritage.org.uk/visit/places/stonehenge/ Then, built a replica/model of Stonehenge using any of the ideas below: https://stufftodoathome.com/make-a-stonehenge-model/

Making Connections

The Stone Age, the period of human history in which people were nomadic, traveled in smaller groups, and used bone and stone for tools, began to change during the discovery of bronze. Not all civilizations entered the Bronze at the same time (some skipped it altogether, such as in the case of the First Americans), but with it brought changes such as the advent of food production, permanent villages, and animal domestication.

Lesson 2: The Bronze Age
(3300 BC – 1200 BC)

Lesson 2: The Bronze Age (3300 BC – 1200 BC)

Introduction

The beginning of the Bronze Age is marked by the first time a civilization discovers and uses metal (specifically when they transition from copper to bronze). The Sumerians, living in the Fertile Crescent, may have been the first to experience the Bronze Age. This period sees the invention of the wheel, as well as writing, textiles, and the potters' wheel. It corresponds to the development of cities and kingdoms, such as Babylonia in Mesopotamia and Athens. Ancient Greece boasted Thebes, Sparta, Athens, and the beginning of Greek mythology emerged. One of the most interesting thing about the Bronze Age is how it ended: no one exactly knows why, but the end of the Bronze Age was quick, dramatic, and potentially violent. Cities and trade routes were abandoned, and literacy declined.

Questions to Ask

1. How did advanced metal work alter the way people lived during this era?
2. Why would the invention of the horse-drawn plow be so revolutionary?
3. How might the development of writing during the Bronze Age help historians if they were already able to learn about what people lived like through archeology?
4. Why was the Epic of Gilgamesh an important document for people then and historians now?

Primary Sources

- Eyewitness to History: The Ancient World:
  http://www.eyewitnesstohistory.com/awfrm.htm

- Internet Ancient History Sourcebook (Fordham University):
  https://sourcebooks.fordham.edu/ancient/asbook.asp

- Ancient History Primary Sources Guide (University of Washington):
  https://guides.lib.uw.edu/research/ancient/primary

General Spines, Series, and Reference Books

DK Eyewitness Books: Ancient China (Cotterell)
DK Eyewitness Books: Ancient Civilizations (Fullman)
DK Eyewitness Books: Ancient Egypt (Hart)
Explore! Stone, Bronze, and Iron Ages (Newland)
Life in the Stone Age, Bronze Age and Iron Age (Ganeri)
Rand McNally's Historical Atlas of the World
Streams of Civilization series (Stanton)
The Usborne Internet-Linked Ancient World (Chandler)
Usborne Timelines of World History (Chisholm)
World History Encyclopedia: A Complete and Comprehensive Guide to the History
of the World (Ganeri)
Going to War in Ancient Times (Butterfield)
Everyday Life in the Ancient World (Tagholm)

Documentaries

The Lost Gardens of Babylon (13+)
Lost Cities with Albert Lin (PG)
Petra: Secrets of the Ancient Builders (PG)
Chasing the Equinox (PG)

Web resources

- Britannica:
  https://www.britannica.com/event/Bronze-Age

- History Channel:
  https://www.history.com/topics/pre-history/bronze-age

- World History Encyclopedia:
  https://www.worldhistory.org/Bronze_Age_Collapse/

- The Bronze Age (Surrey County Archeological Unit download):
  www.surreycc.gov.uk/__data/assets/pdf_file/0019/228241/Downloadable-
  Resource-3-Bronze-Age_compressed.pdf

YouTube videos

Elementary:

- The Bronze Age (Our Cozy World)

- KS2 Prehistory -Bronze Age (Museum of London

- The Bronze Age Collapse: Before the Storm (Extra History #1)

Middle:

- The Bronze Age Collapse - Mediterranean Apocalypse (Fall of Civilizations)

- The Bronze Age Summarized (Geography People and Resources) by Epimetheus

- Bronze Age 1: Rise of Civilization by old_45 (user)

- Bronze Age 2 - Masters of Trade

- Bronze Age 3 - Conquest and Collapse

High:

Crash Course:

- The Agricultural Revolution: Crash Course World History #1

- Indus Valley Civilization: Crash Course World History #2

- Mesopotamia: Crash Course World History #3

- Ancient Egypt: Crash Course World History #4

Fiction & Nonfiction Books

Title	Author	Age	Period
A Child's Introduction to Egyptology	Alexander	8+	Bronze Age
Ancient Egypt	Eyewitness Books	6+	Bronze Age
Ancient Egypt	National Geographic Reader	7+	Bronze Age
Ancient Egypt for Kids	Ruzicka	6+	Bronze Age
Maia of Thebes	Turner	9+	Bronze Age
Bible Infographics for Kids	Harvest Kids	6+	Ancient Period
Bronze Age Adventures	Metal Man	7+	Bronze Age
Bronze Age and Iron Age Hill Forts	Finch	7+	Ancient Period
Mega Meltdown	Tite	7+	Ancient Period
See Inside Ancient Egypt	Usborne	6+	Bronze Age
The Boy with the Bronze Axe	Fidler	8+	Bronze Age
The Wolf King	Turnbull	14+	Bronze Age
The World of the Old Testament	Olson	9+	Ancient Period
The Gilgamesh Trilogy series	Zeman	5+	Bronze Age
The Babylonians	Landau	9+	Bronze Age
The Wise King Hammurabi of Babylon and His Code of Law	Dissected Lives	NA	Bronze Age
Mesopotamia for Kids: Ziggurat Edition	Baby Professor	8+	Bronze Age

Terms to Know

1. <u>bronze</u>: a yellowish-brown alloy of copper with up to one-third tin.

2. <u>bronzesmith</u>: an artisan who works bronze into useful artifacts.

3. <u>excavation</u>: the action of excavating something, especially an archaeological site.

4. <u>ingots</u>: a block of steel, gold, silver, or other metal, typically oblong in shape.

5. <u>hoard</u>: a stock or store of money or valued objects, typically one that is secret or carefully guarded.

6. <u>pyramid</u>: a monumental structure with a square or triangular base and sloping sides that meet in a point at the top, especially one built of stone as a royal tomb in ancient Egypt.

7. <u>mummy</u>: (especially in ancient Egypt) a body of a human being or animal that has been ceremonially preserved by removal of the internal organs, treatment with natron and resin, and wrapping in bandages.

8. <u>sphinx</u>: mythological creature with a lion's body and a human head, an important image in Egyptian and Greek art and legend.[6]

People to Know:
Hatshepsut
Thutmose III ("Napoleon of Ancient Egypt")
Ramesses II
Tutankhamun
Sargon the Great (Sumerian emperor)

Biblical Figures
Noah
Abraham
Isaac
Joseph
Moses
Joshua
the Judges through Samuel

Places to Know:
Egypt
Mesopotamia
Phoenicia
Canaan

---

[6] Britannica

Cyprus
Greece
Hittite Empire (modern day Turkey)
Syria
Palestine
Sumeria
Archeological locations
Stonehenge (England)
Hili Archeological Park (United Arab Emirates)
Su Nuraxi di Barumini (Sardinia)
Jabel Hafit Tombs (Abu Dhabi)
Tanum Rock Carvings (Sweden)
Akrotiri (Greece)
Great Orme Ancient Mines (Wales)
Qatna Archaeological Park (Syria)
Al-Khor Island (Qatar)
Babylon (Al-Hillah, Iraq)
Great Ziggurat of Ur (Baghdad)

Enrichment Activities

General Enrichment Ideas:

- Letters from the Past: write a letter during each lesson from the perspective of a person living during that time period. Be sure to include the date, mention anything historically relevant, and try to understand the perspective of the person in which you're writing. Keep the letters in a folder or binder.
- Book of Eras: Create a timeline for each lesson, illustrating key people and events, and writing the dates chronologically. When the year is over, you have a whole history book you created yourself!
- Book of Bios: Focus specifically on the people you've learned about this year. Create a bio for one or more important people from each lesson and think of creative ways to document their lives and roles in the past. (Ex: create a social media "profile" for each person, or a text/conversation between two or more people.)
- A Taste of History: For each lesson or time period, research a recipe from that era and write it on a notecard. Save your recipes in a recipe box and

cook your way through the past. Another idea is to keep a blog or YouTube channel documenting each recipe, how it was typically prepared (comparing/contrasting it to modern day methods), and any other historical tidbit you find interesting.

- Travel Thru History: For each lesson, create a travel brochure depicting important areas of interest in the area. (It can be funny or serious.)
- Diorama: Choose one (or more) period to illustrate with a diorama.
- Fashion through the Ages: Design a fashion magazine using what you've learned about each era's dress and style.

Specific to this lesson:

- Recreate Stonehenge from the Clonehenge website:
  https://clonehenge.com/

- Look up Grimspound, a Bronze-Age settlement discovered in Dartmoor, England. Then, create the settlement (as it is today, or as it would have been) with clay:
  http://www.stone-circles.org.uk/stone/grimspound.htm

- Explore the web article, "What Was Life Like in the Bronze Age". Then, complete one of the interactive activities listed there:
  https://www.bbc.co.uk/bitesize/topics/z82hsbk/articles/z874kqt

- Visit the following website and create an illustrated timeline of the Bronze Age:
  https://www.worldhistory.org/timeline/Bronze_Age/

- Read the following article about the Epic of Gilgamesh. Then, **answer** the following: What evidence credits Gilgamesh with building the walls of Uruk? What documents prove his existence? How old was he (according to the Sumerian King List) and why would this be a factor in his reputation? Why did ancient kings seek to associate their lineage with him? Why do historians believe he had a fear of death? https://www.worldhistory.org/gilgamesh/

- Learn about ziggurats on the website below. Then, construct your own using clay, Legos, or any other medium.
  https://www.ducksters.com/history/mesopotamia/ziggurats.php

Making Connections

The decrease of access of tin in trading routes led to the eventual collapse of the Bronze Age. The transition from the Bronze Age to the Iron Age occurred when civilizations used iron or steel enough to replace bronze in common, everyday use (although iron was harder to work with). This happened for different places at different times, and although it's not a perfect way to measure eras, it gives historians a picture of when and where civilizations and cultures developed over time. This was also a period in which the ancient world developed complex ancient states (some of which turned into empires).[7] Four regions (Greece, Anatolia, Canaan, Mesopotamia, and Egypt) contained Bronze Age civilizations we think of today: the Hittites, Babylonian empire, Assyrians, Minoans, and Mycenaeans, Canaanites, the Hebrews, and the Phoenicians.[8]

---

[7] https://pressbooks.nscc.ca/worldhistory/chapter/chapter-3-the-bronze-age-and-the-iron-age/
[8] Ibid.

Lesson 3: The Iron Age
(1300 BC - 90 BC)

Lesson 3: The Iron Age (1300 BC - 90 BC)

Introduction

This period began around 1200 BC and included the use of iron and the development of steel. While the early Iron Age left little artifacts and a spotty written record, the later Iron Age brought us Classical Greece: democracy, the Parthenon, and philosophy. Persia, too, developed and under the rule of Cyrus the Great, became a large empire. It was also the period in which the Celts appeared in Europe. Herodotus, the "Father of History", wrote his book *The Histories* around 550 BC, which marks the end of the Iron Age. (Note: The Ancient period, which consists of the Stone, Bronze, and Iron Ages, begin and end at different times depending upon when they were developed in specific regions. For example, China didn't enter the Iron Age until 600 BC, Scotland in 700 BC, and the Middle East in 1200 BC.) The Iron Age saw major feats such as the building of the Agora in Athens, and the use of iron transformed weaponry and farming.

Questions to Ask

1. Why would the development of iron move civilizations into more permanent homes and cities?
2. Did steel impact culture and society? If so, in what ways?
3. How might the invention of iron help populations grow? How did larger populations impact government systems?
4. Why did it take so long for the use of iron to spread around the world?

Primary Sources

- Asia for Educators: Primary Source Database (Columbia University): http://afe.easia.columbia.edu/main_pop/ps/ps_china.htm

- Ancient Egypt and Mesopotamia: Primary Sources (University of Texas): https://libguides.utep.edu/c.php?g=429735&p=2931027

- Primary Sources: Ancient History: Persian Empire (Christopher Newport University): https://cnu.libguides.com/primaryancient/persianempire

- Irish Studies (Primary Sources from Hesburgh Library):
  https://libguides.library.nd.edu/irish-studies/primary-sources

General Spines, Series, and Reference Books

DK Eyewitness Books: Ancient China (Cotterell)
DK Eyewitness Books: Ancient Civilizations (Fullman)
DK Eyewitness Books: Ancient Egypt (Hart)
Explore! Stone, Bronze, and Iron Ages (Newland)
Life in the Stone Age, Bronze Age and Iron Age (Ganeri)
Rand McNally's Historical Atlas of the World
Streams of Civilization series (Stanton)
The Usborne Internet-Linked Ancient World (Chandler)
Usborne Timelines of World History (Chisholm)
World History Encyclopedia: A Complete and Comprehensive Guide to the History
of the World (Ganeri)
Going to War in Ancient Times (Butterfield)
Everyday Life in the Ancient World (Tagholm)

Documentaries/movies

The Lost Tomb of Alexander the Great (PG)

Web resources

- Britannica:
  https://www.britannica.com/event/Iron-Age

- History Channel:
  https://www.history.com/topics/pre-history/iron-age

- Study:
  https://study.com/academy/lesson/iron-age-lesson-for-kids-facts-history.html

- National Library of Medicine: Iron Trade in Western Roman Empire:
  https://www.ncbi.nlm.nih.gov/pmc/articles/PMC9113607/

YouTube videos

Elementary

- Common Core History: The Iron Age (A Kid Explains History)

- The Iron Age: Characteristics and Importance of the Iron Age (Our Cozy World)

- Life in the Iron Age (Lauren Learns History)

Middle
- What Happened After the Bronze Age Collapse? (Epimetheus)

- Mankind: The Story of All of Us (S1, E2) | Rise of the Iron Age (History Channel)

High
- The Persians & Greeks: Crash Course World History #5

- The End of Civilization (In the Bronze Age): Crash Course World History

- Lecture 08 The Iron Age by Chad Ryan Thomas

Fiction & Nonfiction Books

Title	Author	Age	Period
Children of the Wise Oak	Tooley	12+	Iron Age
Discover the Celts (Every Day Life)	Watts	7+	Iron Age
Discover the Celts (Warriors & Weapons)	Butterfield	7+	Iron Age
Farming in the Iron Age	Reynolds	11+	Iron Age

Iron Age Kids (free download)[9]	Nicolay	10+	Iron Age
Life and Death in an Iron Age Hill Fort	Kerrigan	8+	Iron Age
Little Book of Iron Age Skills	Llawerch	7+	Iron Age
Maroo of the Winter Caves	Turnbull	8+	Iron Age
The Iron Age	Bone (Usborne Beginners)	2+	Iron Age
The Windeby Puzzle	Lowry	10+	Iron Age

Terms to Know

1. <u>Celts</u>: a member of a group of peoples inhabiting much of Europe and Asia Minor in pre-Roman times. Their culture developed in the late Bronze Age around the upper Danube and reached its height in the La Tène culture (5th to 1st centuries BC) before being overrun by the Romans and various Germanic peoples.

2. <u>ironworking</u>: architectural features of buildings, artwork, utensils, and weapons made of iron.[10]

3. <u>hill forts</u>: A general term used to describe a fortification on a hilltop, the best known of which are the later prehistoric examples mainly of later Bronze Age and Iron Age[11]

4. <u>torques</u>: a neck ornament consisting of a band of twisted metal, worn especially by the ancient Gauls and Britons.
5. <u>bracae</u>: pants, trousers

6. <u>broch</u>: one of the prehistoric circular stone towers found on the Orkney and Shetland islands and the Scottish mainland and usually consisting of double walls enclosing small apartments about a central court[12]

---

[9] Free Iron Age Kids magazine download: https://www.interreg-danube.eu/uploads/media/approved_project_output/0001/23/809607afffae4525b7fd449dc037d34853515faa.pdf
[10] Britannica
[11] Oxford Reference
[12] Merriam-Webster

People to Know
- Alexander the Great
- Socrates
- Hippocrates
- Plato
- Aristotle
- Biblical figures: Samuel, Saul, David, Solomon, the prophets

Places to Know
- Phoenicia
- Arabia
- Assyria
- Black Sea
- India
- Iran

(for these locations, visit: https://timemaps.com/history/world-1000bc/)

Enrichment Activities

General Enrichment Ideas:

- Letters from the Past: write a letter during each lesson from the perspective of a person living during that time period. Be sure to include the date, mention anything historically relevant, and try to understand the perspective of the person in which you're writing. Keep the letters in a folder or binder.
- Book of Eras: Create a timeline for each lesson, illustrating key people and events, and writing the dates chronologically. When the year is over, you have a whole history book you created yourself!
- Book of Bios: Focus specifically on the people you've learned about this year. Create a bio for one or more important people from each lesson and think of creative ways to document their lives and roles in the past. (Ex: create a social media "profile" for each person, or a text/conversation between two or more people.)
- A Taste of History: For each lesson or time period, research a recipe from that era and write it on a notecard. Save your recipes in a recipe box and

cook your way through the past. Another idea is to keep a blog or YouTube channel documenting each recipe, how it was typically prepared (comparing/contrasting it to modern day methods), and any other historical tidbit you find interesting.

- <u>Travel Thru History</u>: For each lesson, create a travel brochure depicting important areas of interest in the area. (It can be funny or serious.)
- <u>Diorama</u>: Choose one (or more) period to illustrate with a diorama.
- <u>Fashion through the Ages</u>: Design a fashion magazine using what you've learned about each era's dress and style.

Specific to this lesson:

- Choose an Iron Age recipe from this article from Teach It: https://www.teachit.co.uk/resources/primary/iron-age-recipes

- Explore this website to learn about hill forts, a common building invented in the Iron Age: https://www.dkfindout.com/uk/history/iron-age/hill-forts/

- Read about the famous Iron Age bog bodies found in Europe. Answer the questions: Why are these bodies so well preserved? What do scientists and archeologists hope to learn from them? How are bog bodies different from regular mummies? (Grades 9-12) https://education.nationalgeographic.org/resource/bog-bodies/

- Download this free lesson on the Iron Age. https://www.northdowns.surrey.sch.uk/attachments/download.asp?file=5770 &amp

Answer the following:
1. How did iron impact war?
2. Define the term *oppida.*
3. Which new crops were being farmed at this time?
4. What were some characteristics of the religious beliefs of Iron Age Europeans?
5. How might the lathe have changed the way people lived?

- Read the following article about the Iron Age. Answer the questions: What reason is given as to why iron was used? Who was the Father of History? What other main event coincides with the end of the Iron Age?: https://www.worldhistory.org/herodotus/

- Read this lesson on the Iron Age from the World History Project on Khan Academy's website. https://www.khanacademy.org/humanities/whp-origins/era-3-cities-societies-and-empires-6000-bce-to-700-c-e/32-long-distance-trade-betaa/a/read-the-iron-age-beta

Write an essay about the Iron Age, explaining:
1. The comparison between Bronze Age metallurgy and the development of iron.
2. The invasion of the "Sea Peoples" and its impact on society.
3. The role and importance of trade during this period.
4. The connection between cast iron and the population of China

- Learn the story of the Trojan war, and then learn to draw a Trojan horse using this website: https://www.drawandwrite.com/FreeArtLesson.html

Making Connections

The discovery and implementation of iron transformed the way people lived: people groups which were able to create high-temperature furnaces had a leg up on Bronze Age groups, both in terms of farming technology and weapons. This impacted the power dynamic between regions, as well as boosted population growth: the more civilizations implemented inventions like axes and iron plows, the more food they could grow, which in turn increased their populations. The need for wood as fuel to heat iron increased, which caused rapid deforestation. Empires, such as the Roman Empire, grew large and powerful, spreading over vast areas of land. The end of the Iron Age corresponds to the dawn of the Roman Empire.

For more information on the relationship between the Iron Age and Rome, create a free Study.com account and read this article: https://study.com/academy/lesson/the-iron-age-in-the-roman-empire-history-conquest.html

Lesson 4: Classical Antiquity
(700 BC – 450 AD)

Lesson 4: Classical Antiquity (700 BC – 450 AD)

Introduction

This period overlaps with the Iron Age, beginning in the 8th Century BC with Homer's first writings and ending at the fall of the Western Roman Empire in 476 AD. When you think of the Classical Period, think of a blending of Greek and Roman culture around the Mediterranean—but remember that Rome eventually annexed Greece into its large empire in 146 BC. Greco-Roman culture greatly influenced Western Civilization through its art, poetry, philosophy, government, architecture, and more. The Classical Period also saw the origins of Christianity: the birth of Jesus Christ, His death and resurrection, the early church (as well as the Apostolic Fathers), persecution of Christians, the gradual legalism of Christianity and its expansion into Europe and other regions were all a part of this era.

The Roman Empire made a lasting cultural, political, and technological impact on the world—especially in regards to Western Civilization. Although there was much more going on in the world during this time period, the rest of Chronos will focus on the development of Western Civilization beginning with the Classical period. (Note: World history is extremely important, so be sure to use a world history curriculum as well.)

Questions to Ask:

1. Why was the Roman Empire considered an empire? What lands did they acquire?
2. How did the Roman Empire affect the people they conquered? (Daily life, trade, etc.)
3. What is the lasting impact or legacy of Roman culture, ideals, government systems, and beliefs?
4. How did Christianity change the Roman Empire?
5. What were the reasons of the fall of the Western Roman Empire? Why didn't the East fall at the same time?

Primary Sources:

- The Internet Classics Archive: https://jcf.org/resources/internet-classics-archive/

- Perseus Digital Library (Tufts University):
  http://www.perseus.tufts.edu/hopper/collection%3Fcollection%3DPerseus:collection:Greco-Roman

- Early Christianity: Primary Sources and Translations (Southeastern University): https://library.sebts.edu/c.php?g=264648&p=1775511

- Christian Classics Ethereal Library: https://www.ccel.org/

General Spines, Series, and Reference Books

D'Aulaire's Book of Greek Myths
Herodutus and the Road to History (Bendick)
The Kingfisher Book of the Ancient World

Documentaries/movies

The Roman Empire (PG)

Rome: Empire without Limit (16+)

Web resources

- Britannica: https://www.britannica.com/event/Classical-antiquity

- Khan Academy: https://www.khanacademy.org/humanities/big-history-project/agriculture-civilization/first-cities-states/a/greco-roman

- New World Encyclopedia: https://www.newworldencyclopedia.org/entry/Classic_Age

- New World Encyclopedia (Roman Empire): https://www.newworldencyclopedia.org/entry/Roman_Empire

- Penfield.edu: https://www.penfield.edu/webpages/jgiotto/onlinetextbook.cfm?subpage=1647293

- Timeline: https://people.umass.edu/dfleming/english704-timeline.html

- <u>Greek Gods</u>: <u>https://www.history.com/topics/ancient-greece/greek-mythology</u>

- <u>Early Church History</u>: <u>https://earlychurchhistory.org/</u>

YouTube videos

Elementary

- <u>Ancient Rome for Kids (Learn Bright)</u>

- <u>Ancient Rome for Kids (Homeschool Pop)</u>

- <u>Ancient Greece for Kids (Learn Bright)</u>

- <u>Ancient Greece for Kids (Homeschool Pop)</u>

- <u>The Story of Hanukkah (Learn Bright)</u>

Middle

- <u>Mankind: The Story of All of Us (S1, E3) | Fall of the Roman Empire (History Channel)</u>

- <u>History of the Jews- Summary on a Map (Geo History)</u>

- <u>Building the Early Church: The Gospel Project</u>

- <u>Church History in Ten Minutes (TrueTube)</u>

High

- <u>Church History: Complete Documentary AD 33 to Present by Church History</u>

- <u>Church History Full Series: 1st-5th Century (Theology Academy)</u>

- <u>Christian Apologists and Early Heresies (Ryan Reeves)</u>

- <u>Roman Empire and Christianity (Khan Academy)</u>

Crash Course:

- Alexander the Great: Crash Course World History #8

- Plato and Aristotle: Crash Course History of Science #3

- The Roman Empire. Or Republic. Or...Which Was It?: Crash Course World History #10

- Christianity from Judaism to Constantine: Crash Course World History #11

Tom Richey:

- Plato and Aristotle (Introduction to Greek Philosophy)

- The Ancient Greek Sophists (Greek Philosophy)

Fiction & Nonfiction Books

Title	Author	Age	Period
(ANCIENT GREECE)			
A Traveler's Guide to Ancient Greece	MacDonald	7+	1000 BC- 300 BC
The Children's Homer	Colum	10+	1000 BC- 300 BC
All About the 15 Famous Greek Philosophers	Baby Professor	12+	1000 BC- 300 BC
Amazing and Extraordinary Facts: The Olympics	Halliday	8+	1000 BC- 300 BC
Ancient Greece	Eyewitness Books	8+	1000 BC- 300 BC
Truth with Socrates, Love with Plato, and Happiness with Aristotle (series)	Rosenthal	2+	1000 BC- 300 BC
The Wanderings of Odysseus	Sutcliff	12+	1000 BC- 300 BC
Archimedes and the Door of Science	Bendick	7+	1000 BC- 300 BC
Black Ships Before Troy	Sutcliff	7+	1000 BC- 300 BC
Through the Olympics	Platt	6+	1000 BC- 300 BC

Cleopatra	Stanley	4+	51-30 BC
If You Were Me and Lived in Ancient Greece	Roman	4+	1000 BC- 300 BC
King Leonidas and His Spartan Army: History of Sparta	Baby Professor	8+	1000 BC- 300 BC
Our Little Athenian Cousin of Long Ago	Cowles	8+	1000 BC- 300 BC
Our Little Spartan Cousin of Long Ago	Cowles	8+	1000 BC- 300 BC
The History of the Peloponnesian War	Crawley	16+	1000 BC- 300 BC
The Journeys of Hannibal	Rosen	8+	1000 BC- 300 BC
National Geographic: The Greeks	Cline	14+	1000 BC- 300 BC
The Parthenon	Mann	9+	1000 BC- 300 BC
(ANCIENT ROME)			
Battles of Rome	Baby Professor	8+	700 BC – 600 AD
Everything You Need to Know About the Rise and Fall of the Roman Empire In One Fat Book	Baby Professor	8+	7000-476 AD
Roman Forts	Mulvihill	8+	700 BC – 600 AD
Brave Cloelia	Curry	6+	700 BC – 600 AD
Ancient Rome for Kids	Fet	8+	700 BC – 600 AD
Atticus of Rome	Denenburg	9+	30 BC
City: a Story of Roman Planning and Construction	Macaulay	10+	700 BC – 600 AD
Who was Alexander the Great	Waterfield	8+	336 BC
One Day in Ancient Rome	Kirtland	6+	700 BC – 600 AD
Rome and Romans	Usborne	8+	700 BC – 600 AD
Romulus and Remus	Rockwell	6+	700 BC – 600 AD
See Inside Ancient Rome	Daynes (Usborne)	5+	700 BC – 600 AD
The Story of Rome	Usborne	9+	700 BC – 600 AD
Pompeii: Buried Alive	Kunhardt	6+	79 AD
Who Was Julius Caesar?	Medina	8+	64 BC
(EARLY CHURCH)			
The Christ Child as Told by Matthew and Luke	Peterham	5+	6 or 5 BC
The Easter Story	Wildsmith	5+	30 or 33 AD
Tabitha's Travels: A Family Story for Advent	Ytreeide	4+	6 or 5 BC

The Very First Christians	Maier	5+	6 or 5 BC
The World of the Very First Christians	Olson	8+	30 AD – 100 AD

Terms to Know

(Ancient Greece)

1. acropolis: a citadel or fortified part of an ancient Greek city, typically built on a hill.

2. agora: (in ancient Greece) a public open space used for assemblies and markets.

3. city-state: a city that with its surrounding territory forms an independent state.

4. democracy: a system of government by the whole population or all the eligible members of a state, typically through elected representatives.

5. Hellenistic Period: the period between the death of Alexander the Great in 323 BCE and the conquest of Egypt by Rome in 30 BCE[13]

6. hoplite: a heavily armed foot soldier of ancient Greece

7. helots: a member of a class of serfs in ancient Sparta, intermediate in status between slaves and citizens.

8. oligarchy: a small group of people having control of a country, organization, or institution.

9. Olympics: a sporting event held every four years at the sacred site of Olympia, in the western Peloponnese, in honour of Zeus, the supreme god of the Greek religion. The games, held from 776 BCE to 393 CE, involved participants and spectators from all over Greece and even beyond.[14]

10. Titans: any of a family of giants in Greek mythology born of Uranus and Gaea and ruling the earth until overthrown by the Olympian gods[15]

---

[13] Britannica
[14] Worldhistory.org
[15] Merriam-Webster

11. <u>trireme</u>: an ancient Greek or Roman war galley (ship) with three banks of oars.

(For other terms, visit: https://www.ducksters.com/history/ancient_greece/glossary_and_terms.php)

(Ancient Rome)

12. <u>aqueduct</u>: an artificial channel for conveying water, typically in the form of a bridge across a valley or other gap.

13. <u>emperor</u>: a sovereign ruler of great power and rank, especially one ruling an empire.

14. <u>forum</u>: (in an ancient Roman city) a public square or marketplace used for judicial and other business.

15. <u>gladiator</u>: (in ancient Rome) a man trained to fight with weapons against other men or wild animals in an arena.

16. <u>mosaic</u>: a picture or pattern produced by arranging together small colored pieces of hard material, such as stone, tile, or glass.

17. <u>patrician</u>: an aristocrat or nobleman.

18. <u>plebeian</u>: of or belonging to the commoners of ancient Rome.

19. <u>republic</u>: a state in which supreme power is held by the people and their elected representatives, and which has an elected or nominated president rather than a monarch.

20. <u>Byzantine Empire</u>: the eastern half of the Roman empire

21. <u>colosseum</u>: a large theater or stadium.

22. Biblical canon: the collection of books that comprise the sacred scriptures or Bibles of Jews and Christians.[16]

(For other terms, visit: https://www.ducksters.com/history/ancient_rome/glossary_and_terms.php)

---

[16] OxfordBibliographies.com

Areas to Know

(Ancient Greece)
- Athens
- Macedonia
- Peloponnese

(Ancient Rome)
- Rome
- Pompeii

(The Early Church)
- Bethlehem
- Jerusalem
- Judea
- Samaria
- Antioch

People to Know

(Ancient Greece)
- Alexander the Great
- Aristotle
- Homer
- Pericles
- Plato
- Socrates

(Ancient Rome)
- Julius Caesar
- Caesar Augustus
- Gaius Marius
- Cicero
- Spartacus the Gladiator

(The Early Church)
- Jesus Christ

- The Apostles (Simon Peter, Andrew, James and John--sons of Zebedee, Philip and Bartholomew, Thomas, Matthew, James son of Alphaeus, Thaddaeus, Simon the Cananaean, Judas Iscariot)
- Saul (Paul the Apostle)
- Mary the mother of Jesus
- Mary Magdalene
- King Herod
- Nero
- Constantine
- Linus

(Early Church Fathers/Patriarchs)[17]

- Clement of Rome
- Ignatius of Antioch
- Polycarp of Smyrna
- Irenaeus
- St. Augustine
- John Chrysostom
- Tertullian

Enrichment Activities

General Enrichment Ideas:

- Letters from the Past: write a letter during each lesson from the perspective of a person living during that time period. Be sure to include the date, mention anything historically relevant, and try to understand the perspective of the person in which you're writing. Keep the letters in a folder or binder.
- Book of Eras: Create a timeline for each lesson, illustrating key people and events, and writing the dates chronologically. When the year is over, you have a whole history book you created yourself!
- Book of Bios: Focus specifically on the people you've learned about this year. Create a bio for one or more important people from each lesson and think of creative ways to document their lives and roles in the past. (Ex:

---

[17] For more information about early church leaders, visit: https://www.gotquestions.org/early-church-fathers.html

create a social media "profile" for each person, or a text/conversation between two or more people.)

- A Taste of History: For each lesson or time period, research a recipe from that era and write it on a notecard. Save your recipes in a recipe box and cook your way through the past. Another idea is to keep a blog or YouTube channel documenting each recipe, how it was typically prepared (comparing/contrasting it to modern day methods), and any other historical tidbit you find interesting.
- Travel Thru History: For each lesson, create a travel brochure depicting important areas of interest in the area. (It can be funny or serious.)
- Diorama: Choose one (or more) period to illustrate with a diorama.
- Fashion through the Ages: Design a fashion magazine using what you've learned about each era's dress and style.

Specific to this lesson:

- Read about the first Olympic Games. Then, create a Venn diagram to compare and contrast the ancient games with the ones we see today: https://kids.nationalgeographic.com/history/article/first-olympics

- You can also make your own Olympic wreath here: https://www.dltk-kids.com/sports/mleaf-crown.htm

- Classical Antiquity also covers the end of the Iron Age, and the earliest years of the Christian church. Read the book, *The World of the First Christians* (Olson) to learn about what life was like for them.

- Create a Roman mosaic using construction paper (or pottery pieces). *julesmadden.blogspot.com/2017/02/mosaicing-with-kids-how-to-with-tips*

- Review this PDF of the history of the Christian church. https://www.saintjohnchurch.org/differences-between-orthodox-and-catholic/

  Answer the following:
  1. What event, foretold by Christ, came to pass in 70 AD?
  2. When was the New Testament canon closed?
  3. The First Ecumenical Council was _____.
  4. When did Russia begin to accept Christianity?
  5. When do Russian missionaries arrive in Alaska, and which version of Christianity do they spread?
  6. When does Gutenberg print the Bible for the first time?

7. When did Christian schools start appearing in Antioch?

Making Connections

The fall of Rome left a void of power in the West which destabilized Europe, playing a huge role in this period precisely because it was gone; with no emperor in the West, roads, and water supply networks (to say nothing of art and culture) fell into disrepair. Decentralized power in Europe after the fall of Rome led to rival "political, military, economic and religious constituencies began to fight, bargain and compromise and—in the process—rebuilt society along different lines."[18] These grabs for power and influence led to the formation of countries and distinct monarchy within Europe, and the Early Middle Ages.

---

[18] https://news.stanford.edu/2019/10/23/fall-rome-europes-lucky-break

Lesson 5: Early Middle Ages
(500 AD – 1050 AD)

Lesson 5: Early Middle Ages (500 AD – 1050 AD)

Introduction

Once called the "Dark Ages", the Early Middle Ages refer to the period immediately following the fall of the Western Roman Empire. Amidst constant warfare, urban areas depopulated and relatively few records were left for historians to decipher. (Note: It's important to note that Late Antiquity, a period between 200-600, is considered by historians to be a bridge between the Classical Antiquity and the Middle Ages.) It's in this period that the legends of Arthur begin, although historians are dubious of his existence.[19] From the late 6th Century forward, Britain was Christianized by missionaries from Rome or Ireland.

Another key event during the Early Middle Ages was the emergence of Islam around 610 AD. Islam spread through various regions in Africa, Europe, and the Middle East, leading to major conflicts with Christian countries in the High and Late Middle Ages.[20] Charlemagne, a Frankish noble who became King of the Franks in 768, would unify previously Roman territories over the course of thirty years and become the first Holy Roman Emperor.[21] The end of this period also saw the Christianization of the Vikings after a few hundred years of raiding their European neighbors.

Questions to Ask

1. What were the benefits for Europe being under Roman control? What happened to the West when Rome fell?
2. Why is the term "Dark Ages" no longer used by historians?
3. Why would the Early Middle Ages be called the "migration period"?
4. What challenges did Europeans face in this era?

Primary Sources

- Internet Medieval Sourcebook (Fordham University):
  https://sourcebooks.fordham.edu/sbook.asp

---

[19] https://www.english-heritage.org.uk/learn/story-of-england/early-medieval/
[20] https://math.ucr.edu/~res/math153-2019/historical-maps2.pdf
[21] https://courses.lumenlearning.com/atd-herkimer-westerncivilization/chapter/the-rise-of-charlemagne/

- The Account Given by Wulfstan:[22]
  http://anglosaxon.archeurope.info/index.php?page=the-account-given-by-wulfstan

- De Re Militari: https://deremilitari.org/primary-sources/

General Spines, Series, and Reference Books

Rulers of the Middle Ages (History Makers)
Feudalism and Daily Life in the Middle Ages (Padrino)
It's a Feudal, Feudal World (Shapiro)
How Would You Survive in the Middle Ages (MacDonald)
Kids in the Medieval World (Johnson)
The Thrifty Guide to Medieval Times (Stokes)

Documentaries

Secrets of the Castle (13+)
The Norse: An Arctic Mystery (13+)

Web resources

- Britannica: https://www.britannica.com/event/Dark-Ages

- Study: https://study.com/academy/lesson/early-middle-ages-in-europe-definition-overview.html

- Eyewitness to History: http://www.eyewitnesstohistory.com/fallofrome.htm

- History Channel: https://www.history.com/topics/middle-ages

- English Heritage: https://www.english-heritage.org.uk/learn/story-of-england/early-medieval/

- Britannica (Middle Ages): https://www.britannica.com/event/Middle-Ages

- Encyclopedia (timeline): https://www.encyclopedia.com/history/encyclopedias-almanacs-transcripts-and-maps/timeline-events-middle-ages

---

[22] Wulfstan lived just before the official start of this historic period, but his first-hand accounts of the early Vikings are a good addition to this lesson.

- Medievalists: https://www.medievalists.net/2018/04/most-important-events-middle-ages/

- Time Map (map of Europe in 979 AD): https://timemaps.com/history/europe-979ad/

YouTube videos

Elementary

- Life in a Medieval Village (Simple History)

Middle

- Charlemagne: How He Changed History Forever (Captivating History)

- What Was Life Like in the Middle Ages? (Captivating History)

- Fall of the Roman Empire | Mankind: The Story of All of Us (S1, E3) | Full Episode | History

- Everyday Village Life in the Middle Ages (Captivating History)

- What Did Medieval Peasants Eat? (Tasting History With Max Miller)

High

- The Early Middle Ages (Part 1) - Lesson #3 of Introduction to Medieval History | Online Course (The Medieval Historian)

- The Dark Ages...How Dark Were They, Really?: Crash Course World History #14

- The rise and fall of the medieval Islamic Empire (Petra Sijpesteijn & Birte Kristiansen)

- Feudalism in Medieval Europe (What is Feudalism?) Tom Richey

Fiction & Nonfiction Books

Title	Author	Age	Period
Clovis, King of the Franks	Rice	10+	466-511
Ancient Civilizations of Islam	Baby Professor	5+	600+
The World in the Time of Charlemagne	MacDonald	9+	747-814
Charlemagne and the Early Middle Ages	Greenblat	11+	747-814
Stories of Charlemagne	Westwood	9+	747-814
The Holy Roman Emperor and Charlemagne in the Early Middle Ages	Sypeck	10+	747-814
Who Were the Vikings?	Usborne	8+	700s+
Viking	Eyewitness Book	8+	700s+
Life as a Viking	Lassieur	8+	700s+
Guts & Glory: The Vikings	Thompson	8+	700s+
Vikings	Margeson	5+	700s+
The Story of Beowulf	Marshall	9+	700-1000
Alfred the Great	Abbott	10+	871-886

Terms to Know

1. Frankish kingdom: Dominating present-day northern France, Belgium, and western Germany, the Franks established the most powerful Christian kingdom of early medieval western Europe. The name France (Francia) is derived from their name.[23]

2. Holy Roman Emperor: the ruler of various lands in western and central Europe, a title held first by Frankish and then by German kings from 800 to 1806.[24]

3. Islam: the religion of the Muslims, a monotheistic faith regarded as revealed through Muhammad as the Prophet of Allah.

---

[23] Britannica
[24] Ibid.

4. caliphate: the rule or reign of a caliph or chief Muslim ruler.

5. barbarian: a member of a community or tribe not belonging to one of the great civilizations.

6. monastery: a building or buildings occupied by a community of monks living under religious vows.

7. missionary: a person sent on a religious mission, especially one sent to promote Christianity in a foreign country.

8. Anglo-Saxon: a Germanic inhabitant of England between the 5th century and the Norman Conquest.

9. Norman Invasion of 1066: the 11th-century invasion and occupation of England by an army made up of thousands of Norman, Breton, Flemish, and French troops, all led by the Duke of Normandy, later styled William the Conqueror.[25]

10. Viking Age: the peak period of the Vikings, between 800-1050 AD

11. cathedral: cathedral is the church which contains the official "seat" or throne of a bishop[26]

Areas to Know

- Kievan Rus (area near modern-day Russia)
- Scandinavia
- Mediterranean Sea
- Gaul (area near modern-day France)

People to Know

- Justinian

---

[25] Wikipedia
[26] www.TheMiddleAges.net

- Charlemagne
- Clovis
- Muhammad
- Alfred the Great

Enrichment Activities

General Enrichment Ideas:

- <u>Letters from the Past</u>: write a letter during each lesson from the perspective of a person living during that time period. Be sure to include the date, mention anything historically relevant, and try to understand the perspective of the person in which you're writing. Keep the letters in a folder or binder.
- <u>Book of Eras</u>: Create a timeline for each lesson, illustrating key people and events, and writing the dates chronologically. When the year is over, you have a whole history book you created yourself!
- <u>Book of Bios</u>: Focus specifically on the people you've learned about this year. Create a bio for one or more important people from each lesson and think of creative ways to document their lives and roles in the past. (Ex: create a social media "profile" for each person, or a text/conversation between two or more people.)
- <u>A Taste of History</u>: For each lesson or time period, research a recipe from that era and write it on a notecard. Save your recipes in a recipe box and cook your way through the past. Another idea is to keep a blog or YouTube channel documenting each recipe, how it was typically prepared (comparing/contrasting it to modern day methods), and any other historical tidbit you find interesting.
- <u>Travel Thru History</u>: For each lesson, create a travel brochure depicting important areas of interest in the area. (It can be funny or serious.)
- <u>Diorama</u>: Choose one (or more) period to illustrate with a diorama.
- <u>Fashion through the Ages</u>: Design a fashion magazine using what you've learned about each era's dress and style.

Specific to this lesson:

- Feudalism was brought to England by the Normans and was used in Europe for several hundred years. Learn about it using this activity by Angelic Scalliwags: https://angelicscalliwagshomeschool.com/feudalism-in-the-middle-ages/?amp=1)

- Learn about the Vikings by creating a longship from TeachBesideMe: https://teachbesideme.com/learning-about-vikings/

- Print this map of the Viking world and compare it to a modern map today. https://layers-of-learning.com/viking-people/

- Read about Charlemagne. **Answer**: Who was he? What did he accomplish? What kind of influence did he have? How did Europe change because of him? https://kids.britannica.com/kids/article/Charlemagne/352939

- Learn about the Viking Age here: https://en.natmus.dk/historical-knowledge/denmark/prehistoric-period-until-1050-ad/the-viking-age/ Then, create a story about a fictional Viking based on what you've learned.

Making Connections

As the Early Middle Ages progressed, the power of the Roman Catholic Church grew. Western civilization, which began during the Roman Empire, formed a unique culture in Europe which would last for centuries. It was during this transition from Early to High which Europe saw the revival of trade, towns, and increased resources.[27] A major mark of the transition from Early to High is the start of the Crusades.

---

[27] https://yalebooks.yale.edu/2020/08/18/the-high-middle-ages

Lesson 6: High Middle Ages
(1050 - 1300 AD)

Lesson 6: High Middle Ages (1050 - 1300 AD)

Introduction

The High Middle Ages, between 1000-1300, represent the most recognizable aspects of the medieval period: knights, princesses, the Crusades (beginning in 1095), and chivalry. This period saw clearer social and economic structures, the building of universities, professionalism of certain occupations (like doctors and lawyers), more centralized power in European kingdoms, and the rise of guilds. It also saw the Catholic Church reform and grow in power under new leaders.

Questions to Ask

1. Why would the development of a cash economy cause towns and cities to grow?
2. What was the ultimate goal of the Crusades? How did this goal conflict with that of the Seljuk Turks?
3. What are modern criticisms of the Crusades, and are they fair? Why/why not?

Primary Sources

- Medieval and Renaissance Periods (500AD-17th Century): https://cnu.libguides.com/psmedievalandrenaissance

- Internet Medieval Sourcebook: https://sourcebooks.fordham.edu/sbook1d.asp

- Icelandic Saga Database: https://sagadb.org/

- Medieval Illuminated Manuscripts: https://chnm.gmu.edu/worldhistorysources/r/21/whm.html

- International Dunhuang Project (Silk Road): https://chnm.gmu.edu/worldhistorysources/r/99/whm.html

- Medieval Law (Catholic University of America): http://legalhistorysources.com/

- Internet Medieval Sourcebook (Selected Sources: The Crusades): https://sourcebooks.fordham.edu/sbook1k.asp

Bodleian Library Broadside Ballads:
https://chnm.gmu.edu/worldhistorysources/r/64/whm.html

General Spines, Series, and Reference Books

Rulers of the Middle Ages (History Makers)
Feudalism and Daily Life in the Middle Ages (Padrino)
It's a Feudal, Feudal World (Shapiro)
How Would You Survive in the Middle Ages (MacDonald)
Kids in the Medieval World (Johnson)
The Thrifty Guide to Medieval Times (Stokes)
Historical Atlas of the Crusades (Konstam)

Web resources

- Yale University Press: https://yalebooks.yale.edu/2020/08/18/the-high-middle-ages/

- NCSS: https://pressbooks.nscc.ca/worldhistory/chapter/chapter-1-the-high-middle-ages/

- Khan Academy: https://www.khanacademy.org/humanities/world-history/medieval-times/european-middle-ages-and-serfdom/v/overview-of-the-middle-ages

- Course Hero: https://www.coursehero.com/study-guides/atd-fscj-earlyhumanities/high-middle-ages/

- History: https://www.history.com/topics/ancient-middle-east/silk-road

YouTube videos

Elementary

- The Middle Ages in 3 ½ Minutes (Margreet de Heer) (**Note**: Her explanation

  of the Crusades are wrong, but everything else is good)

- [The Middle Ages Explained in 10 Minutes (Captivating History)](#)

- [Art in the Middle Ages (Happy Learning English)](#)

- [What Was the Feudal System: Middle Ages Feudal System Story for Kids (The Ancient Library)](#)

- [The Crusades in 5 Minutes (Real Crusades History)](#)

Middle

History Channel:

- [The Crusades and the Dark Ages | Mankind: The Story of All of Us (S1, E4)](#)

- [Modern Marvels: Massive Medieval Castles and Deadly Dungeons - (S10, E2)](#)

- [What Was Feudalism? (History Hub)](#)

High

- [Unit 7: The High and Late Middle Ages (The Medieval Historian)](#)

- [Timeline of High Middle Ages (Atomo)](#)

- [13-2 Europe in Transition: The High Middle Ages (Joseph Prezzavento)](#)

Fiction and Nonfiction Books

Wulf the Saxon: The Story of the Norman Conquest	Henty	8+	1066-1087
William the Conqueror Becomes King of England	Baby Professor	8+	1066

Crusades: The Battle for Jerusalem	DK Books	8+	1095-1291
The Crusader: The Story of Richard the Lionheart	Power-Waters	8+	1189
Richard the Lionheart: The Life of a King and Crusader	West	8+	1189
The Magna Carta	Barrington	10+	1215
The Magna Carta Chronicle	Skipworth	8+	1215
Cross-Sections Castle	Stephen Biesty	5+	1050+
Arms and Armor	Eyewitness	6+	800+
The Age of Feudalism	Davenport	8+	1050+
A Concise History of the Catholic Church	Bokencotter	12+	400+
A Medieval Feast	Aliki	6+	500+
The Adventures of Marco Polo	Freedman	10+	1254
The Hawk of the Castle: A Story of Medieval Falconry	Smith	8+	500+
St. George and the Dragon	Hodges	5+	800+
Good Masters! Sweet Ladies! Voices from a Medieval Village	Schlitz	5+	800+
The Knight at Dawn	Osborne	8+	1000+
Castle: Fast Forward	Dennis	6+	800+
Knights & Castles: Exploring History Through Art	Martin	10+	1066
Knights	Steele	10+	1066
The Door in the Wall	De Angeli	9+	1066
Castle Diary: Journal of Tobias Burgess	Platt	10+	1066
Marco Polo: The Boy Who Traveled the Medieval World	McCarty	8+	1254
William Wallace: The Battle to Free Scotland	MacPherson	4+	1270

Terms to know

1. feudal system: the dominant social system in medieval Europe, in which the nobility held lands from the Crown in exchange for military service, and

vassals were in turn tenants of the nobles, while the peasants (villeins or serfs) were obliged to live on their lord's land and give him homage, labor, and a share of the produce, notionally in exchange for military protection.

2. Crusades: each of a series of medieval military expeditions made by Europeans to the Holy Land in the 11th, 12th, and 13th centuries.

3. Knights Templar: a large organization of devout Christians during the medieval era who carried out an important mission: to protect European travelers visiting sites in the Holy Land while also carrying out military operations.[28]

4. Fall of Constantinople: the capture of the capital of the Byzantine Empire by the Ottoman Empire.

5. Silk Road: a network of routes which connected people, goods, and cultures from East to West for over 1,500 years and covered 4,000 miles

6. guild: a medieval association of craftsmen or merchants, often having considerable power.

7. Magna Carta[29]: a document guaranteeing English political liberties that was drafted at Runnymede, a meadow by the River Thames, and signed by King John on June 15, 1215, under pressure from his rebellious barons. By declaring the sovereign to be subject to the rule of law and documenting the liberties held by "free men," it provided the foundation for individual rights in Anglo-American jurisprudence.

8. Parliament: By 1236, royal clerks used the word "parliament" to refer to the king's meetings with his Great Council. This term comes from the French verb "to talk or discuss." French, not English, was the language spoken by the kings and ruling elite, who were the descendants of the Norman conquerors.[30]

Areas to Know

- Antioch
- Jerusalem

---

[28] History.com
[29] Encyclopedia Britannica
[30] https://www.crf-usa.org/bill-of-rights-in-action/bria-25-2-king-and-parliament-in-medieval-england.html

- Jaffa
- Constantinople

People to Know

- William the Conqueror
- Henry II
- Richard the Lionheart
- Marco Polo
- William Wallace
- Pope Urban II
- Alexius Comnenus

Enrichment Activities

General Enrichment Ideas:

- Letters from the Past: write a letter during each lesson from the perspective of a person living during that time period. Be sure to include the date, mention anything historically relevant, and try to understand the perspective of the person in which you're writing. Keep the letters in a folder or binder.
- Book of Eras: Create a timeline for each lesson, illustrating key people and events, and writing the dates chronologically. When the year is over, you have a whole history book you created yourself!
- Book of Bios: Focus specifically on the people you've learned about this year. Create a bio for one or more important people from each lesson and think of creative ways to document their lives and roles in the past. (Ex: create a social media "profile" for each person, or a text/conversation between two or more people.)
- A Taste of History: For each lesson or time period, research a recipe from that era and write it on a notecard. Save your recipes in a recipe box and cook your way through the past. Another idea is to keep a blog or YouTube channel documenting each recipe, how it was typically prepared (comparing/contrasting it to modern day methods), and any other historical tidbit you find interesting.
- Travel Thru History: For each lesson, create a travel brochure depicting important areas of interest in the area. (It can be funny or serious.)
- Diorama: Choose one (or more) period to illustrate with a diorama.

- <u>Fashion through the Ages</u>: Design a fashion magazine using what you've learned about each era's dress and style.

Specific to this lesson:

- Make a codex using this link from Tina's Dynamic Homeschool: https://tinasdynamichomeschoolplus.com/how-to-make-a-codex/

- As the Catholic Church grew more prominent in the Middle Ages, their church buildings did, too. Make this stained glass project from Having Fun At Home: http://www.havingfunathome.com/2013/10/stained-glass-kids-medieval-project.html

- Learn about the various machines used during this period with one of these STEM challenges: https://www.teachstudentsavvy.com/2018/07/early-medieval-europe-stem-challenges.html

- Build a medieval village by visiting High Hill Education: http://highhillhomeschool.blogspot.com/2014/07/make-your-own-medieval-village.html

- Review this article about the Knights Templar. Then, write your own "code of conduct" (such as the one used by the Knights, *The Rule of the Templars*). https://www.history.com/topics/middle-ages/the-knights-templar

- Read about the Silk Road here: https://education.nationalgeographic.org/resource/silk-road/ Then. watch this video on how the Silk Road operated: How did The Silk Road Actually Work? (Knowledgia) Print this free document to test your knowledge: https://www.cloverleaflocal.org/Downloads/Silk%20Road%20Worksheet.pdf

- Read this chapter about the High Middle Ages shared by Portland Community College. Then, **answer** the following questions: https://blogs.nvcc.edu/westernciv/history-of-western-civilization/western-civilizations-his-101/volume-2-chapter-1-the-high-middle-ages/

1. Why would the development of a cash economy cause towns and cities to grow?

2. What was the ultimate goal of the Crusades? How did this goal conflict with that of the Seljuk Turks?

3. Why would Pope Urban II need to summon the knights of Europe to protect Christians "in and near" the Holy Land?

4. Explain the possible reasons the Crusaders had to answer the Pope's call.

5. Which two groups of "monk-knights" took monastic vows by authorization of the Church?

6. When Jerusalem was lost in 1187, what happened to the Templars?

7. Were the Crusades successful?

8. Which three consequences and effects of the Crusades are listed as "particularly important"?

9. Who were the Teutonic Knights and which people groups did they lead crusades against? What was their legacy?

10. Review the map, *The State of the Teutonic Order after 1466.* How long did the influence of the Northern Crusaders last? Into which historical period did it last?

11. Describe the Middle East after the Caliphates.

12. The Turks were effective in warfare but generally _____ at establishing stable governments.

13. Describe the economy of the Early Middle Ages compared with that of the High Middle Ages.

14. What is a "carruca" and how did it change agriculture? List other innovations which had an impact on farming.

15. The centuries between 1000-1300 AD were relatively _____ for many European peasants.

16. By the 12th Century, many cities were expanding rapidly for the first time since the _____.

17. Explain the views and stereotypes of Jews during this period.

18. What was the average life expectancy for Europeans during the High Middle Ages?

19. Describe the role of men and women during this period?

20. Explain the relationship between the growth of monasteries and convents, and that of church corruption.

Making Connections

The High Middle Ages saw the development of agriculture, growth of cities, and expansion of Christianity. The Late Middle Ages, however, began with several crises: climate change (known as the Little Ice Age), the bubonic plague, and the Hundred Years' War were just some of the dramatic events which marked the end of the Middle Ages.

Lesson 7: Late Middle Ages
(1300 - 1500 AD)

Lesson 7: Late Middle Ages (1300 - 1500 AD)

Introduction

The Late Middle Ages, the period between 1300-1500, overlaps the beginning of the Renaissance. It began with a series of crises which would soon spell the end of the Middle Ages. A "Little Ice Age" cooled the temperatures in Europe, causing a decrease of food production and therefore, widespread food insecurity and even starvation. It also includes the event of the Black Plague (caused by the bacterium, Yersinia pestis) which killed between 1/3 and 1/2 of the population of Europe. England and France fought a series of wars known as the Hundred Years' War, killing potentially millions. There were also peasant uprisings and urban rebellions which added to the instability in Europe.[31] The end of the High Middle Ages saw the beginning of Age of Exploration and the arrival of Christopher Columbus to the New World.

Primary Sources

(See previous lists from lessons 5 and 6)

General Spines, Series, and Reference Books

Rulers of the Middle Ages (History Makers)
Feudalism and Daily Life in the Middle Ages (Padrino)
It's a Feudal, Feudal World (Shapiro)
How Would You Survive in the Middle Ages (MacDonald)
Kids in the Medieval World (Johnson)
The Thrifty Guide to Medieval Times (Stokes)

Documentaries/movies

Tudor Monastery Farm (7+)

---

[31] http://facstaff.bloomu.edu/mhickey/late_middle_ages.htm (Parents, please read to be sure your child can handle some of this material.)

Web resources

- Encyclopedia.com: https://www.encyclopedia.com/history/encyclopedias-almanacs-transcripts-and-maps/late-middle-ages-0

- History: https://www.history.com/topics/middle-ages/black-death

- Britannica: https://www.britannica.com/event/Hundred-Years-War

- University of Pennsylvania: *facstaff.bloomu.edu/mhickey/late_middle_ages.htm*

YouTube videos

Elementary:

(None suggested for this particular lesson: continue to find and watch videos about the Middle Ages from YouTube channels such as Free School, HiHo Kids, Brain Pop, etc.)

Middle:

- The Crisis of the Later Middle Ages (Kevin Roberts)

- How the Plague Doctor's Mask Protected Them (The Infographics Show)[32]

- The rise and fall of the Byzantine Empire (Leonora Neville)

- What Made The Black Death (The Plague) so Deadly? (The Infographics Show)

- Plague 101 | National Geographic

- Century of Crisis - Why the 1300s Were the Worst (Kings and Generals)

High:

---

[32] This video briefly mentions how masks can protect us from another pandemic and showed people at the grocery store wearing masks.

- Humanity vs. the Plague | Mankind: The Story of All of Us (S1, E5) | History

- The Late Middle Ages (by Whaptors)

- The Plague That Ravaged London (Timeline-World History Documentaries)

- The Crisis of the Late Middle Age Church - Episode 28 - 100+ Moments in History with Mike Woodruff (Press On)

- Late Medieval Background to the Reformation (Ryan Reeves)

- History of Civilization 38: The Late Medieval Period (Dr. John Stevenson)

- Lecture 1b - The Late Middle Ages (Brett Olmstead: KPHS)

Fiction and Nonfiction Books

Dante's Divine Comedy: As Told for Young People	Tusiani	6+	1308
Plague!: Epidemics and Scourages Through the Ages	Farndon	8+	1346-1352
What Was the Plague?	Edwards	8+	1346-1352
The Black Death	Usbourne Young Reading	8+	1346-1352
Plague: Outbreak in London	Bradman	8+	1346-1352
The Story of Joan of Arc	Dover Classics	9+	1412
The Western Schism of 1378: The History and Legacy of the Papal Schism that Split the Catholic Church	Charles River Editors	16+	

Terms to Know

1. plague: a contagious bacterial disease characterized by fever and delirium, typically with the formationof buboes (bubonic plague) and sometimes infection of the lungs (pneumonic plague)

2. famine: severe and prolonged hunger in a substantial proportion of the population of a region or country, resulting in widespread and acute malnutrition and death by starvation and disease.[33]

3. Great Famine of 1315-1322: was the first of a series of large-scale crises that struck Europe early in the 14th century.

4. Peasant's Revolt: also named Wat Tyler's Rebellion or the Great Rising, was a major uprising across large parts of England in 1381 against King Richard II; it signaled the potential power which peasants had

5. 100 Years War: a series of armed conflicts between the kingdoms of England and France during the Late Middle Ages.

6. Great Schism (East-West Schism): On July 16, 1054, Patriarch of Constantinople Michael Cerularius was excommunicated, starting the "Great Schism" that created the two largest denominations in Christianity—the Roman Catholic and Eastern Orthodox faiths.

7. communion: Christian sacrament commemorating the death of Jesus Christ with bread and wine

8. Eastern Orthodox: loose affiliation of several Christian denominations (including Russian Orthodox, Greek Orthodox, etc.) which follow early church hierarchy.[34]

9. heretic: a person believing in or practicing religious heresy.

10. heresy: belief or opinion contrary to orthodox religious (especially Christian) doctrine.

11. Western Schism: the period from 1378 to 1417, when there were two, and later three, rival popes, each with his own following, his own Sacred College of Cardinals, and his own administrative offices[35]

---

[33] Britannica
[34] National Geographic
[35] Britannica

12. The Jacquerie: the name of French peasants who organized a mass rebellion to protest tax increases.

13. flagellants: pious Christians who, believing the tragedies of the Late Middle Ages were God's judgement against sin, participated in self-mutilation and self-harm as an act of penance.

14. Lollards: Christian followers of the theology of John Wyclif

15. Hussites: Christian followers of Jan Hus

16. War of the Roses: a war fought in the 15th century between two royal families in England (the royal house of Lancaster, and the royal house of York) to decide which one would rule.

Areas to Know

- Avignon, France
- Rome, Italy
- London, Essex, Kent, Canterbury (England)

People to Know

- King Edward III
- King Philip Valois
- King Charles IV of France
- French King John II
- King Richard II of England
- John Wyclif
- Pope Boniface VII
- Jan Hus (proto-Reformer from Bohemia)
- Joan of Arc
- (prospective) French King Charles VII
- King Henry VI
- King Henry VII

- Geoffrey Chaucer
- "Black Prince" Edward

Enrichment Activities

General Enrichment Ideas:

- <u>Letters from the Past</u>: write a letter during each lesson from the perspective of a person living during that time period. Be sure to include the date, mention anything historically relevant, and try to understand the perspective of the person in which you're writing. Keep the letters in a folder or binder.
- <u>Book of Eras</u>: Create a timeline for each lesson, illustrating key people and events, and writing the dates chronologically. When the year is over, you have a whole history book you created yourself!
- <u>Book of Bios</u>: Focus specifically on the people you've learned about this year. Create a bio for one or more important people from each lesson and think of creative ways to document their lives and roles in the past. (Ex: create a social media "profile" for each person, or a text/conversation between two or more people.)
- <u>A Taste of History</u>: For each lesson or time period, research a recipe from that era and write it on a notecard. Save your recipes in a recipe box and cook your way through the past. Another idea is to keep a blog or YouTube channel documenting each recipe, how it was typically prepared (comparing/contrasting it to modern day methods), and any other historical tidbit you find interesting.
- <u>Travel Thru History</u>: For each lesson, create a travel brochure depicting important areas of interest in the area. (It can be funny or serious.)
- <u>Diorama</u>: Choose one (or more) period to illustrate with a diorama.
- <u>Fashion through the Ages</u>: Design a fashion magazine using what you've learned about each era's dress and style.

Specific to this lesson:

- Play the Black Plague simulation game from The Homeschool Den: https://homeschoolden.com/2016/01/25/middle-ages-in-the-1300s-black-plague-simulation-worksheets-on-the-crusades-hundred-years-war/

- Homeschool Share has a free, downloadable unit study on the Black Plague, which covers everything from the specifics of the illness to the impact on society: https://www.homeschoolshare.com/plague-lapbook

- Read the following article on some of the causes of the end of the Middle Ages. **Answer**: What's the difference between an intellectual movement and a historical period? How do they influence each other? What was Pope Urban II's reaction when Emperor Komnenos asked for help from the invading Ottomans? Describe how rediscovering Aristotle influenced the end of the Middle Ages. How did the death of nobility during the Black Plague change the mobility of the middle classes? What was the result of "Greek-speaking scholars" fleeing to the west? https://welltrainedmind.com/a/five-events-began-renaissance-ended-middle-ages/

- Visit the following websites. Then, summarize how and why the Middle Ages ended:
  History for Kids: https://www.historyforkids.net/late-middle-ages.html
  Schoolwork Helper: www.schoolworkhelper.net/reasons-for-the-downfall-of-the-middle-ages

- Watch this video from Kings and Generals, and answer the question: Why was the Thirty Years' War so devastating?
  Kings and Generals: Why the Thirty Years' War Was So Devastating - European Wars of Religion

- Learn about the Great Famine of 1315-1322 here:
  https://geoalliance.asu.edu/sites/default/files/LessonFiles/Godfrey/Famine/GodfreyFamineS.pdf

  Create a cause & effect web which demonstrates the cause and effect of the famine on Europe during this period.
  To learn more about cause and effect, read this article:
  www.literacyideas.com/teaching-cause-effect-in-english

- Read about the Peasants' Revolt, then create an illustration (like the painting in the article) of what happened. **Answer**: What were the storm and long-term effects of the revolt?
  https://www.bbc.co.uk/bitesize/topics/z93txbk/articles/zyb77yc#:~:text

- Read about the Great Schism. Then, create a Venn diagram comparing and contrasting the Greek Orthodox church and the Roman Catholic church.
  https://education.nationalgeographic.org/resource/great-schism/
  To help make your diagram, use this website:
  https://www.saintjohnchurch.org/differences-between-orthodox-and-catholic/

- Learn about the "Little Ice Age" and a period known as "the Crisis" using the following resources. Write an essay explaining the term and how this cooling period influenced Europe, the Middle Ages, and the development of the Modern Era:

  Websites:
  o science.smith.edu/climatelit/the-effects-of-the-little-ice-age/
  o nationalgeographic.com/history/article/111003-science-climate-change-little-ice-age

  Youtube:
  The 17th Century Crisis: Crash Course European History #11

- Read about the Late Middle Ages from this document created by a professor at the University of Pennsylvania. Then, answer the questions below:
  http://facstaff.bloomu.edu/mhickey/late_middle_ages.htm

  1. Describe the crises which impacted the Late Middle Ages.
  2. Explain the role and consequences of epizootics between 1300-1320.
  3. How did the Plague enter Europe? What was the result?
  4. Define the Hundred Years' War in your own words.
  5. Explain how famine, disease, and war affected the urban economy.
  6. What caused peasant uprisings in France and England?
  7. Why might people blame God, or their own sin, for the series of crises during the Late Middle Ages?
  8. List the heresies and heretics mentioned in this article. Why were they a threat to the Catholic church?
  9. Define the Babylonian Captivity in your own words.
  10. Create a timeline of events between 1400-1450: how did the "demographic disasters of the 1300s" help "revive the agricultural economy"?
  11. What was the Conciliarist Controversy?
  12. Explain the War of the Roses in your own words.

Making Connections

The Late Middle Ages contained several tragic events which prompted the concept of humanism, especially during the Renaissance. Humanism in this period essentially caused people of this era to look inward (towards self, reason, human achievements, etc.) rather than to religion for answers. Historians differ on the "end" of the Middle Ages: some consider Christopher Columbus' travels to the New World during the Age of Exploration as the end, while others believe it was the Protestant Reformation (beginning in 1517). Still others claim that it was when the Eastern Roman Empire (the Byzantine Empire) fell to the Ottomans in 1453. The important thing to know about the Late Middle Ages isn't the exact end date, but that the traumatic events led to a questioning of papal authority and a burst of new ideas (Renaissance) and personal beliefs about God, the Bible, and salvation (the Reformation).

Lesson 8: The Renaissance
(1300 AD - 1600)

Lesson 8: The Renaissance (1300 AD – 1600 AD)

Introduction

The Renaissance, beginning in Italy in the 14th Century, occurred during the Late Middle Ages. It emphasized humanism, but also (as Greek Christians fled the Muslims from Constantinople in 1453) Greek philosophy was introduced to European cities, spreading ideas through the newly invented printing press. Scientific interest stimulated new studies and theories, some of which conflicted with earlier ideas (which at the time were synonymous with accepted Christian theology). The spreading of ideas and information helped to stir the social, cultural, and religious waters which would later cause the Protestant Reformation.

Additional notes

There are several instances in this curriculum guide which occur at the same time, and this event is one of those times. The Renaissance, Reformation, Age of Exploration, and American colonial period overlap during the years 1300-1600.

Questions to Ask

1. What were the causes of the Renaissance?
2. Why did it begin in Italy instead of another nation?
3. What role did the Renaissance have on the power and influence of the church (and vice versa)?
4. What ideas, philosophies, and values were a direct result of the Renaissance, and what was the legacy of these?

Primary Sources

- Perseus Collection: Renaissance Materials:
  https://www.perseus.tufts.edu/hopper/collection?collection=Perseus:collection:Renaissance

- Internet Medieval Sourcebook: Renaissance (Fordham University):
  https://sourcebooks.fordham.edu/sbook.asp

General Spines, Series, and Reference Books

The Renaissance for Kids (Fet)
The Renaissance Thinkers (Taylor)
The Renaissance Inventors (Klepeis)
The Renaissance Artists (Taylor)
Essential History of Art (Payne)

Web resources

- Britannica: https://www.britannica.com/event/Renaissance

- Study: https://study.com/academy/topic/the-renaissance.html

- History Channel: https://www.history.com/topics/renaissance/renaissance

- Khan Academy: https://www.khanacademy.org/humanities/whp-origins/era-5-the-first-global-age/52-old-world-webs-betaa/a/read-renaissance

YouTube videos

Elementary

- Adventure into the Renaissance: History for Kids (Smile and Learn English)

- The Renaissance: World Ahoy 1x22 (World Ahoy)

- Exploring the Renaissance (Nationalgalleryie)

- Leonardo da Vinci for Children: Biography for Kids (Free School)

Middle

- The Renaissance: The Age of Michelangelo and Leonardo da Vinci (DW Documentary: parts ½ and 2/2)

- The Renaissance Period Explained: All You Need to Know (Captivating History)

- The Tudors Explained in 13 Minutes (Captivating History)

High
- All About the Renaissance (Full Program) (Chris Gorski)

Crash Course:
- The Renaissance: Was it a Thing? -Crash Course World History #22

- Florence and the Renaissance: Crash Course European History #2

- The Northern Renaissance: Crash Course European History #3

Tom Richey:
- The Italian Renaissance (AP Euro Review)

- Renaissance Art (AP Euro Review)

- Headbanger Humanism (August Burns Red and the Renaissance)

- The Book of the Courtier (Castiglione's Guide for the Renaissance Man)

- The Northern Renaissance (AP Euro Review)

- Italian Renaissance vs. Northern Renaissance (AP European History)

- AP Euro Review Live Hangout #1 (Renaissance & Reformation)

Fiction & Nonfiction Books

Title	Author	Age	Period
Every Day Life in Ottoman Turkey	Lewis	12+	1299

Everyday Life in the Renaissance	Hinds	11+	1300+
Renaissance: Eyewitness Books	Langley	8+	1300+
Life and Times: Leonardo and the Renaissance	Harris	8+	1452
Your Travel Guide to Renaissance Europe	Day	9+	1300+
Gutenberg's Gift	Willard	7+	1393
Johann and the Printing Press	Smith	9+	1393
Fine Print: Johann and the Printing Press	Burch	9+	1393
The Tudors: Kings, Queens, Scribes, and Ferretts	Williams	8+	1485+
The Tudors: A Very Peculiar History	Pipe	8+	1485+
Tudor and Stuart Life	Guy	9+	1500s-1600s
Henry VIII: Royal Beheader	Price	11+	1509
You Wouldn't Want to Sail in the Spanish Armada!	Malam	8+	1558
Royal Diaries: Elizabeth 1	Lasky	10+	1558
A Stage Full of Shakespeare Stories	McAllister	6+	1649
Poetry for Kids: William Shakespeare	Tassi	8+	1618
Thirty Years' War: A History from Beginning to End	Hourly History	12+	1618

Terms to Know

1. <u>humanism</u>: an intellectual movement typified by a revived interest in the classical world and studies which focused not on religion but on what it is to be human[36]

2. <u>printing press</u>: a machine for printing text or pictures from type or plates.

3. <u>realism</u>: to paint and sculpt subjects realistically to give them more emotion

---

[36] Worldhistory.org

4. <u>naturalism</u> (in art): a true-to-life style which involves the representation or depiction of nature (including people)[37]

5. <u>Renaissance</u>: the revival of art and literature under the influence of classical models in the 14th–16th centuries.

Areas to Know

- Florence
- Venice
- Milan
- Bologna
- Ferrara

People to Know

- Medici family
- Leonardo da Vinci
- Desiderius Erasmus
- Rene Descartes
- Galileo
- Nicolaus Copernicus
- Thomas Hobbes
- Geoffrey Chaucer
- Petrarch
- Dante
- Niccolo Machiavelli
- Titian
- William Byrd
- John Milton
- William Shakespeare
- Bonatello
- Sandro Botticelli
- Raphael
- Michelangelo

---

[37] Visual Arts Cork

- Filippo Brunellschi

Enrichment Activities

General Enrichment Ideas:

- <u>Letters from the Past</u>: write a letter during each lesson from the perspective of a person living during that time period. Be sure to include the date, mention anything historically relevant, and try to understand the perspective of the person in which you're writing. Keep the letters in a folder or binder.
- <u>Book of Eras</u>: Create a timeline for each lesson, illustrating key people and events, and writing the dates chronologically. When the year is over, you have a whole history book you created yourself!
- <u>Book of Bios</u>: Focus specifically on the people you've learned about this year. Create a bio for one or more important people from each lesson and think of creative ways to document their lives and roles in the past. (Ex: create a social media "profile" for each person, or a text/conversation between two or more people.)
- <u>A Taste of History</u>: For each lesson or time period, research a recipe from that era and write it on a notecard. Save your recipes in a recipe box and cook your way through the past. Another idea is to keep a blog or YouTube channel documenting each recipe, how it was typically prepared (comparing/contrasting it to modern day methods), and any other historical tidbit you find interesting.
- <u>Travel Thru History</u>: For each lesson, create a travel brochure depicting important areas of interest in the area. (It can be funny or serious.)
- <u>Diorama</u>: Choose one (or more) period to illustrate with a diorama.
- <u>Fashion through the Ages</u>: Design a fashion magazine using what you've learned about each era's dress and style.

Specific to this lesson:

- Use the following website to learn about the most influential people of the Renaissance. Then, create an "artist study" of someone who interests you on a poster. Include: a short biography, their most important works, their immediate impact on society, and their lasting impact on Western civilization: https://kids.kiddle.co/Renaissance

- Using the same link as above, write a 1-page essay on the subject on humanism. Include: a definition of humanism, where the idea came from during this period, it's relationship with Christianity and the church at the time, and any ways in which humanism influenced the arts and sciences during the Renaissance.

- Read the following article on the importance of Gutenberg's printing press upon the rest of the world. Answer: How did the printing press impact news and the way in which information was transmitted? How did it "help" the cause of the Renaissance? https://www.history.com/news/printing-press-renaissance

- Using this article from Nomad Press, create a Styrofoam printing project: https://nomadpress.net/wp-content/uploads/2018/02/REN-Inventors_Project.pdf

- Visit the following website. Read the summary, and the create a piece of art similar to the styles of one of the artists listed: https://www.ducksters.com/history/renaissance.php

- Watch the Youtube video, Going Back In Time To Work In The Tudor Era | Tudor Monastery (by Absolute History). What was life like for workers in the Tudor Era? What role did the church play in everyday life? (Create a reenactment video, either funny or serious, using highlights of the video above.)

Making Connections

Think of the Renaissance as a springboard for the Reformation and the Enlightenment. It fostered a renewed interest in education and literacy (including reading the Bible), and as a result, caused an intellectual movement. Humanism placed mankind in a more central place, questioning the supreme authority of the Roman Catholic church. The Reformation helped further individualism along through its emphasis on personal salvation (possible outside the church). Later, the emphasis on knowledge, humanism, and new discoveries about science would build the foundation of the Enlightenment. For more information on how these subjects are intertwined, visit: https://byjusexamprep.com/upsc-exam/difference-between-renaissance-and-enlightenment

Lesson 9: The Reformation
(1517 AD – 1648 AD)

Lesson 9: The Reformation (1517 AD – 1648 AD)

Introduction

The Reformation officially began in 1517 with a German priest and professor, Martin Luther (however, there was an earlier proto-Reformation which argued many of the same points as later reformers). Reformers found fault with the Roman Catholic Church for a variety of theological reasons and used the printing press to air their grievances. The Protestant Reformation launched what would eventually become hundreds of different Christian denominations around the world, and also allowed for King Henry VIII to split from the Roman Catholic Church.

Questions to Ask

1. Did the Renaissance inspire or influence the Reformation? If so, how?
2. What were the reasons for the Protestant Reformation?
3. In which ways did the Reformers find "success" in their reforms?
4. How did the Roman Catholic church react to the Reformation and its aftermath?
5. What are some long-lasting impacts of the Reformation?

Primary Sources

- Project Wittenberg: https://www.projectwittenberg.org/

- Reformation Europe (Fordham University): https://sourcebooks.fordham.edu/mod/modsbook02.asp

- Europe: Religious Reformation: https://eudocs.lib.byu.edu/index.php/Europe:_Religious_Reformation

- The Council of Trent and Catholic Reformation: https://college.cengage.com/history/world/resources/students/primary/trent.htm

General Spines, Series, and Reference Books

Church History (Carr)
Stories of the Reformation in Germany and England (Johns)
History of the Reformation of the 16th Century (D'Aubigne) (free download)[38]

Documentaries/movies

Luther (2003, 13+)
God's Outlaw: The Story of William Tyndale (NR)

Web resources

- History Channel: https://www.history.com/topics/religion/reformation

- MTSU: https://www.mtsu.edu/first-amendment/article/1064/protestant-reformation

- British Library: https://www.bl.uk/sacred-texts/articles/henry-viii-and-the-reformation

- Britannica: https://www.britannica.com/event/Counter-Reformation

- New World Encyclopedia: https://www.newworldencyclopedia.org/entry/Calvinism

YouTube videos

Elementary

- A Fun, Animated History of the Reformation and the Man Who Started it All (National Geographic)

- The Torchlighters: The Martin Luther Story (2016) Episode 15 (Vision Video)

---

[38] Free download: https://www.monergism.com/history-reformation-sixteenth-century-ebook

Middle

- The Protestant Reformation explained (Explainity Channel)

- Basic Protestant Christian Beliefs (Ready to Harvest)

- Why Did the Reformation Actually Happen? (Knowledgia)

- Reformation (Mr. Byrd)

- Introduction to the Protestant Reformation: Martin Luther (Smarthistory)
  (Note: There are 4 videos in this series.)

- Martin Luther Special Feature-Drive Thru History (Drive Thru History with Dave Stotts)

High

Ryan Reeves:

- Martin Luther and the 95 Theses

- Ignatius Loyala and the Catholic Reformation

Crash Course:

- Luther and the Protestant Reformation: Crash Course World History #218

- The Protestant Reformation: Crash Course European History #6

- Reformation and Consequences: Crash Course European History #7

Tom Richey:

- Calvinism (Introduction to John Calvin's Reformed Theology)

- The English Reformation (Henry VIII and the Church of England)

- Free Will and the Reformation

(Compare the following two views of the Reformation)

- Luther: The Life and Legacy of the German Reformer (Ligonier Ministries)
- Was Martin Luther Right? Catholic Perspective on Protestant Reformation (Augustine Institute: Catholic Church Explained)

Fiction & Nonfiction Books

Title	Author	Age	Period
Morningstar of the Reformation	Thomson	12+	1328
For God and His People	D'Aubigne	16+	1328+
Heralds of the Reformation	Hannula	12+	1328+
Reformation Heroes	Kleyn	10+	1328+
Characters of the Reformation	Belloc	10+	1328+
Martin Luther: A Man Who Changed the World	Maier	8+	1483
The Life of Martin Luther	Traini	4+	1483
The Hawk That Dare Not Hunt by Day	O'Dell	12+	1483+
John Calvin	(Carr)	7+	1509
John Knox	(Carr)	8+	1514

Terms to Know

1. Reformation: a 16th-century movement for the reform of abuses in the Roman Catholic Church ending in the establishment of the Reformed and Protestant Churches.

2. doctrine: a belief or set of beliefs held and taught by a Church, political party, or other group.

3. indulgence: (in the Roman Catholic Church) a grant by the Pope of remission of the temporal punishment in purgatory still due for sins after absolution.

The unrestricted sale of indulgences by pardoners was a widespread abuse during the later Middle Ages.

4. pilgrim: a person who journeys to a sacred place for religious reasons.

5. Protestant: a member or follower of any of the Western Christian churches that are separate from the Roman Catholic Church and follow the principles of the Reformation, including the Baptist, Presbyterian, and Lutheran churches.

6. reform: make changes in (something, typically a social, political, or economic institution or practice) in order to improve it.

7. separatist: a person who supports the separation of a particular group of people from a larger body on the basis of ethnicity, religion, or gender.

8. anabaptist: "re-baptizer"; a belief in adult baptism during the Reformation, at a time when most people baptized infants

9. annulment: a declaration by a Church tribunal (a Catholic Church court) that a marriage thought to be valid according to Church law actually fell short of at least one of the essential elements required for a binding union[39]

10. Puritan: a member of a group of English Protestants of the late 16th and 17th centuries who regarded the Reformation of the Church of England under Elizabeth as incomplete and sought to simplify and regulate forms of worship.

11. Church of England: the official church of England, created by King Henry VIII after his split from the Roman Catholic Church in 1534

12. denomination: a recognized autonomous branch of the Christian Church.

13. papal: relating to a pope or to the papacy.

14. Counter-Reformation: efforts in the 16th and early 17th centuries to oppose the Protestant Reformation and reform the Catholic church.[40]

15. Inquisition: an ecclesiastical tribunal established by Pope Gregory IX c. 1232 for the suppression of heresy. It was active chiefly in northern Italy and

---

[39] www.USCCB.org
[40] Britannica

southern France, becoming notorious for the use of torture. In 1542 the papal Inquisition was re-established to combat Protestantism, eventually becoming an organ of papal government.[41]

16. <u>Diet of Worms</u>: meeting of the Diet (assembly) of the Holy Roman Empire held at Worms, Germany, in 1521, made famous by Martin Luther's appearance before it to respond to charges of heresy.[42]

17. <u>95 Theses</u>: the theses of Luther against the sale of indulgences in the Roman Catholic Church, posted by him on the door of a church in Wittenberg, October 31, 1517.[43]

18. <u>excommunication</u>: the action of officially excluding someone from participation in the sacraments and services of the Christian Church.

19. <u>Swiss Reformation</u>: a reformation movement which emerged in Switzerland around the same time as Luther's in Germany; it was led by John Calvin and Huldrych Zwingli

20. <u>Council of Trent</u>: (1545-1563) was a meeting of Catholic clerics convened by Pope Paul III (served 1534-1549) in response to the Protestant Reformation; launched the Catholic Counter-Reformation[44]

21. <u>purgatory</u>: (in Roman Catholic doctrine) a place or state of suffering inhabited by the souls of sinners who are expiating their sins before going to heaven.

Areas to Know

- Wittenberg
- Geneva

---

[41] Ibid.

[42] Ibid.

[43] www.Dictionary.com

[44] www.Worldhistory.org

People to Know

- Martin Luther
- John Calvin
- Huldrych Zwingli
- Henry VIII
- Friedrich the Wise, elector of Saxony

Enrichment Activities
General Enrichment Ideas:

- Letters from the Past: write a letter during each lesson from the perspective of a person living during that time period. Be sure to include the date, mention anything historically relevant, and try to understand the perspective of the person in which you're writing. Keep the letters in a folder or binder.
- Book of Eras: Create a timeline for each lesson, illustrating key people and events, and writing the dates chronologically. When the year is over, you have a whole history book you created yourself!
- Book of Bios: Focus specifically on the people you've learned about this year. Create a bio for one or more important people from each lesson and think of creative ways to document their lives and roles in the past. (Ex: create a social media "profile" for each person, or a text/conversation between two or more people.)
- A Taste of History: For each lesson or time period, research a recipe from that era and write it on a notecard. Save your recipes in a recipe box and cook your way through the past. Another idea is to keep a blog or YouTube channel documenting each recipe, how it was typically prepared (comparing/contrasting it to modern day methods), and any other historical tidbit you find interesting.
- Travel Thru History: For each lesson, create a travel brochure depicting important areas of interest in the area. (It can be funny or serious.)
- Diorama: Choose one (or more) period to illustrate with a diorama.
- Fashion through the Ages: Design a fashion magazine using what you've learned about each era's dress and style.

Specific to this lesson:

- Read the following web article. Then, create a timeline of the main events of the Reformation:
  https://education.nationalgeographic.org/resource/protestant-reformation/

- Learn about the leaders of the Protestant Reformation. **Answer**: How was the Swiss Reformation different than the one which took place in Germany? Explain the differences between these leaders. Then, write a letter from the perspective of one of these men to another, agreeing or disagreeing with their ideas.
  1. https://kids.britannica.com/kids/article/Huldrych-Zwingli/627267
  2. https://kids.britannica.com/kids/article/Luther-Martin/353401
  3. https://kids.britannica.com/kids/article/John-Calvin/352901

- The Reformation is still very important to Christians today, and theology found in modern Protestant denominations are still hotly debated. Whether you're a person of faith or not, it's interesting to study how and why these issues are so important to Christians. For older students, consider exploring theological differences between Calvinism and other Protestant views. These two systems of theology "attempt to explain the relationship between God's sovereignty and man's responsibility". Watch the following videos and offer a debate in video form or in a persuasive essay.
  Calvinism vs. Arminianism- which view is correct?
  The Heart of the Calvinist-Arminian Divide (Desiring God)
  The BEST Argument Against Calvinism w/Dr. Braxton Hunter
  Lutheran, Reformed, Methodist & Baptist: What's the Difference?
  Anglicans, Lutherans, Moravians and Reformed-What's the Difference?

Making Connections

The Renaissance championed the expression of the individual, and in a sense, the Reformation championed the idea of individual *salvation*—apart from an orthodox institution like the Roman Catholic or Greek Orthodox church. The invention of the printing press helped spread the messages of the reformers but also the translations of the Bible itself, creating divisions within the Christian world in regard to how it should be interpreted. Some historians believe the Enlightenment would not have been possible without the Reformation, stating that the concept that you can determine truth for yourself is the foundation of the Age of Reason and a catalyst for the American Revolution. [45] Regardless, the end of the Reformation resulted in a division of the European church, leading to religious wars, various denominations, and religious persecution which would eventually send English Separatists across the ocean on the Mayflower.

---

[45] https://hwpi.harvard.edu/files/pluralism/files/enlightenment_and_revolution_0.pdf

Lesson 10: Discovery and the New World

(1492 – 1600s)

Lesson 10: Discovery & the New World (1492 AD – 1600s)

Introduction

The Age of Discovery, known also as the Age of Exploration, started initially as a result of Western trade routes being no longer being safe to travel. Finding alternative routes to the East was necessary for European nations to continue trading, and this drove exploration efforts. Portugal and Spain were at the forefront of exploration efforts, and Portugal established a strong presence along the western coast of Africa. After Columbus sailed to the Caribbean, Spain and Portugal fought for control over South America and Mesoamerica, while other European nations began to explore North America. The European discovery and settlement of the New World meant a new way of life for Europeans, and a dramatic shift in life for indigenous people already living there.

Questions to Ask

1. How did the European discovery and settlement of the New World impact Europe?
2. What were the relationships between Europeans and indigenous people during this period? How did those relationships differ from region to region and nation to nation?
3. What is the Columbian exchange and why is it significant?
4. What was the lasting impact of the settlement of the Americas?
5. Which nations created colonies in the New World?
6. What was the relationship between European countries during this period?
7. Who were the Pilgrims?

Primary Sources

- Library of Congress: Religion and the Founding of the American Republic: https://www.loc.gov/exhibits/religion/

- Cornell University Witchcraft Collection: https://rmc.library.cornell.edu/witchcraftcoll/

- Plymouth Colony Archive Project:
- http://www.histarch.illinois.edu/plymouth/

- Early Americas Digital Archive:
  http://eada.lib.umd.edu/

- Salem Witch Trials Documentary Archive and Transcription Project:
  https://salem.lib.virginia.edu/home.html

General Spines, Series, and Reference Books

Land Ho! Fifty Glorious Years in the Age of Exploration (Parker)
Into the Unknown: How Great Explorers Found Their Way by Land, Sea, and Air (Ross)
What Was the Age of Exploration (Daly)
European Explorers for Kids (Fet)
See Inside: Exploration and Discovery (Usbourne)
Kids During the Age of Exploration (MacGregor)
The Colony Books (series by Kevin Cunningham)
The Story of North America's First Explorers (Burgan)
Did Christopher Columbus Really Discover America?: And Other Questions About the New World (Berne)
Early American History Primary Teacher Guide (Grades K-3) (Beautiful Feet) (Manor)
How it All Began!: The Creation and Expansion of British Colonies in America

Web resources

- Study.com:
  https://study.com/academy/lesson/age-of-exploration-lesson-for-kids.html?

- Britannica:
  www.britannica.com/topic/European-exploration/The-Age-of-Discovery

- History:
  https://www.history.com/topics/exploration/exploration-of-north-america
  www.history.com/topics/colonial-america

YouTube videos

Elementary

- The New World: European Age of Exploration in the Americas (Miacademy Learning Channel)

- Pilgrim Life with Scholastic News (Scholastic)

- The Wampanoag Way (Scholastic)

Middle

- European conquest of America - Summary on a Map (Geo History)

- The Jamestown Colony (The Daily Bellringer)

- Chapter 1 | The Pilgrims | American Experience | PBS

- The Fall of the Aztec Empire | Mankind: The Story of All of Us (S1, E7) (History)

High

- AP US History Study Guide: Period 1-1491- to 1607 (gilderlerhman)

Crash Course:

- The Age of Exploration: Crash Course European History #4

- Expansion and Consequences: Crash Course European History #5

- The Columbian Exchange: Crash Course World History #23

- The Spanish Empire, Silver, & Runaway Inflation: Crash Course World History #25

- The Columbian Exchange: Crash Course History of Science #16

Tom Richey:

- Pilgrims, Puritans, and Separatists

- Religious Freedom in Colonial New England (APUSH)

Fiction & Nonfiction Books

Title	Author	Age	Period
Leif Ericksson, Norwegian Explorer	Our People	9+	960[46]
Henry the Navigator: Prince of Portuguese Exploration	Ariganello	10+	1450s
Anaoana (Royal Diaries)	Danticat	9+	1490
In 1492	Marzollo	5+	1492
I, Columbus, My Journal	Roop	8+	1492
Isabella of Castile	Bridges	9+	1400s
Encounter	Yolen	6+	1492
The World in 1492	Fritz	12+	1492
Who Was Ponce de Leon?	Pollack	8+	1513
Magellan's World	Waldman	9+	1519
Who Was Ferdinand Magellan?	Kramer	8+	1519
The Sea King	Marrin	12+	1577
America: As Seen by its First Explorers	Bakeless	NA	1585+
The Discovery of the Americas	Maestro	6+	1585+
The First Book of Early Settlers	Rich	6+	1585+
The New Americans: Colonial Times 1620-1689	Maestro	6+	1585+
The Lost Colony of Roanoke	Fritz	7+	1585
Searching for Virginia Dare	Hudson	NA	1585
Roanoke: The Mystery of the Lost Colony	Miller	18+	1585
Jamestown	National Geographic Explorer! Collection	7+	1607

---

[46] The reason I placed Leif here rather than the Early Middle Ages is to acknowledge that there were explorers in North America before the 15th Century.

1607: A New Look at Jamestown	Lange	9+	1607
Elizabeth's Our Strange New Land (My America): Elizabeth's Jamestown Colony Diary	Hermes	7+	1607
Blood on the River: Jamestown 1607	Carbone	9+	1607
Poison in the Colony: Jamestown 1622	Carbone	8+	1622
Surviving Jamestown: The Adventures of Young Sam Collier	Karwoski	8+	1607
Mayflower 1620: A New Look at a Pilgrim Voyage	National Geographic	8+	1620
1621: A New Look at Thanksgiving	Grace	8+	1621
Almost Home: A Story Based on the Life of the Mayflower's Mary Chilton	Lawton	8+	1621
If You Sailed on the Mayflower	McGovern	6+	1620
Tattered Sails	Kay	3+	1620
P is for Pilgrim	Crane	6+	1620
Pilgrims of Plymouth	Goodman	8+	1621
Samual Eaton's Day	Waters	4+	1621
Sarah Morton's Day	Waters	4+	1621
Squanto, Friend of the Pilgrims	Bulla	7+	1621
Thanksgiving on Thursday	Osborne	7+	1621
Squanto's Journey: The Story of the First Thanksgiving	Bruchac	7+	1621
Three Young Pilgrims	Harness	7+	1621
John Winthrop, Oliver Cromwell, and the Land of Promise	Aronson	7+	1630
Shadows in the Glass House	McDonald	10+	1630
I Walk in Dread: The Diary of Deliverance, Witness to Salem Witch Trials	Fraustino	8+	1692
The Witch of Blackbird Pond	Speare	10+	1692
The Salem Witch Trials	Yolen	6+	1692

Terms to Know

1. <u>Treaty of Tordesillas</u>: New World into Spanish and Portuguese spheres of influence[47]

2. <u>Age of Exploration</u>: a period from 1400 to 1600 in which Europeans traveled the rest of the world in search of goods, raw materials, land, and trade partners.[48]

3. <u>quadrant</u>: an instrument used for taking angular measurements of altitude in astronomy and navigation, typically consisting of a graduated quarter circle and a sighting mechanism.

4. <u>cross-staff</u>: a navigational tool used to measure the angle between the horizon and a celestial body such as the sun or stars.[49]

5. <u>compass</u>: a navigational tool with a magnetic needle that points towards the magnetic north pole[50]

6. <u>caravel</u>: a small, fast Spanish or Portuguese sailing ship of the 15th–17th centuries.

7. <u>trading posts</u>: a store or small settlement established for trading, typically in a remote place.

8. <u>navigation</u>: the process or activity of accurately ascertaining one's position and planning and following a route.

9. <u>mutiny</u>: an open rebellion against the proper authorities, especially by soldiers or sailors against their officers.

10. <u>expedition</u>: a journey or voyage undertaken by a group of people with a particular purpose, especially that of exploration, scientific research, or war.

11. <u>colony</u>: a country or area under the full or partial political control of another country, typically a distant one, and occupied by settlers from that country.

---

[47] www.Britannica.com
[48] www.Cambridge.org
[49] www.Marinersmuseum.com
[50] Ibid.

Areas to Know

- Newfoundland
- Greenland
- Explored by Columbus: Bahamas (San Salvador), Cuba, Haiti, Puerto Rico, Virgin Islands, Jamaica, and Trinidad

People to Know

- Prince Henry the Navigator
- Pedro Alvares Cabral (discovered Brazil for Portugal)
- Christopher Columbus (1492-1504)
- Ferdinand and Isabella of Spain
- Amerigo Vespucci
- John Cabot (Newfoundland) 1497
- Juan Ponce de Leon (Florida in 1513)
- Vasco Nunez de Balboa (Isthmus of Panama/Pacific Ocean)
- Ferdinand Magellan (1519-1522)
- Hernan Cortes (Mexico/Aztec) 1519
- Giovanni da Verrazzano (Northwest Passage search 1524)
- Francisco Pizarro (Peru/Incan)1529
- Jacques Cartier (St Lawrence River 1534)
- Pedro de Mendoza (1535) Argentina
- Cabeza de Vaca (North American Southwest)
- Francisco Vasquez de Coronado (Southwest) 1539-1542
- Jean Ribault (St Johns River, FLA 1562)
- Sir Walter Raleigh (Newfoundland, Virginia) 1585
- Samuel de Champlain (Quebec, Port Royal, Nova Scotia, Cape Cod) 1608
- Henry Hudson (Hudson River to NY) 1609

Enrichment Activities

General Enrichment Ideas:

- Letters from the Past: write a letter during each lesson from the perspective of a person living during that time period. Be sure to include the date, mention anything historically relevant, and try to understand the perspective of the person in which you're writing. Keep the letters in a folder or binder.

- Book of Eras: Create a timeline for each lesson, illustrating key people and events, and writing the dates chronologically. When the year is over, you have a whole history book you created yourself!
- Book of Bios: Focus specifically on the people you've learned about this year. Create a bio for one or more important people from each lesson and think of creative ways to document their lives and roles in the past. (Ex: create a social media "profile" for each person, or a text/conversation between two or more people.)
- A Taste of History: For each lesson or time period, research a recipe from that era and write it on a notecard. Save your recipes in a recipe box and cook your way through the past. Another idea is to keep a blog or YouTube channel documenting each recipe, how it was typically prepared (comparing/contrasting it to modern day methods), and any other historical tidbit you find interesting.
- Travel Thru History: For each lesson, create a travel brochure depicting important areas of interest in the area. (It can be funny or serious.)
- Diorama: Choose one (or more) period to illustrate with a diorama.
- Fashion through the Ages: Design a fashion magazine using what you've learned about each era's dress and style.

Specific to this lesson:

- Create an Astrolabe from Uplifting Mayhem:
  https://www.upliftingmayhem.com/quadrant-used-for-early-navigation/

- Create a sailor's meal similar to that of the early explorers:
  https://adventuresinmommydom.org/sailors-food/

- Visit this website. Then, choose a person or subject and write a paper explaining the importance of this person/subject in the larger picture of exploration and discovery.
  https://www.history.com/topics/exploration

- Learn about how early explorers traveled using Portolan navigation:
  https://adventuresinmommydom.org/portolan-navigation/

- Play this printable Age of Exploration game:
  https://adventuresinmommydom.org/age-of-exploration-game/

- Review the theories about the "lost colony of Roanoke" and write a persuasive essay about which theory is most likely true:
  https://thriveingradefive.com/teaching-the-lost-colony-of-roanoke/

- Visit this blog for a free, downloadable unit study on the Jamestown settlement: https://blessmybudget.com/2018/08/12/complete-free-american-history-lesson/

- Visit one or all of the interactive (free) websites and "tour" Plymouth, the Mayflower, or the journey across the Atlantic in this article by Free Tech 4 Teachers: https://www.freetech4teachers.com/2012/11/touring-mayflower-and-daily-life-in.html

- Recreate any of these authentic dishes from the first Thanksgiving:
  www.delishably.com/holidays/colonial-thanksgiving

Making Connections

Although American history begins at this point for most of us today, there were already tribes of indigenous Americans living in North America during the Age of Discovery. Historians have grappled with the moral implications of European exploration and settlement in the New World for decades, and it is a particularly sensitive subject at the time of this writing. The most important thing to note is that the arrival of the Europeans meant the decline (either rapid or gradual) of the American Indian and launched a complex relationship between the descendants of both groups. The discovery and settlement of North America was conducted by different groups for varying reasons but eventually led to the identification of most colonists as being "British subjects".

Lesson 11: The First Americans
(14,000 BC – 1491 AD)

Lesson 11: The First Americans (14,000 BC – 1491 AD)

Introduction

Although the America's first settlers didn't enter the story of Western Civilization until the European explorers discovered them in the New World, it had been an old world to them. This lesson explores the paths of the indigenous people before the arrival of the Europeans.

Historians generally agree that the first Americans came either by the Bering Strait land bridge or by water travel from the Far East during the last ice age. Initially they began as small tribes hunting food, (gathering mainly along the western coast), they began to spread out as large land animals were hunted to extinction. General, broad cultures of indigenous people developed, followed by the evolution of tribes as we know them today. Much of what we know of the first Americans has been discovered through archeological evidence or first-hand accounts of European settlers and explorers, since written records did not exist in the Americas until that time. Major efforts have been made through the National Archives, Library of Congress, and the tribes themselves to keep their history alive, and many resources are available to learn about the proud, painful, and lasting legacy of the American Indians.

Questions to Ask

1. How did indigenous Americans arrive in the Americas?
2. What developments did the American Indians experience in the centuries leading to European settlement?
3. How did they adapt to their climate and region?
4. What were the political structures of tribes (generally speaking)?
5. What was the nature of Native American alliances and/or relationships with other tribes?

Primary Sources

National Archives: Published Primary Sources Relating to American Indians: https://www.archives.gov/research/native-americans/published-resources.html

- UC San Diego: Guide to Online Primary Sources: Native Americans: https://ucsd.libguides.com/primarysources/nativeamericans

- Sam Houston State University: U.S. History Primary Source Collections Online: https://shsulibraryguides.org/c.php?g=86715&p=558322

- Arctic Studies Center (Smithsonian): https://naturalhistory.si.edu/research/anthropology/programs/arctic-studies-center

- Mesoweb: Mesoamerican Culture: https://www.mesoweb.com/

- Primary Sources, US history: Native Americans (Lonestar College): https://kwlibguides.lonestar.edu/PrimarySources-History/nativeamericans

General Spines, Series, and Reference Books

National Geographic Kids: Encyclopedia of the American Indian
Series by Sonia Bleeker (series of native American tribes)
Charles River Editors book series (various tribes)

Web resources

- History: https://www.history.com/topics/native-american-history

- National Archives: https://www.archives.gov/news/topics/native-american-heritage-month

- GALE: https://www.gale.com/native-american-history

- EDSITEment!: American Indian History and Heritage: https://edsitement.neh.gov/teachers-guides/american-indian-history-and-heritage

- NIH Timeline: https://www.nlm.nih.gov/nativevoices/timeline/index.html

YouTube videos

Elementary

- Native American History for Kids | An insightful look into the history of the Native Americans (Learn Bright)

- Native Americans Before European Colonization (Miacademy Learning Channel)

Middle

- Pre-Columbian Civilizations playlist: Kings & Generals

- Lecture 2 Native Americans of Pennsylvania (HIH2016 A History of Pennsylvania):

- The First Southerners: Creeks and Cherokees in Early Georgia [Lecture]: Ingram Library (University of West Georgia)

- In Search of the First Americans: Museum of Natural and Cultural Archeology

- The Fall of the Aztec Empire | Mankind: The Story of All of Us (S1, E7) (History)[51]

High

- Native American Cultures (1491-1607) - (APUSH Period 1 / APUSH Chapter 1): Tom Richey

---

[51] This video was listed in a previous lesson, but it also would be valuable in this one.

- The Black Legend, Native Americans, and Spaniards: Crash Course US History #1: Crash Course

- Native American societies before contact | Period 1: 1491-1607 | AP US History: Khan Academy

- Ancient Civilizations of the Americas by Anna Guengerich 1.22.2015: Vanderbilt University

- An "Idiot's Guide" to the American Upper Paleolithic: The Archeological Conservancy

- The Gault Site and the Peopling of the Americas: The Archeological Conservancy

Fiction & Nonfiction Books

Title	Author	Age
A True Book: American Indians (The Navajo)	Cunningham	8+
A True Book: American Indians (The Wampanoag)	Cunningham	8+
A True Book: American Indians (the Iroquois)	Dolbear	8+
Many Nations	Goetzl	10+
A True Book: American Indians (The Inuit)	Cunningham	8+
Brown Paper School US Kids History: Book of the American Indians	Egger-Bovat	8+
Flaming Arrows	Steele	8+
Getting to Know the Native American Indian Tribes	Baby Professor	5+
Native American History for Kids	Gibson	9+

Native Americans	Kavin	9+
The Very First Americans	Ashrose	4+
If You Lived with the Iroquois	Levine	7+
Apache: American Indian Art and Culture	Kissok	9+
The Cherokee	Petra Press	7+
Indians of the Great Plains: Traditions, History, Legends, and Life	Sita	8+
Native Homes	Kalman	8+
The Navajo Nation	Pasqua	9+
North American Indian	Eyewitness Books	8+
The History of the American Indians	Adair	12+
The Indian Book	Childcraft Annual	10+
FOLK LORE/ LEGEND		
The Legend of Blue Jacket	Spradlin	5+
Children of the Earth and Sky	Krensky	8+
The Sea-Ringed World: Sacred Stories of the Americas	Esperon	8+
Native American Stories for Kids: 12 Traditional Stories from Indigenous Tribes Across North America	Weso	6+
Favorite Native American Indian Legends	Dover Children's Classics	8+
Native American Animal Stories	Bruchac III	7+
The Girl Who Helped Thunder	Bruchac	8+
The Legend of Mackinac Island	Wargin	6+
Brave Wolf and the Thunderbird	Crow	7+
Coyote and the Fire Stick	Goldin	4+
The Tree of Life	Guillain	4+
The Legend of the Old Man Mountain	Ortakales	8+
Dragonfly's Tale	Rodanas	4+

Terms to Know

1. <u>Adobe:</u> a kind of clay used as a building material, typically in the form of sun-dried bricks.

2. <u>tribe:</u> a social division in a traditional society consisting of families or communities linked by social, economic, religious, or blood ties, with a common culture and dialect, typically having a recognized leader.

3. <u>buckskin:</u> the skin of a male deer used for making shoes or clothes

4. <u>canoe:</u> a narrow, keelless boat with pointed ends, propelled by a paddle or paddles.

5. <u>cradleboard:</u> a board to which an infant is strapped, traditionally used by some North American Indian peoples.

6. <u>hogan:</u> a traditional Navajo hut of logs and earth.

7. <u>igloo:</u> a type of dome-shaped shelter built from blocks of solid snow, traditionally used by Innuits.

8. <u>chickee:</u> a rough, open structure consisting of palm or palmetto thatching on a log frame with a raised floor, adapted for beach use from the original Seminole design.

9. <u>potlatch:</u> (among North American Indian peoples of the northwest coast) an opulent ceremonial feast at which possessions are given away or destroyed to display wealth or enhance prestige.

10. <u>moccasins:</u> a soft leather slipper or shoe, strictly one without a separate heel, having the sole turned up on all sides and sewn to the upper in a simple gathered seam in a style originating among North American Indians.

11. <u>powwow:</u> a North American Indian ceremony involving feasting, singing, and dancing.

12. <u>pueblo:</u> a North American Indian settlement of the southwestern US, especially one consisting of multistoried adobe houses built by the Pueblo people.

13. <u>reservation</u>: an area of land set aside for occupation by North American Indians or Australian Aboriginal people.

14. <u>teepee</u>: a portable conical tent made of skins, cloth, or canvas on a frame of poles, used by North American Indians of the Plains and Great Lakes regions.

15. <u>wampum</u>: small cylindrical beads traditionally made by some North American Indian peoples from shells, strung together and worn as decoration or used as money.

16. <u>wigwam</u>: a hut or tent with a domed or conical roof made by fastening bark, hides, or reed mats over a framework of poles (as used traditionally by some North American Indian peoples).

Areas to Know

- Bering Strait
- General areas listed on this historical map:
  http://www.emersonkent.com/map_archive/united_states_indian_tribes.htm

People to Know

Native Americans in History: A History Book for Kids (Beason) 8+

Enrichment Activities

General Enrichment Ideas:

- <u>Letters from the Past</u>: write a letter during each lesson from the perspective of a person living during that time period. Be sure to include the date, mention anything historically relevant, and try to understand the perspective of the person in which you're writing. Keep the letters in a folder or binder.

- Book of Eras: Create a timeline for each lesson, illustrating key people and events, and writing the dates chronologically. When the year is over, you have a whole history book you created yourself!
- Book of Bios: Focus specifically on the people you've learned about this year. Create a bio for one or more important people from each lesson and think of creative ways to document their lives and roles in the past. (Ex: create a social media "profile" for each person, or a text/conversation between two or more people.)
- A Taste of History: For each lesson or time period, research a recipe from that era and write it on a notecard. Save your recipes in a recipe box and cook your way through the past. Another idea is to keep a blog or YouTube channel documenting each recipe, how it was typically prepared (comparing/contrasting it to modern day methods), and any other historical tidbit you find interesting.
- Travel Thru History: For each lesson, create a travel brochure depicting important areas of interest in the area. (It can be funny or serious.)
- Diorama: Choose one (or more) period to illustrate with a diorama.
- Fashion through the Ages: Design a fashion magazine using what you've learned about each era's dress and style.

Specific to this lesson:

- Learn about the different type of Native American traditional homes. Then, recreate your favorite one, or create an informative poster comparing the homes. https://study.com/learn/lesson/native-american-houses-buildings-types-facts.html

- Read the following web article and choose a craft from one of the 9 listed: https://artsycraftsymom.com/9-native-american-crafts-for-kids/

- Choose a Native American folktale story listed in this blog post. Then, create a comic strip of your favorite character: https://www.whatdowedoallday.com/native-american-folktales-for-kids/

- Design a North American map similar to the one in this article: https://mrsschmelzer.blogspot.com/2010/11/native-americans.html

- Use this NPR article & map to see where indigenous tribes used to live in pre-Columbian times:

- Learn about the Bering Strait land bridge:
  https://education.nationalgeographic.org/resource/bering-land-bridge/
  Then, use clay (or another medium) to simulate the land bridge in this blog
  post: http://spencespace.blogspot.com/2012/10/understanding-bering-strait-land-bridge.html

- Find a federally recognized Indian tribe using this US government database.
  Then, research the tribe of your choice. Find out the following:

  1. A brief history of the tribe: where did they come from? Did they split
     from another tribe in the past? Who were their enemies? Were they a
     part of a confederacy? Were they relocated from their original location
     by the US government?
  2. Current information from their website: how is their government set
     up (do they have elders, chiefs, etc.)? What's the current tribe
     population? What kind of struggles or challenges does the tribe face (if
     any), and what kinds of outreach or educational opportunities does the
     tribe offer (if any)?

Making Connections

Since the development of the academic discipline of history (around 1880 in the
United States), professional historians have placed Native Americans in various
areas of American history. To Consensus historians of the 1940s and 1950s, they
are sort of in the background, while New Left historians of the 1960s move them to
the front using "bottom up" history writing (a style of history writing which focuses
on everyday people, including women and marginalized groups). Studying
indigenous history is important for all Americans to truly understand what
European settlement and Westward Expansion meant for everyone involved.

Lesson 12: The American Colonies
(1585 – 1783 AD)

Lesson 12: The American Colonies (1585 – 1783)

Introduction

The American colonial period begins at the founding of the Roanoke settlement and ends at the end of the American Revolution. Although the colonial period encompasses French, Spanish, Dutch, and English colonies, the bulk of this lesson will focus on the English ones (even New York, which was originally New Netherland and founded by the Dutch). As people left Europe for the New World, the colonies grew. Certain colonies were known for religious toleration (such as Maryland and Pennsylvania), and others for their religious strictness (such as Massachusetts Bay). The colonial period saw major events such as the Salem Witch Trials, First Great Awakening, the French and Indian War, and of course, the coming American Revolution.

Questions to Ask

1. Why was each colony established? How did the intentions of the colonial founders impact the beliefs, behaviors, expectations, and governments of each colony?
2. What was life like for colonists? How did this differ between colonies?
3. Did the colonies have "relationships" with other colonies? (Trade, etc.)
4. Did certain groups migrate to established colony for a specific purpose?

Primary Sources

- JCB Archive of Early American Images:
  https://jcb.lunaimaging.com/luna/servlet/JCB~1~1

- The Avalon Project: 17th Century Documents:
  https://avalon.law.yale.edu/images/avalon_logo2.gif

- The Avalon Project: 18th Century Documents:
  https://avalon.law.yale.edu/subject_menus/18th.asp

- Colonial North America at Harvard Library:
  https://colonialnorthamerica.library.harvard.edu/spotlight/cna

General Spines, Series, and Reference Books

Child Life in Colonial Days (Earle)
A Visual Dictionary of a Colonial Community (Kalman)
The Thirteen British Colonies in the United States (Baby Professor)
Colonial America (Lassieur)
The English Colonies Before 1750: 13 Colonies for Kids
The Great Awakening: The Roots of Evangelical Christianity in Colonial America
(Kidd)[52]

Web resources

- History:
  https://www.history.com/topics/colonial-america

- National Geographic:
  https://education.nationalgeographic.org/resource/resource-library-society-and-culture-colonial-america/

- Library of Congress:
  https://www.loc.gov/classroom-materials/united-states-history-primary-source-timeline/colonial-settlement-1600-1763/

- Baruch College:
  https://guides.newman.baruch.cuny.edu/c.php?g=188261&p=1243339

---

[52] This book is suitable for adults who want to understand the First Great Awakening and its role in the development of the US.

YouTube videos

Elementary

- Colonial America: 3 Regions of Colonies - US History for Kids! (Miacademy)

- Colonial Times (1585 - 1776): Harmony Square

- 13 American Colonies | US History: Kids Academy

- Winters in Colonial America (Townsends)

- A Day in the Life of a Colonial Kid (Historic Bath State Historic Site)

- CW Kids Ask How did different kids fit into colonial America? (Colonial Williamsburg)

Middle

- America: The Story of Us: Rebels | Full Episode (S1, E1): History

- 13 Colonies: Comparing Regions New England, Middle, and Southern (Mr. Raymond's Social Studies Academy)

High

- AP US History Study Guide: Period 2-1607-1754 (Gilderlehrman)

- First Great Awakening: Ryan Reeves

Tom Richey:
- The Thirteen Colonies (Colonial America - US History EOC Review - USHC 1.1)

- Spanish Colonization of the Americas (New Spain / APUSH Period 1 / Colonial America)

- French Colonization of North America (New France Colonial America APUSH):

- New Netherland (Dutch Colonization - Colonial America) APUSH

- The Colonists, the Indians, and General Patton (APUSH Review)

- The Virginia Colony (APUSH Period 1 & 2 / Chapter 1 & 2)

- The Virginia Colony (Part 2: Indentured Servitude, Slavery, and the 1622 Massacre)

- Religious Freedom in Colonial New England (APUSH)

- Roger Williams: America's First Baptist (Religious Freedom in Colonial New England: Part II)

- Anne Hutchinson: Religious Dissenter (Religious Freedom in Colonial New England: Part III)

- The Pennsylvania Colony (Colonial America)

- First Great Awakening (APUSH - Need to Know)

- The American Enlightenment

Fiction & Nonfiction Books

Title	Author	Age	Period
A Kid's Life in Colonial America	Machajewski	8+	1585 – 1783
Enemy in the Fort	Buckley	9+	1585 – 1783
Homespun Sarah	Kay	4+	1585 – 1783
If You Lived in Williamsburg in Colonial Days	Brenner	7+	1585 – 1783

Standing in the Light: The Captive Diary of Catherine	Dear America Series	9+	1585 – 1783
Molly Banaky	McGill	4+	1585 – 1783
Colonial Days	King	8+	1585 – 1783
School in Colonial America	Thomas	4+	1585 – 1783
The Amazing Mr. Franklin (The Boy Who Read Everything)	Ashby	7+	1585 – 1783
Colonial America (How'd They Do That In)	Sherman	9+	1585 – 1783
Would I Survive Colonial Living?	Baby Professor	7+	1585 – 1783
The Southern Colonies: The First and Last of 13	Rodgers	9+	1585 – 1783
You Wouldn't Want to be and American Colonist!	Morely	8+	1585 – 1783
Ox-cart Man[53]	Hall	4+	1585 – 1783
Colonial Voices: Hear Them Speak	Winters	8+	1585 – 1783
A Horse's Tale: A Colonial Williamsburg Adventure	Lubner	3+	1585 – 1783
Our Colonial Year	Harness	5+	1585 – 1783
Hornbooks and Inkwells	Kay	5+	1585 – 1783
The Sign of the Beaver	Speare	9+	1585 – 1783
Fever 1793	Anderson	11+	1585 – 1783
Colonial Kids	Carlson	5+	1585 – 1783
Colonial Times Picture Book: An Alphabetical Journey Through Colonial America for Kids	Savage	7+	1585 – 1783

Terms to Know

1. charter colony: a colony, such as Virginia or Massachusetts, created by royal charter under the control of an individual, trading company, etc, and exempt from interference by the Crown.[54]

---

[53] Technically this book takes place in the early 19th Century, but it feels appropriate to place it here.
[54] Collins Dictionary

2. breeches: short trousers fastened just below the knee, now chiefly worn for riding a horse or as part of ceremonial dress.

3. doublet: a man's short close-fitting padded jacket, commonly worn from the 14th to the 17th century.

4. governor: British rule in the colonies was enforced by the colonial governor. He was usually appointed by the King, and he served as the chief law enforcement officer in the colony[55]

5. meetinghouse: a building where religious and sometimes public meetings take place.

6. Middle Colonies: Delaware, New Jersey, New York, Pennsylvania

7. musket: an infantryman's light gun with a long barrel, typically smooth-bored, muzzleloading, and fired from the shoulder.

8. New England: Connecticut, Massachusetts Bay, New Hampshire, Rhode Island

9. plantation: an estate on which crops such as coffee, sugar, and tobacco are cultivated by resident labor.

10. Puritans: a member of a group of English Protestants of the late 16th and 17th centuries who regarded the Reformation of the Church of England under Elizabeth as incomplete and sought to simplify and regulate forms of worship.

11. Pilgrims: one of the English colonists settling at Plymouth in 1620[56]

12. Quaker: a member of the Religious Society of Friends, a Christian movement founded by George Fox c. 1650 and devoted to peaceful principles. Central to the Quakers' belief is the doctrine of the "Inner Light," or sense of Christ's direct working in the soul. This has led them to reject both formal ministry and all set forms of worship.

13. Southern Colonies: Georgia, Maryland, North Carolina, South Carolina, Virginia

---

[55] https://www.digitalhistory.uh.edu/teachers/lesson_plans/pdfs/unit1_3.pdf
[56] Merriam-Webster

Areas to Know

- The original 13 colonies listed in this web article:
  https://www.ducksters.com/history/colonial_america/thirteen_colonies.php

People to Know

- John Smith (Virginia)
- John Mason and John Wheelwright (New Hampshire)
- George and Cecil Calvert (Maryland)
- Thomas Hooker (Connecticut)
- George Fox
- Roger Williams (Rhode Island)
- Peter Minuit (Delaware)
- William Penn (Quakers/Pennsylvania)
- James Oglethorpe (Georgia)
- Queen Elizabeth
- King Charles I
- King George II

Enrichment Activities

General Enrichment Ideas:

- Letters from the Past: write a letter during each lesson from the perspective of a person living during that time period. Be sure to include the date, mention anything historically relevant, and try to understand the perspective of the person in which you're writing. Keep the letters in a folder or binder.
- Book of Eras: Create a timeline for each lesson, illustrating key people and events, and writing the dates chronologically. When the year is over, you have a whole history book you created yourself!
- Book of Bios: Focus specifically on the people you've learned about this year. Create a bio for one or more important people from each lesson and think of creative ways to document their lives and roles in the past. (Ex:

create a social media "profile" for each person, or a text/conversation between two or more people.)

- A Taste of History: For each lesson or time period, research a recipe from that era and write it on a notecard. Save your recipes in a recipe box and cook your way through the past. Another idea is to keep a blog or YouTube channel documenting each recipe, how it was typically prepared (comparing/contrasting it to modern day methods), and any other historical tidbit you find interesting.
- Travel Thru History: For each lesson, create a travel brochure depicting important areas of interest in the area. (It can be funny or serious.)
- Diorama: Choose one (or more) period to illustrate with a diorama.
- Fashion through the Ages: Design a fashion magazine using what you've learned about each era's dress and style.

Specific to this lesson:

- Choose one game from this link by Education Possible:
  https://educationpossible.com/colonial-games-children/

- Create an ink and quill set with this blog post by There's Just One Mommy:
  https://theresjustonemommy.com/colonial-america-kids-activity-make-a-quill-and-ink/

- There were no cameras during the colonial period, and silhouettes were a common way to memorialize people. Make your own with this tutorial by Southern State of Mind:
  www.southernstateofmindblog.com/diy-silhouettes

- Read about the 13 colonies here:
  https://www.dkfindout.com/us/history/american-revolution/british-america-thirteen-colonies/ Then, Download and print this free 13 colonies worksheet:
  https://www.thecleverteacher.com/13-colonies-map-worksheet/

Making Connections

The colonial period reflects the diversity of the colonies and their inhabitants. Eventually these communities would become states of a new nation, but in the meantime, they developed unique social and religious cultures which impacted the US long after the American Revolution. For more on this, read:
sagepub.com/sites/default/files/upm-binaries/23122_Chapter_3.pdf

Lesson 13: The American Revolution (1775 - 1783 AD)

From Colonies to *country*

French & Indian War
1754-1763

Sugar Act
1764

Stamp Act
1765

1775
April: Shot heard 'round the world
(Lexington/Concord)
May: 2nd Continental Congress
June: Battle of Bunker Hill
July: Olive Brand Petition sent

Townshend Acts
1767

British troops arrive to enforce laws
1768

Boston Massacre
1770

1776
August: Battle of Long Island
December: Battle of Trenton

Boston Tea Party
1773

Intolerable Acts
1774

1777
September: British capture Philadelphia
October: Battle of Saratoga
November: Articles of Confederation
December: Winter at Valley Forge

Revolutionary War begins
1775

Declaration of Independence
July 4, 1776

1778
February: Treaty of Alliance with
France
June: British leave Philadelphia

1777

1778

1780   October: Battle of King's Mountain

1781   October: Cornwallis surrenders at Yorktown

1783   War ends with Treaty of Paris

1787   Federalist Papers written (1787-1788)

1788   Constitution ratified

1789   Washington becomes first president

1791   Bill of Rights ratified

 thehomeschoolhistorian

Lesson 13: The American Revolution (1775 - 1783)

Introduction

The war which began in 1775 had been brewing for over a decade, under growing resistance and resentment to the British crown. Having been largely independent already (in business, culture, and religion), the colonists also benefited from British protection from the French and native tribes: all this would change after the French and Indian War. Although the British won the war, wars are expensive; in addition to other perceived injustices, England decided to increase taxes upon the American colonists. Events such as the Boston Massacre, Boston Tea Party, and parliamentary legislation only fueled the rage between the crown and the colonists. In the years leading up to the Revolution, the Great Awakenings had the effect of making salvation a personal (not communal) experience: combined with Enlightenment ideas of natural law and personal liberty, these concepts melded to create a truly unique (and powerful) American spirit. The Patriots used the power of the pen (and the distribution efforts of the printing press) to spread the ideas of Revolution along the colonies. The American Revolution launched a period in history known as the Age of Revolutions, in which nations like France, Ireland, Haiti, Latin America, and other European nations began to challenge their individual governments.

Questions to Ask

1. What events led to the American Revolution?
2. Which people or groups were hesitant to fight a war with England, and why?
3. In what way did the American Revolution impact other countries during this period?

Primary Sources

- Digital Public Library of America: Primary Source Sets:
  https://dp.la/primary-source-sets

- Eyewitness to History: 17th Century:
  http://eyewitnesstohistory.com/17frm.htm

- French and Indian War Primary Sources:
  https://cnu.libguides.com/primarywars/frenchandindian

- The American Revolution and the New Nation
  (Library of Congress primary sources):
  https://loc.gov/rr/program/bib/ourdocs/newnation.html

- Founders Online: Archives.gov: https://founders.archives.gov/

- A Century of Lawmaking for a New Nation: 1774-1875:
  https://memory.loc.gov/ammem/amlaw/lawhome.html

  America 1775-1815 (Library of Congress):
  www.loc.gov/rr/program/bib/ourdocs/newnation.html

General Spines, Series, and Reference Books

Battle for a New Nation: Causes and Effects of the Revolutionary War (Radomski)
A Kid's Guide to the American Revolution (KidCaps)
American Revolution (Eyewitness Books)

Web resources

- History:
  https://www.history.com/topics/american-revolution

- Library of Congress:
  www.loc.gov/classroom-materials/united-states-history-primary-source-timeline/american-revolution-1763-1783

- National Museum of American History:
  https://americanhistory.si.edu/american-revolution

YouTube videos

Elementary

The American Revolution (History Heroes)

Liberty's Kids: American Revolution, Full Series (Liberty's Kids-Wild Brain)

Middle

History Channel:

- Washington Leads the Revolution | America: The Story of Us (S1, E2)

- Into the Wilderness | The Men Who Built America: Frontiersmen (S1, E1)

- Revolution Transforms the Globe | Mankind: The Story of All of Us

- American Revolutionary War - Timelines and Maps - Animated US History (History on Maps)

High

- AP US History Study Guide: Period 3-1754 to 1800 (Gilderlehrman)

Crash Course:

- The Seven Years War and the Great Awakening: Crash Course US History #5

- Tea, Taxes, and The American Revolution: Crash Course World History #28

Tom Richey:

- Parliament vs the Colonies (US History EOC Review - USHC 1.2)

- The French and Indian War as a Turning Point (APUSH Period 3)

- Parliament Taxes the Colonies (Sugar Act, Stamp Act, Townshend Acts)

- Road to Revolution (Boston Tea Party, Intolerable Acts, Lexington & Concord)

- The Declaration of Independence (Recited by Tom Richey in London)

- Treaty of Paris 1783 (American Revolutionary War)

- What is Enlightenment? (Immanuel Kant)

Fiction & Nonfiction Books

Title	Author	Age	Period
(Leading to the Revolution)			
Trouble in the Colonies (the Beginnings of the Revolution)	Baby Professor	7+	1760s
Struggle for a Continent: The French and Indian Wars	Maestro	6+	1689-1763
(The Revolution)			
A Rebel Among Redcoats: A Revolutionary War Novel	Gunderson	9+	1775-1783
A Revolutionary Field Trip	Katz	6+	1775-1783
America's Black Founders	Sanders	9+	1775-1783
Forge	Anderson	10+	1775-1783
George VS George	Schanzer	8+	1775-1783
Give Me Liberty	Freedman	7+	1775-1783
Guns for General Washington	Reit	10+	1775-1783
If You Were a Kid During the American Revolution	Mara	7+	1775-1783
In 1776	Marzollo	7+	1776
Johnny Tremain	Forbes	8+	1775-1783
Moon of Two Horses	Keehn	10+	1775-1783
My Brother Sam is Dead	Collier	10+	1775-1783
My Name is America: The Journal of William Thomas Emerson	Denenberg	9+	1775-1783
Paul Revere's Ride	Longfellow	NA	1775-1783

Redcoats and Petticoats	Kirkpatrick	6+	1775-1783
Revolutionary Friends: General George Washington and the Marquis de Lafayette	Castrovilla	8+	1775-1783
Revolutionary War on Wednesday	Magic Tree House	7+	1775-1783
Sam the Minuteman	Benchley	6+	1775-1783
The American Revolution	Bliven	8+	1775-1783
The Boston Tea Party	Freedman	7+	1773
The Crossing	Murphy	9+	1776
The Daily Life of Colonists During the Revolutionary War	Baby Professor	8+	1775-1783
The Declarations from A-Z	Johnson	6+	1776
The Declaration of Independence: The Words that Made America	Fink	2+	1776
The Liberty Tree	Penner	8+	1775-1783
The Life of a Soldier During the Revolutionary War	Baby Professor	7+	1775-1783
The Matchlock Gun	Edmonds	6+	1775-1783
The Revolutionary War Begins	Landau	8+	1775-1783
The Scarlet Stockings Spy	Noble	6+	1775-1783
The Treaty of Paris	Jedson	10+	1783
The Winter of Red Snow	Gregory	9+	1777-1778
This Country of Ours	Marshall	16+	1775-1783
Toliver's Secret	Brady	10+	1775-1783
Dangerous Crossing	Krensky	5+	1778

Terms to Know

1. Articles of Confederation: an agreement between the thirteen colonies to form a single government under the United States of America: it was replaced by the US Constitution.

2. bayonet: a blade that may be fixed to the muzzle of a rifle and used to stab an opponent in hand-to-hand fighting.

3. <u>Bill of Rights</u>: the first ten amendments to the US Constitution, ratified in 1791 and guaranteeing such rights as the freedoms of speech, assembly, and worship.

4. <u>Confederation</u>: an organization which consists of a number of parties or groups united in an alliance or league.

5. <u>Continental Congress</u>: An assembly of delegates from the thirteen colonies

6. <u>minutemen</u>: (in the period preceding and during the American Revolution) a member of a class of American militiamen who volunteered to be ready for service at a minute's notice.

7. <u>Declaration of Independence</u>: the founding document of the United States, was approved by the Continental Congress on July 4, 1776, and announced the separation of 13 North American British colonies from Great Britain. It explained why the Congress on July 2 "unanimously" (by the votes of 12 colonies, with New York abstaining) had resolved that "these United Colonies are, and of right ought to be Free and Independent States.[57]

8. <u>occupation</u>: the action, state, or period of occupying or being occupied by military force.

9. <u>"Shot heard 'round the world"</u>: The first shots fired at the 1775 Battle of Lexington and Concord, which marked the beginning of the American Revolution.[58]

10. <u>democracy</u>: a system of government by the whole population or all the eligible members of a state, typically through elected representatives.

11. <u>republic</u>: a state in which supreme power is held by the people and their elected representatives, and which has an elected or nominated president rather than a monarch.

12. <u>Hessians</u>: refers to the approximately 30,000 German troops hired by the British to help fight during the American Revolution.[59]

---

[57] Britannica
[58] The Free Dictionary
[59] www.MountVernon.org

13. Patriot: colonists who rebelled against British control during the American Revolution.[60]

14. Loyalist: a colonist of the American revolutionary period who supported the British cause.

15. monarchy: a form of government with a monarch at the head.

16. Red-coat: a British soldier (sometimes also called "lobsters")

17. revolution: a forcible overthrow of a government or social order, in favor of a new system.

18. Stamp Act: an act of the British Parliament in 1765 which imposed a stamp duty on newspapers and other legal documents.

Areas to Know

- Cowpens National Battlefield (South Carolina)
- Kings Mountain (South Carolina)
- Washington Crossing (Delaware river, PA)
- Bunker Hill (Massachusetts)
- Saratoga National Park (New York)
- Valley Forge (Pennsylvania)
- Yorktown, Virginia
- Minute Man National Historic Park (location of Lexington and Concord, Massachusetts)
- Philadelphia, PA

People to Know[61]

- George Washington
- John Adams
- Thomas Jefferson
- Samuel Adams

---

[60] https://americanexperience.si.edu/wp-content/uploads/2014/07/Loyalists-and-Patriots.pdf
[61] For more information on these key people, visit: https://guides.lib.jjay.cuny.edu/c.php?g=288395&p=1922291

- Patrick Henry
- John Hancock
- John Dickinson
- Light-Horse Harry Lee
- Paul Revere
- Nathan Hale
- John Paul Jones
- Ethan Allen
- Benjamin Franklin
- Alexander Hamilton
- James Madison
- John Jay
- Marquis de Lafayette
- Betsy Ross
- King George III
- Benedict Arnold
- General William Howe
- General John Burgoyne
- General Charles Cornwallis
- Thomas Paine

Enrichment Activities

General Enrichment Ideas:

- <u>Letters from the Past</u>: write a letter during each lesson from the perspective of a person living during that time period. Be sure to include the date, mention anything historically relevant, and try to understand the perspective of the person in which you're writing. Keep the letters in a folder or binder.
- <u>Book of Eras</u>: Create a timeline for each lesson, illustrating key people and events, and writing the dates chronologically. When the year is over, you have a whole history book you created yourself!
- <u>Book of Bios</u>: Focus specifically on the people you've learned about this year. Create a bio for one or more important people from each lesson and think of creative ways to document their lives and roles in the past. (Ex: create a social media "profile" for each person, or a text/conversation between two or more people.)
- <u>A Taste of History</u>: For each lesson or time period, research a recipe from that era and write it on a notecard. Save your recipes in a recipe box and

cook your way through the past. Another idea is to keep a blog or YouTube channel documenting each recipe, how it was typically prepared (comparing/contrasting it to modern day methods), and any other historical tidbit you find interesting.

- Travel Thru History: For each lesson, create a travel brochure depicting important areas of interest in the area. (It can be funny or serious.)
- Diorama: Choose one (or more) period to illustrate with a diorama.
- Fashion through the Ages: Design a fashion magazine using what you've learned about each era's dress and style.

Specific to this lesson:

- Read about the timeline of the American Revolution. Then illustrate your own timeline on a posterboard:
  nps.gov/subjects/americanrevolution/timeline.htm

- Watch this video from YouTube about the timeline of the American Revolution:
  American Revolutionary War - Timelines and Maps - Animated US History: History on Maps
  Then, download and print this free timeline activity:
  https://www.thecleverteacher.com/revolutionary-war-timeline-for-kids/

- Learn about the events which led to the Revolution here:
  https://www.ducksters.com/history/american_revolution/causes_revolutionary_war.php
  Then, visit this link to make a triarama:
  https://excellenceinteachingsocialstudies.blogspot.com/2013/10/social-studies-triarama.html

- Go on a virtual field trip to the Museum of the American Revolution and explore the website here: https://www.amrevmuseum.org/learn-and-explore/for-students-and-educators/beyond-the-battlefield-a-virtual-field-trip

- Launch this interactive experience from the Museum of the American Revolution: www.amrevmuseum.org/interactives/season-of-independence

- Learn about the American Revolution from the British perspective. Then, write a persuasive essay about your personal interpretation of the

Revolution. **Answer**: Were the colonists justified in declaring independence? What did the British fear would happen as a result of American independence? Were these fears justified?

www.battlefields.org/learn/articles/british-perspective-american-revolution

Youtube: King George III and the American Revolution (George Washington's Mount Vernon)

Making Connections

Following the American Revolution there was a period of uncertainty in which the Founding Fathers had to grapple with how the new nation would be managed. The Articles of Confederation was found to be insufficient for the new government, causing the writing of the Federalist Papers to encourage Americans to vote for the new Constitution. Another key economic change in the US was the end of mercantilism with England; this led to a boom in manufacturing and the economic growth of the states. For more on these changes, read:

https://courses.lumenlearning.com/suny-ushistory1ay/chapter/the-consequences-of-the-american-revolution/

Lesson 14: The New Nation
(1783 – 1812 AD)

Lesson 14: The New Nation (1783-1812)

Introduction

The Revolution was over, the United States was born, and changes were happening. The Constitution replaced the Articles of Confederation, the first President was inaugurated, political parties began to form, and under Thomas Jefferson, the size of the United States exploded through the Louisiana Purchase. Lewis and Clark's expedition uncovered new people, lands, plants and animals, and the fledging nation faced another war with Britain: The War of 1812.

Questions to Ask

1. What challenges did the United States face in the decades following the American Revolution?
2. How and why did political parties begin to take shape?
3. How did the Louisiana Purchase impact the United States?
4. What was the Northwest Ordinance of 1787 and the Land Ordinance of 1785, and how did these affect American citizens?
5. How did the Cherokee, Creek, and Choctaw tribes react to white encroachment in the Northwest Territory, and how did this impact American/Native relations?

US Presidents during this era

President	Vice President	Years
George Washington	John Adams	1789-1797
John Adams	Thomas Jefferson	1797-1801
Thomas Jefferson	Aaron Burr/George Clinton	1801-1809
James Madison	George Clinton	1809-1812

States Admitted to the Union (1783-1812)

Delaware	1787
Pennsylvania	1787

New Jersey	1787
Georgia	1788
Connecticut	1788
Massachusetts	1788
Maryland	1788
South Carolina	1788
New Hampshire	1788
Virginia	1788
New York	1788
North Carolina	1789
Rhode Island	1790
Vermont	1791
Kentucky	1792
Tennessee	1796
Ohio	1803
Louisiana	1812

Primary Sources

- Primary Sources: George Washington (Christopher Newport University): https://cnu.libguides.com/primarypresidents/georgewashington

- Primary Sources: John Adams (Christopher Newport University): https://cnu.libguides.com/primarypresidents/johnadams

- Thomas Jefferson: A Resource Guide (Library of Congress): https://guides.loc.gov/thomas-jefferson/digital-collections

- Primary Sources: James Madison (Christopher Newport University): https://cnu.libguides.com/primarypresidents/jamesmadison

- Bill of Rights Institute Primary Sources: https://www.billofrightsinstitute.org/primary-sources

General Spines, Series, and Reference Books

Our Nation's Documents (America Handbooks, a TIME for Kids Series)
The Louisiana Purchase: A History Just for Kids (Kid Caps)

US Growth and Change in the 19th Century (Howell)
The Big Book of Presidents (Hajewski)

Web resources

- Library of Congress: https://www.loc.gov/classroom-materials/united-states-history-primary-source-timeline/new-nation-1783-1815/overview/

- John Jay College: www.guides.lib.jjay.cuny.edu/c.php?g=288395&p=1922311

- American Revolution: The Aftermath: https://guides.lib.jjay.cuny.edu/c.php?g=288395&p=1922311

Suggested movies/documentaries

John Adams: HBO Miniseries

YouTube videos

Elementary

US Presidents playlist (History Heroes) *(Note: This series is good for rest of the lessons from this point)*

George Washington for Kids (Homeschool Pop)

Who Is George Washington? (Twinkl Teaching Resources)

Who Are the Founding Fathers? (Learn Bright)

History of the Star-Spangled Banner for Kids (Free School)

Middle

History:
- George Washington: From General to President | The Revolution (S1, E13)

- Native Americans Battle Pioneers | The Men Who Built America: Frontiersmen (S1, E2)

- America's Westward Expansion | America: The Story of Us (S1, E3)

- Battle for the Modern World | Mankind: The Story of All of Us (S1, E9)

High

- The American vs French Revolutions: John Anderson

- AP US History Study Guide: Period 4-1800 to 1848 (Gilderlehrman)

- The Federalist Papers Explained (AP US Government and Politics): Marco Learning

- George Washington: America's First President & the Birth of a Nation | Full Documentary: Biography

- APUSH Review: 1st and 2nd Great Awakening (Adam Norris)

Crash Course:
- The French Revolution: Crash Course World History #29

- Napoleon Bonaparte: Crash Course European History #22

- Thomas Jefferson & His Democracy: Crash Course US History #10

- The Constitution, the Articles, and Federalism: Crash Course US History #8

- Where US Politics Came From: Crash Course US History #9

Professor Dave Explains:
- John Adams: His Rotundity (1797 - 1801)

- James Madison: Father of the Constitution (1809 - 1817)

Tom Richey:

- George Washington's Foreign Policy (Neutrality, Citizen Genet, Jay Treaty, Pinckney's Treaty)

- The Adams Administration

- The Election of 1800

- Thomas Jefferson's Agrarian Vision (APUSH Review)

- Thomas Jefferson vs Alexander Hamilton (AP US History - APUSH Review

- The Anti-Federalists

- Jefferson and the Constitution: NOT Love at First Sight

- Jefferson, the Louisiana Purchase, and the Constitution

- James Madison: Father of the Constitution (1809 - 1817)

Fiction & Nonfiction Books

Title	Author	Age	Period
United States Civics: Articles of Confederation for Kids	Baby Professor	8+	1777
(Post-Revolutionary War)			
A More Perfect Union	Maestro	6+	1789
A New Kind of Government: Articles of Confederation to Constitution	Baby Professor	8+	1777-1789
Farmer George Plants a Nation	Thomas	7+	1732
If You Were There When They Signed the Constitution	Levy	6+	1789
Shh! We're Writing the Constitution	Fritz	8+	1789

Who Was George Washington?	Edwards	7+	1732
John Adams Speaks for Freedom	Hopkinson	6+	1735
The Revolutionary John Adams	Harness	7+	1735
John Adams: Independence Forever	Benge	9+	1735
(1800-1812)			
Who Was Alexander Hamilton?	Pollack	7+	1755-1804
Napoleon and the Napoleonic Wars	Marrin	13+	1800-1815
History for Kids: The Illustrated Life of Napoleon Bonaparte	Charles River Editors	7+	1769
Who Was Marie Antoinette?	Rau	8+	1755
Who Was Napoleon?	Gigliotti	8+	1769
In the Reign of Terror: A Story of the French Revolution	Henty	8+	1789-1799
The French Revolution: Terror and Triumph	Schwartz	10+	1789-1799
Who Was Thomas Jefferson?	Fradin	7+	1743
The Worst of Friends	Jermain	6+	1775
12 Incredible Facts About the Louisiana Purchase	Yasuda	8+	1803
A Picture Book of Lewis and Clark	Adler	4+	1804
Animals on the Trail with Lewis and Clark	Patent	10+	1804
Building an Empire: The Louisiana Purchase	Thompson	9+	1803
How We Crossed the West	Schabzer	5+	1804
Louisiana Purchase	Roop	7+	1803
Plants on the Trail with Lewis and Clark	Patent	10+	1804
Sacagawea of the Shoshone	Yim	9+	1804
Girl of the Shining Mountains: Sacagawea's Story	Roop	8+	1804
Sacajawea	Bruchac	12+	1804
Seaman's Journey: On the Trail with Lewis and Clark	Eubank	6+	1804

The Amazing Lewis and Clark Expedition	Johmann	8+	1804
Thomas Jefferson Builds a Library	Rosenstock	7+	1815
Thomas Jefferson: A Picture Book Biography	Giblin	8+	1743
Thomas Jefferson: President and Philosopher	Meacham	10+	1743
York's Adventures with Lewis and Clark	Blumberg	8+	1804
James Madison and the Making of the United States	Maloof	8+	1751

Terms to Know

1. Constitutional Convention of 1787: a formal meeting held in 1787 for the purpose of creating a constitution for the United States.[62]

2. Constitution: the basic written set of principles and precedents of federal government in the US, which came into operation in 1789 and has since been modified by twenty-seven amendments

3. Federalist Papers: The Federalist Papers were a series of eighty-five essays urging the citizens of New York to ratify the new United States Constitution.[63]

4. Democratic-Republican: an early 19th century American political party preferring strict interpretation of the constitution and emphasizing states' rights.[64]

5. Federalist: an early 19th Century American political party which favored a strong central government (led by Alexander Hamilton)

6. Shay's Rebellion: a 1786 attempt by western Massachusetts farmers to seize an armory and overthrow the government.

---

[62] Dictionary.com
[63] https://guides.loc.gov/federalist-papers
[64] Merriam-Webster

7. <u>Northwest Ordinance</u>: chartered a government for the Northwest Territory, provided a method for admitting new states to the Union from the territory, and listed a bill of rights guaranteed in the territory[65]

8. <u>Bill of Rights</u>: the first ten amendments to the US Constitution, ratified in 1791 and guaranteeing such rights as the freedoms of speech, assembly, and worship.

Areas to Know

- Mississippi River
- Rocky Mountains
- New Orleans
- Gulf of Mexico
- Minnesota
- North Dakota
- Montana
- Canada
- Appalachian Mountains
- Northwest Territory
- The area of the Louisiana Purchase as shown on this map: *docsteach.org/documents/document/map-louisiana-purchase*
- The general path taken by Lewis and Clark as shown on this interactive map: *gilderlehrman.org/history-resources/online-exhibitions/lewis-and-clark-expedition-interactive-map*

People to Know

- George Washington
- John Adams
- Thomas Jefferson
- James Madison
- John Jay
- Patrick Henry

---

[65] www.Archives.gov

- Meriwether Lewis
- William Clark
- Sacagawea

Enrichment Activities

General Enrichment Ideas:

- Letters from the Past: write a letter during each lesson from the perspective of a person living during that time period. Be sure to include the date, mention anything historically relevant, and try to understand the perspective of the person in which you're writing. Keep the letters in a folder or binder.
- Book of Eras: Create a timeline for each lesson, illustrating key people and events, and writing the dates chronologically. When the year is over, you have a whole history book you created yourself!
- Book of Bios: Focus specifically on the people you've learned about this year. Create a bio for one or more important people from each lesson and think of creative ways to document their lives and roles in the past. (Ex: create a social media "profile" for each person, or a text/conversation between two or more people.)
- A Taste of History: For each lesson or time period, research a recipe from that era and write it on a notecard. Save your recipes in a recipe box and cook your way through the past. Another idea is to keep a blog or YouTube channel documenting each recipe, how it was typically prepared (comparing/contrasting it to modern day methods), and any other historical tidbit you find interesting.
- Travel Thru History: For each lesson, create a travel brochure depicting important areas of interest in the area. (It can be funny or serious.)
- Diorama: Choose one (or more) period to illustrate with a diorama.
- Fashion through the Ages: Design a fashion magazine using what you've learned about each era's dress and style.

Specific to this lesson:

- Print this free one-sheet about the Louisiana Purchase. **Answer**: Why did Jefferson buy this land? List the potential challenges or problems the US might have faced in buying this territory: https://online.kidsdiscover.com/infographic/infographic-the-louisiana-purchase

- Download and print this free Lewis and Clark unit study (k-2): https://wholechildhomeschool.com/lewis-clark-primary/

- Read about the Louisiana Purchase with this free lesson plan by iCivics for 6th grade+ (create a free profile to sign in): https://www.icivics.org/teachers/lesson-plans/louisiana-purchase-1803

- Download and print this Westward Expansion map lesson (note: save it for future lessons this year, and color them in when you learn about each area): https://www.thecleverteacher.com/westward-expansion-free-lesson/

- Visit KidsKonnect.com to learn about how to teach about the Constitution Day for kids. Choose one or more activities: https://kidskonnect.com/articles/constitution-day-activities/

  Download this free We the Civics Kids PDF to learn more about the Bill of Rights: https://constitutioncenter.org/media/files/CK130001_CivicsKids-2013-PAGES-FNL-Lesson3.pdf

- Read this article about the difference between Federalists or Anti-Federalists. **Answer**: Would you have been a Federalist? Why or why not? https://billofrightsinstitute.org/would-you-have-been-a-federalist-or-an-anti-federalist

  (Parents: You can register for free at iCivics.org, and download this lesson about the Federalism debate: https://www.icivics.org/teachers/lesson-plans/federalists-anti-federalists)

- Watch the video, American Influence on the French Revolution (feat. Atun-Shei Films), from The Cynical Historian. Write a summary of the video, outlining the differences between these revolutions.

Making Connections

With the expansion of the United States came conflict with Native Americans as well as domestic conflict over the roles and powers of the government (something still debated today) which resulted in the growth of political parties. The issue of slavery became a more pressing issue during this era, setting a precedence for future conflicts surrounding abolition. The end of this period also saw the beginning of the Second Great Awakening, a religious revival between 1795-1835 which encouraged social reform and religious fervor.

Lesson 15: US Expansion & Reform (1812 - 1841 AD)

Lesson 15: US Expansion and Reform (1812 – 1841)

Introduction

At this point in the curriculum guide, certain aspects of American history will be intentionally introduced thematically. Although chronology is at the heart of Chronos, several things were happening at the same time, but they must be treated separately so they can be fully understood.

The War of 1812 (a war fought by the US against the British, ending in a sort of stalemate which was considered a victory by the Americans) helped to legitimize the US around the world. In the years following the War of 1812, there was rapid expansion happening, new states were being added to the Union, immigrants were still coming to the New World, political parties were deepening, slavery was a growing concern, and reform movements were launched from the Second Great Awakening. These reform movements created missionary and Bible societies, sought to improve public education, and offered strong support for temperance, women's rights, and other social issues.

Questions to Ask

1. What was the War of 1812 and how did it impact the international reputation of the United States?
2. What was the immediate effect of the end of the war?
3. How did the Second Great Awakening impact reform efforts?
4. What was Westward Expansion?
5. How did the Erie canal (and subsequent canals) impact the economy?
6. What was the Monroe Doctrine and how did it shape American foreign policy?
7. Who was Tecumseh and what was he trying to do? Was he successful?
8. How did the Missouri Compromise affect the issue of slavery?
9. What happened at the Alamo?
10. What was Manifest Destiny and what was its result?

US Presidents during this era

President	Vice President	Years
James Madison	Vacant/ Elbridge Gerry	1812-1817
James Monroe	Daniel D. Tompkins	1817-1825

John Quincy Adams	John C. Calhoun	1825-1829
Andrew Jackson	John C. Calhoun	1829-1832
Andrew Jackson	Martin Van Buren	1833-1837
Martin Van Buren	Richard M. Johnson	1837-1841
William Henry Harrison	John Tyler	1841

States Admitted to the Union

Louisiana	1812
Indiana	1816
Mississippi	1817
Illinois	1818
Alabama	1819
Maine	1820
Missouri	1821
Arkansas	1836
Michigan	1837

Primary Sources

- Primary Sources: James Monroe (Christopher Newport University): https://cnu.libguides.com/primarypresidents/jamesmonroe

- Primary Sources: John Quincy Adams (Christopher Newport University): https://cnu.libguides.com/primarypresidents/johnquincyadams

- Primary Sources: Andrew Jackson (Christopher Newport University): https://cnu.libguides.com/primarypresidents/andrewjackson

- Primary Sources: Martin Van Buren (Christopher Newport University): https://cnu.libguides.com/primarypresidents/martinvanburen

- Primary Sources: William Henry Harrison (CN University): https://cnu.libguides.com/primarypresidents/williamhenryharrison

- Primary Sources: Tecumseh (CN University): https://cnu.libguides.com/pspeoplenativeamericans/tecumseh

- Missouri Compromise (Archives.org): https://www.archives.gov/milestone-documents/missouri-compromise

- Texas Revolution (Digital Public Library of America): https://dp.la/primary-source-sets/texas-revolution

General Spines, Series, and Reference Books

The War of 1812: By the Dawn's Early Light - Social Studies Book for Kids (Schwartz)
A Companion to 19th-Century America / Edition 1 (Barney)[66]

Web resources

- History: https://www.history.com/topics/19th-century/war-of-1812

- Britannica: https://www.britannica.com/event/War-of-1812/Final-stages-of-the-war-and-the-aftermath

- Archives.gov (Monroe Doctrine): https://www.archives.gov/milestone-documents/monroe-doctrine

- US History.org: https://www.ushistory.org/us/22c.asp

- American History: The Market Revolution (Georgia Highlands College): https://getlibraryhelp.highlands.edu/c.php?g=677685&p=4779061

- Erie Canalway.org: https://eriecanalway.org/learn/history-culture

- DK Find Out? Steam Locomotives: https://www.dkfindout.com/us/transportation/history-trains/steam-locomotives/

Suggested movies/documentaries

Remember the Alamo (PBS)
God in America: Two: A New Eden (PBS)
Erie: The Canal That Made America (PBS)
The History Channel Presents: The War of 1812

---

[66] This reference book is suitable for adults and teens wanting a more "text" book of this period.

Henry Clay: The Missouri Compromise of 1820 to the Tariff Compromise of 1833 (Amazon)

Andrew Jackson (American Experience)

Ultimate Guide to the Presidents: episodes 1-2 (free with Amazon membership)

YouTube videos

Elementary

- If You Had Lived Then: America Around 1800 (Periscope Film)

- Liberty's Kids 127-The New Frontier

- **Any and all videos from the Youtube Channels:**

  @EarlyAmerican

  @frontierpatriot

Middle

History:

- Chief Tecumseh Leads War Against U.S. | The Men Who Built America: Frontiersmen (S1, E3)

- America Unearthed: Lost Secrets of the Alamo Revealed (S3, E1)

- The War for California | The Men Who Built America: Frontiersmen (S1, E4)

- What Happened at the Alamo? (American History Homeschool Curriculum)

- The History of the Alamo (Daily Bellringer)

High

- The Early Republic (1800-1848) (Khan Academy, play list)

Professor Dave Explains:

- James Monroe: Last Cocked Hat (1817 - 1825)

- John Quincy Adams: Like Father, Like Son (1825 - 1829)

- Andrew Jackson: Founder of the Democratic Party (1829 - 1837)

- Martin Van Buren: Best Mutton Chops Ever (1837 - 1841)

Tom Richey:
- The War of 1812

- The Missouri Compromise of 1820 (APUSH Review - Period 4)

- The Second Great Awakening

Crash Course:
- The War of 1812 - Crash Course US History #11

- The Market Revolution: Crash Course US History #12

- Age of Jackson: Crash Course US History #14

- 19th Century Reforms: Crash Course US History #15

Fiction & Nonfiction Books

Title	Author	Age	Period
A Picture Book of Dolley and James Madison	Adler	4+	1809-1817
Mr. Madison's War: Cause and Effects of the War of 1812	Radomski	8+	1809-1817
The Great Little Madison	Fritz	8+	1809-1817
Dolley Madison and the War of 1812	McNamee	12+	1812-1815
Famous People of the War of 1812	Johnson	10+	1812-1815
The Town That Fooled the British	Papp	6+	1812-1815

The War of 1812: By the Dawn's Early Light	Schwartz	8+	1812-1815
What Caused the War of 1812?	Isaacs	10+	1812-1815
Whispers of War	Dear Canada	8+	1812-1815
Francis Scott Key's Star-Spangled Banner	Kulling	5+	1812-1815
James Madison and the Making of the United States	Maloof	8+	1809-1817
Jeremy and the General	Ibbitson	12+	1812-1815
Jeremy's War: 1812	Ibbitson	10+	1815-1815
Tecumseh: Shawnee War Chief	Fleisher	8+	1763-1813
Tecumseh: Shooting Star of the Shawnee	Zimmerman	5+	1763-1813
James Monroe: 5th President	Venezia	6+	1817-1825
James Monroe	Old	10+	1817-1825
The Monroe Doctrine: The Birth of American Diplomacy	Hamilton	8+	1817-1825
Amazing Impossible Erie Canal	Harness	6+	1817-1825
Bluebird of Brockport	Winters	13+	1817-1825
The Erie Canal	Spier	8+	1817-1825
Building the Erie Canal	Thompson	9+	1817-1825
John Quincy Adams	Walker	8+	1825-1829
The Missouri Compromise: We the People	Burgan	9+	1820
The Missouri Compromise and Its Effects	Baby Professor	9+	1820
Who Let Muddy Boots into the White House?	Quakenbush	9+	1829-1837
Who Was Andrew Jackson?	Yacka	8+	1829-1837
Old Hickory: Andrew Jackson and the American People	Marrin	10+	1829-1837
What Was the Alamo?	Belviso	8+	1836
Susanna of the Alamo	Jakes	6+	1836
The Alamo Cat	Kerr	8+	1836
The Alamo from A to Z	Chemarka	8+	1836
Who Was Davey Crockett?	Herman	8+	1786-1863
Davey Crockett: A Life on the Frontier	Krensky	6+	1786-1863

Martin Van Buren	Jankowski	9+	1837-1841
Martin Van Buren: 8th President of the United States	Rumsch	7+	1837-1841

Terms to Know

1. Second Great Awakening: a Protestant revival which swept the United States between 1795 and 1835 and launched a series of reforms (abolition, rights to education, voting rights, prison reform, temperance[67]

2. abolition: the action or an act of abolishing a system, practice, or institution.

3. temperance: abstinence from alcoholic drink.

4. Erie Canal: a historic American waterway built from Albany to Buffalo between 1817-1825

5. Missouri Compromise: legislation admitted Missouri as a slave state and Maine as a non-slave state at the same time, so as not to upset the balance between slave and free states in the nation. It also outlawed slavery above the 36° 30' latitude line in the remainder of the Louisiana Territory.[68]

6. steam locomotive: steam-powered locomotives invented in the early 1800s which pulled freight and eventually people

7. Battle of the Alamo: a battle during Texas' war for independence from Mexico; it lasted thirteen days

8. The Texas Revolution: also known as the War of Texas Independence in which American and Mexican colonists fought the Mexican army between 1835-1836 and resulted in the Republic of Texas (1836-1845)[69]

9. The Great Famine: a famine caused by a fungus which killed Ireland's potato crops, leading to 1.5 million Irish immigrants coming to the United States between 1845-1855[70]

---

[67] https://apprend.io/apush/period-6/2nd-great-awakening
[68] https://www.archives.gov/milestone-documents/missouri-compromise
[69] https://www.britannica.com/topic/Texas-Revolution
[70] https://www.archives.gov/publications/prologue/2017/winter/irish-births

Areas to Know

- location of the Erie Canal
- location of the Alamo near San Antonio
- a relative understanding of the US during this era:
  http://www.emersonkent.com/map_archive/united_states_1815_1845.htm

People to Know

- Davey Crockett
- Sam Houston
- General Antonio de Santa Anna
- Lucretia Mott
- Elizabeth Cady Stanton
- Francis Scott Key
- Henry Clay
- William Henry Harrison
- Andrew Jackson
- Laulewasikau the Prophet
- Tecumseh

Enrichment Activities

General Enrichment Ideas:

- Letters from the Past: write a letter during each lesson from the perspective of a person living during that time period. Be sure to include the date, mention anything historically relevant, and try to understand the perspective of the person in which you're writing. Keep the letters in a folder or binder.
- Book of Eras: Create a timeline for each lesson, illustrating key people and events, and writing the dates chronologically. When the year is over, you have a whole history book you created yourself!
- Book of Bios: Focus specifically on the people you've learned about this year. Create a bio for one or more important people from each lesson and think of creative ways to document their lives and roles in the past. (Ex:

create a social media "profile" for each person, or a text/conversation between two or more people.)

- A Taste of History: For each lesson or time period, research a recipe from that era and write it on a notecard. Save your recipes in a recipe box and cook your way through the past. Another idea is to keep a blog or YouTube channel documenting each recipe, how it was typically prepared (comparing/contrasting it to modern day methods), and any other historical tidbit you find interesting.
- Travel Thru History: For each lesson, create a travel brochure depicting important areas of interest in the area. (It can be funny or serious.)
- Diorama: Choose one (or more) period to illustrate with a diorama.
- Fashion through the Ages: Design a fashion magazine using what you've learned about each era's dress and style.

Specific to this lesson:

- View this downloadable 1812 lesson from the National Park Service. Adapt the lesson to your child/family as needed: nps.gov/fomc/castyourvote/CastYourVote-curriculum46.pdf

- Download and print this short lesson and worksheet written by students about the War of 1812 (perfect for younger elementary): cyberlearning-world.com/lessons/ushistory/19thcentury/war1812pd3.html

- Watch the PBS Special "The War of 1812" (free through your local PBS station). Then, **answer** the following: Why did the War of 1812 occur? What would have happened if Tecumseh and the Indian resistance were successful? Was the end result of the war a stalemate, or a victory for the US? https://www.pbs.org/video/the-war-of-1812-the-war-of-1812-full-program/

- Read the following article about Tecumseh's role in the War of 1812. Then, **answer** the following: What was Tecumseh's intention in working towards a pan-Indian federation? What was William Henry Harrison's first impression of him? Who was the Shawnee Prophet? Explain the phrase, "Tippecanoe and Tyler, too": https://americanexperience.si.edu/wp-content/uploads/2014/10/Tecumseh-and-the-War-of-1812_.pdf

- Check out the book *Rockets' Red Glare* (Alderman) from your local library. Then, Download and print this free Star-Spangled Banner lesson: http://blessmybudget.com/2018/05/07/1422/

- Read this article, *The Second Great Awakening and Reform in the 19th Century*, by the Constitutional Rights Foundation. Describe how abolition and temperance became intertwined with a Christian-based morality reform. https://www.crf-usa.org/images/pdf/the-second-great-awakening.pdf (For more information about the different Awakenings in the United States, visit: https://press.uchicago.edu/Misc/Chicago/256626.html)

- Read the following article from the Erie Canalway website. Explain the role of the Erie Canal as it relates to social reform (abolition, women's rights, and the Second Great Awakening). https://eriecanalway.org/learn/history-culture/social-reform

Making Connects

This period saw the new United States fight the British again (this time for good), Western Expansion, the Texas Revolution, and the building of canals and railroads. This was also the period when a surge of Irish immigrants arrived at the US, spurred by the Great Famine between 1845-1847. (Gold was also discovered in California, but we will discuss that when we learn about the Frontier.)

As the United States continued to expand, the institution of slavery—which had originally begun to wane before the invention of the cotton gin in 1794—became a growing concern for those on both sides of abolition. Would the new states be slave states or free?

Lesson 16: Slavery and Abolitionism (1619 - 1861)

Lesson 16: Slavery and Abolitionism (1619 – 1861)

Introduction

Although slavery had been around for thousands of years, chattel slavery (such as was seen in North and South America) was different. Indentured servants and slaves were both put to work in colonies like Virginia until it was realized that slave labor was a more economic choice for landowners. The south (due to its agriculture and cash crops) became dependent upon slave labor, while the northern states became more industrialized.

Meanwhile, the abolition movement was growing, thanks to the reform movements discussed in the previous lesson. Books like *Uncle Tom's Cabin* by Harriet Beecher Stowe and the Kansas-Nebraska Act of 1854 served to further the discussion of slavery and abolition.

Questions to Ask

1. How was indentured servitude and chattel slavery similar and different?
2. Why did slavery thrive in southern colonies and states? How did this compare to the north?
3. How did the Columbian Exchange impact slavery?
4. When was the slave trade made illegal in the United States?
5. How did the ideas from the American Revolution affect the way people saw slavery?
6. How did the cotton gin reinforce the south's dependence on slave labor?
7. Were there slave rebellions in America before the Civil War? How did this impact views and treatments of slaves during this period?
8. How did the Underground Railroad operate and how many people were able to escape?

US Presidents during 19ᵗʰ Century Abolitionism

President	Vice President	Years
John Tyler	NA	1841-1845
James K. Polk	George Dallas	1845-1849
Zachary Taylor	Millard Fillmore	1849-1850
Millard Fillmore	NA	1850-1853
Franklin Pierce	King/NA	1853-1857
James Buchanan	John Breckinridge	1857-1861

States Admitted to the Union (1845-1861)[71]

Florida	1845
Texas	1845
Iowa	1846
Wisconsin	1848
California	1850
Minnesota	1858
Oregon	1859
Kansas	1861

Primary Sources

- The African American Odyssey: A Quest for Full Citizenship (LOC): loc.gov/exhibits/african-american-odyssey/abolition.html

- Slavery in the United States: Primary Sources and the Historical Record: www.loc.gov/classroom-materials/slavery-in-the-united-states-primary-sources-and-the-historical-record

- Primary Sources: Slavery and Abolition (Christopher Newport University): https://cnu.libguides.com/primaryslavery/abolition

- Underground Railroad (State Historical Society of Iowa): http://iowaculture.gov/history/education/educator-resources/primary-source-sets/underground-railroad

General Spines, Series, and Reference Books

The Transatlantic Slave Trade: The Forced Migration of Africans to America (1607-1830) (Alexander)

---

[71] See previous lessons for dates of all previous states.

Web resources

- History:
  www.history.com/topics/black-history/slavery
  www.history.com/topics/black-history/abolitionist-movement
  www.history.com/topics/black-history/underground-railroad

- Yale University: https://glc.yale.edu/abolitionism-timeline

- American Abolitionists.com: www.americanabolitionists.com/international-abolition-and-anti-slavery-timeline.html

Suggested movies/documentaries

Digging for Slaves (BBC)
Freedom Seekers: Stories from the Western Underground Railroad (Amazon)
Found Voices: The Slave Narratives
Ghosts of Amistad: In the Footsteps of the Rebels
American Experience: The Abolitionists (PBS)
Amazing Grace (a movie about William Wilberforce)

YouTube videos

Elementary

- The Life of An Enslaved Person - America's Journey Through Slavery on the Learning Videos Channel (Harmony Square)

- Liberty's Kids HD 138-Born Free and Equal (Liberty's Kids- WildBrain)

- Torchlighters: The Harriet Tubman Story (2018) Full Movie (EncourageTV)

Middle

- Slavery-Summary on a Map (GeoHistory)

- Harriet Tubman's Escape to Freedom (Scholastic)

- The Abolitionists, Part 1, Chapter 1 (American Experience)

- The Abolitionists, Part 2, Chapter 1 (American Experience)

History:
- Deepening Division Threatens the Union/ America: The Story of Us (S2:E4)

High

- AP US History Study Guide: Period 4-1800 to 1848 (Gilderlehrman)

Professor Dave Explains:
- John Tyler: His Accidency (1841 - 1845)
- James Polk: Best Mullet Ever (1845 - 1849)
- Zachary Taylor: Old Rough and Ready (1849 - 1850)
- Millard Fillmore: Last of the Whigs (1850 - 1853)
- Franklin Pierce: The Compromise Candidate (1853 - 1857)
- James Buchanan: The Civil War Approaches (1857 - 1861)

Tom Richey:
- The Compromise of 1850
- Bleeding Kansas (The Kansas-Nebraska Act and Its Consequences)
- The Road to Civil War (US History EOC Review - USHC 3.1)

Crash Course: (WARNING: Some mature content included)
- Slavery: Crash Course US History #13
- Slavery in the American Colonies: Crash Course Black American History #2
- The Underground Railroad: Crash Course Black American History #15
- The Dred Scott Decision: Crash Course Black American History #16
- Frederick Douglass: Crash Course Black American History #17

Fiction & Nonfiction Books

Title	Author	Age	Period
A Picture of Freedom	McKissack	8+	1859
Allen Jay and the Underground Railroad	Brill	7+	1842
Aunt Harriet's Underground Railroad in the Sky	Ringgold	3+	1822-1913

Escape North!	Kulling	6+	1822-1913
Freedom Over Me	Bryan	6+	1800-1865
Freedom Train: The Story of Harriet Tubman	Sterling	9+	1822-1913
Freedom's A-Callin' Me	Shange	6+	1800-1865
Henry's Freedom Box	Levine	5+	1800-1865
If You Lived When There was Slavery in America	Johnson	7+	1800-1865
Light in the Darkness	Cline-Ransom	4+	1800-1865
Love Twelve Miles Long	Armand	6+	1820
Midnight Teacher	Halfmann	7+	1800-1865
Escape to Freedom: The Underground Railroad Adventures of Callie and William	Brooks-Simon	8+	1858
Frederick Douglass	National Geographic	5+	1818-1895
North by Night	Ayres	8+	1800-1865
Pink and Say	Polacco	7+	1861-1865
Seven Miles to Freedom	Halfmann	4+	1839-1915
Sweet Clara and the Freedom Quilt	Hopkinson	3+	1800-1865
The Last Safe House	Greenwood	8+	1850s
The Patchwork Path	Stroud	5+	1800-1865
The Story of Slavery	Usborne Young Reading	8+	1800-1865
Two Friends: Susan B. Anthony and Frederick Douglass	Robbins	4+	1818-1906
Unspoken	Cole	8+	1800-1865
Which Way to Freedom?: and Other Questions about the Underground Railroad	Carson	7+	1800-1865
Who Was Frederick Douglas?	Prince	8+	1818-1895

Terms to Know

1. Trans-Atlantic slave trade: segment of the global slave trade that transported between 10 million and 12 million enslaved Africans across the Atlantic Ocean to the Americas from the 16th to the 19th century.[72]

---

[72] Britannica

2. abolition: the action or an act of abolishing a system, practice, or institution.

3. slave codes: any of the set of rules based on the concept that enslaved persons were property, not persons.[73]

4. Missouri Compromise of 1820: an act of Congress (1820) by which Missouri was admitted as a Slave State, Maine as a Free State, and slavery was prohibited in the Louisiana Purchase north of latitude 36°30′N, except for Missouri.[74]

5. Underground Railroad: A network of houses and other places that abolitionists used to help slaves escape to freedom in the northern states or in Canada before the Civil War.[75]

6. emancipation: the fact or process of being set free from legal, social, or political restrictions; liberation.

7. chattel slavery: a system, which allowed people to be bought, sold and owned forever as legal property, was lawful in the United States and elsewhere from the 16th – 18th centuries[76]

8. Creole: a person of mixed European and Black descent, especially in the Caribbean.

9. plantation: an estate on which crops such as coffee, sugar, and tobacco are cultivated by resident labor.

10. triangular trade: used to refer to the trade in the 18th and 19th centuries that involved shipping goods from Britain to West Africa to be exchanged for slaves, these slaves being shipped to the West Indies and exchanged for sugar, rum, and other commodities which were in turn shipped back to Britain.

11. middle passage: the sea journey undertaken by slave ships from West Africa to the West Indies.

---

[73] Ibid.

[74] Dictionary.com

[75] Dictionary.com

[76] https://freedomcenter.org/learn/modern-day-abolition/#:~:text=Chattel%20slavery%20is%20the%20most,from%20the%2016th%20%E2%80%93%2018th%20centuries.

12. human rights: a right that is believed to belong justifiably to every person.
13. indentured servant: a person who signs and is bound by indentures to work for another for a specified time especially in return for payment of travel expenses and maintenance[77]

14. insurrection: a violent uprising against an authority or government.

15. racism: prejudice, discrimination, or antagonism by an individual, community, or institution against a person or people on the basis of their membership in a particular racial or ethnic group, typically one that is a minority or marginalized

16. Dred-Scott Decision: a US Supreme Court decision in 1857 which determined a slave was not a citizen and could not begin a legal case against anyone. Dred Scott was an enslaved man who wanted a court to say he was free because his owner took him to a free state.[78]

Areas to Know

- Mason-Dixson Line
- The general locations important in the Trans-Atlantic Slave Trade as shown on the map from SlaveVoyages.com:
  https://www.slavevoyages.org/blog/tag/intro-maps
- Missouri
- Kansas
- Maine
- The general paths of the Underground Railroad:
  www.nps.gov/nr/travel/underground/routes.htm

People to Know

- Eli Whitney
- Nat Turner
- Frederick Douglass

---

[77] Merriam-Websters dictionary
[78] www.OxfordsLearnersDictionary.com

- William Llyod Garrison
- Harriet Beecher-Stowe
- Harriet Tubman
- Soujourner Truth
- William H. Seward
- John Brown
- Angelina Grimke

Enrichment Activities

General Enrichment Ideas:

- Letters from the Past: write a letter during each lesson from the perspective of a person living during that time period. Be sure to include the date, mention anything historically relevant, and try to understand the perspective of the person in which you're writing. Keep the letters in a folder or binder.
- Book of Eras: Create a timeline for each lesson, illustrating key people and events, and writing the dates chronologically. When the year is over, you have a whole history book you created yourself!
- Book of Bios: Focus specifically on the people you've learned about this year. Create a bio for one or more important people from each lesson and think of creative ways to document their lives and roles in the past. (Ex: create a social media "profile" for each person, or a text/conversation between two or more people.)
- A Taste of History: For each lesson or time period, research a recipe from that era and write it on a notecard. Save your recipes in a recipe box and cook your way through the past. Another idea is to keep a blog or YouTube channel documenting each recipe, how it was typically prepared (comparing/contrasting it to modern day methods), and any other historical tidbit you find interesting.
- Travel Thru History: For each lesson, create a travel brochure depicting important areas of interest in the area. (It can be funny or serious.)
- Diorama: Choose one (or more) period to illustrate with a diorama.
- Fashion through the Ages: Design a fashion magazine using what you've learned about each era's dress and style.

Specific to this lesson:

- View this map of the various escape routes for the underground railroad. Choose one area to research. Write an essay or create a PowerPoint presentation about your findings. Include: important people and places, how many enslaved people likely found freedom from that route, where the route led, how successful the escape attempts were, and any other information you find interesting or important: http://education.nationalgeographic.org/resource/underground-railroad/

- Download this free lesson, Key Figures Who Worked to End Slavery, created by the National Archives: https://www.docsteach.org/activities/teacher/key-figures-who-worked-to-end-slavery

- Read this article about the history of slavery in the United States: https://kids.kiddle.co/Slavery_in_the_United_States Then, download this free worksheet explaining who the leaders of the Underground Railroad were: https://www.education.com/worksheet/article/underground-railroad-leaders/

- Watch the YouTube video of the book, Sweet Clara and the Freedom Quilt by *Rockin' Read Alouds*. Then, Download and print this free Underground Railroad Quilt Code game: https://deceptivelyeducational.blogspot.com/

- Study this map of the Underground Railroad from the New York Public Library. https://digitalcollections.nypl.org/items/863f0211-4262-2898-e040-e00a18060f45
Then, read the book, *The Underground Railroad for Kids: From Slavery to Freedom* (Carson) Choose one of the 21 activities in this book.

- Watch the YouTube video Who were the Abolitionists? by *Compass Learning*. **Answer**: Who was Nat Turner and what did he do? Why did some people want to send slaves back to Africa? Who were the "radical" abolitionists?

- Watch the video Susan B. Anthony for Kids by *Homeschool Pop*. Then read the book *Friends for Freedom* (Slade). Explain the relationship between Douglass and Anthony. How did they work together? What did they accomplish? Then, print this free Susan B Anthony paper doll: https://www.education.com/worksheet/article/susan-b-anthony-for-kids/

- Read the following article about John Brown's Harpers Ferry Raid by the American Battlefield Trust. **Answer**: What was Brown's goal? What role did Robert E. Lee play in this event? What happened to Brown and his fellow abolitionists? Lastly, explain in your own words why Brown was charged with treason: https://www.battlefields.org/learn/topics/john-browns-harpers-ferry-raid

Making Connections

During this era, something called *sectionalism* helped to create the conditions which led to the Civil War. Sectionalism is an idea in which communities (small or large) share cultural and economic loyalties within a larger area.[79] While the nation grew in population and spread to the west, sectionalism appeared in the political sphere: the north sought a stronger central government, the north wanted a stronger state government, and the west wanted resources that the northern states had (mainly, railroads). Economic, cultural, and political differences drove a deeper wedge between the regions, and the issue of slavery inflamed these differences.[80]

Other events, such as the Compromise of 1850, the Fugitive Slave Act, the Dred Scott Decision, the Kansas-Nebraska Act, and the election of 1860 (in which Abraham Lincoln was elected) all pushed the nation towards war.

For more information on the events leading to the war, visit: https://www.battlefields.org/learn/articles/trigger-events-civil-war

---

[79] www.essentialcivilwarcurriculum.com/sectionalism.html
[80] www.studysmarter.us/explanations/history/us-history/sectionalism-in-the-civil-war/

Lesson 17: The American Civil War (1861- 1865) and Reconstruction (1865-1877)

Lesson 17: The American Civil War (1861-1865) and Reconstruction (1865-1877)

Introduction

The Civil War is an enormous subject in American history, proven by the fact that there are more Civil War historians than any other. It's widely researched and even more widely debated, especially when it comes to the causes of the war. Was it really about slavery, or states' rights, or the economy? It's a complex subject and the resources offered here will help you unpack the details.

When you study a subject like this, it's important to know that the North and South were (and to some extent, still are) critically different in terms of culture, values, industries, and interests. At the time of the Civil War, the North was rapidly progressing in terms of industrialization, rail roads, the telegraph, education, and production: Northern states saw an influx of immigration in the years leading up to the war, changing the cultural climate (including the introduction of non-Christian religions and cults). By contrast, Southern states were loyal to orthodox Christianity, lacked diversity in immigration (immigrants moved to large cities in the north to find work, as they couldn't compete with free slave labor), and their economy depended upon agriculture (not industry). The question of states' rights, the role of the federal government, and the plight of millions of enslaved people hung in the balance during the bloodiest war the US has ever seen. In the ten years following the war, Reconstruction attempted to "reconstruct" the South into a post-slave society, but many historians feel it didn't succeed in its mission (for reasons found in this lesson).

Questions to Ask

1. Was the Civil War about slavery, state's rights, or both?
2. Which events led to the Civil War? Could it have been avoided?
3. How different were the north and south, and did this play a part in this conflict?
4. Which battles are worth noting (and why)?
5. Why did Abraham Lincoln want to declare war?
6. What is the "lost cause" ideology? How does it impact how Americans look at the Civil War?
7. Did Reconstruction "fail"? Why/why not?

US Presidents during the American Civil War and Reconstruction

President	Vice President	Years
Abraham Lincoln	Hannibal Hamlin	1861-1865
Abraham Lincoln	Andrew Johnson	1865 (assassinated)
Andrew Johnson	Office vacant	1865-1869

States Added to the Union

Kansas	1861
West Virginia	1863
Nevada	1864

Primary Sources

- Civil War (The Ohio State University):
  ehistory.osu.edu/topics/uscw

- Rose O'neal Greenhouse Papers (Duke University):
  library.duke.edu/rubenstein/scriptorium/greenhow

- Sarah E. Thomson Papers (Duke University):
  library.duke.edu/rubenstein/scriptorium/Thompson

- The Emily Davis Diaries (Villanova University):
  https://davisdiaries.villanova.edu/

- Documenting the American South (University of North Carolina):
  https://docsouth.unc.edu/index.html

- Victoria Regional History Center Archives:
  7006.sydneyplus.com/Archive/Portal

- Civil War Glass Negatives and Related Prints:
  https://www.loc.gov/pictures/collection/cwp/

- Abraham Lincoln Papers at the Library of Congress:
  https://loc.gov/collections/abraham-lincoln-papers/about-this-collection

- Andrew Johnson Papers at the Library of Congress:
  https://loc.gov/collections/andrew-johnson-papers/about-this-collection

- The Collected Works of Abraham Lincoln (Abraham Lincoln Association): https://quod.lib.umich.edu/l/lincoln/

- Ulysses S. Grant Papers at the Library of Congress: https://loc.gov/collections/ulysses-s-grant-papers/about-this-collection

- The American Presidency Project (Ulysses S. Grant): https://www.presidency.ucsb.edu/people/president/ulysses-s-grant

- The American Presidency Project (Abraham Lincoln): https://www.presidency.ucsb.edu/people/president/abraham-lincoln

- Civil War Maps (Library of Congress): https://loc.gov/collections/civil-war-maps/about-this-collection

- Civil War Interactive Map (American Battlefield Trust): https://www.battlefields.org/learn/maps/civil-war-animated-map

General Spines, Series, and Reference Books

The Civil War Visual Encyclopedia (Parker)
The Civil War Art of Mort Kunstler (Kunstler)

Web resources

- History: https://www.history.com/topics/american-civil-war/american-civil-war-history

- American Battlefield Trust: https://www.battlefields.org/learn/articles/brief-overview-american-civil-war

- American War Museum: https://acwm.org/

- US Military Academy: Civil War: https://www.westpoint.edu/academics/academic-departments/history/american-civil-war

- Reconstruction and Its Aftermath (Library of Congress): loc.gov/exhibits/african-american-odyssey/reconstruction.html

Suggested movies/documentaries

The Civil War (Ken Burns)

Grant (History Channel miniseries)

Lincoln (Steven Spielberg)

The Ultimate Civil War Series (13)

Blood and Glory: The Civil War in Color (13)

YouTube videos

Elementary

- Civil War History (Learn Bright)

- Causes of the American Civil War-Educational Social Studies Video for Elementary Students and Kids (Bow Tie Guy and Wife)

- Liberty's Kids 134: Conflict in the South (Liberty's Kids-Wild Brain)

- Abraham Lincoln for Kids (Homeschool Pop)

- The Reconstruction Era (KidsKonnect)

Middle

- Causes of the Civil War (Ryan Hill)

- The Civil War Animated Battle Map: April 12, 1861 – May 9, 1865 (American Battlefield Trust)

- Reconstruction Amendments (The Daily Bellringer)

- The Reconstruction Era 1865-1877: History GCSE (Homeschool History)

History:

- The Civil War Rages | America: The Story of Us (S1, E5)

- Civil War Combat series (free)

High

- Lecture 32: Presidential Reconstruction (Patrick Hayes)

- AP US History Study Guide: Period 6-1865 to 1898 (Gilderlehrman)

- The Lost Cause, a short history (Fultonhistory)

Professor Dave Explains:

- Abraham Lincoln: The Emancipator (1861 - 1865)

- Andrew Johnson: First Impeached (1865 - 1869)

- Ulysses S. Grant: Civil War Hero (1869 - 1877)

Tom Richey:

- The Road to Civil War (US History EOC Review - USHC 3.1)

- The Civil War (US History EOC Review - USHC 3.2)

- The Confederacy as Other (Interpreting the Civil War)

- Was Robert E. Lee a Traitor Like Benedict Arnold?

- Reconstruction: Part I (US History EOC Review - USHC 3.3)

- Reconstruction: Part II (US History EOC Review - USHC 3.4)

Crash Course:

- The Civil War, Part I: Crash Course US History #20

- The Civil War Part 2: Crash Course US History #21

- <u>Reconstruction and 1876: Crash Course US History #22</u>

- <u>Reconstruction: Crash Course Black American History #19</u>

Fiction & Nonfiction Books

Title	Author	Age	Period
A Light in the Storm: The Civil War Diary of Amelia Martin	Hesse	7+	1861-1865
Across Five Aprils	Hunt	12+	1861-1865
B is for Battle Cry	Bauer	6+	1861-1865
Blood and Germs	Jarrow	10+	1861-1865
Calico Girl	Nolen	8+	1861-1865
Civil War on Sunday	Osborne	6+	1861-1865
Clara Barton: Founder of the America Red Cross	Stevenson	8+	1861-1865
Dear America: When Will This Cruel War Be Over?	Denenberg	9+	1861-1865
Great Battles for Boys: The Civil War	Giorello	9+	1861-1865
Hidden Heroes in the Civil War	Smith	8+	1861-1865
Hoopskirts, Union Blues, and Confederate Grays	Havelin	10+	1861-1865
I Survived: The Battle of Gettysburg	Tarshis	8+	1861-1865
If You Lived at the Time of the Civil War	Moore	7+	1861-1865
If You Were a Kid During the Civil War	Mara	7+	1861-1865
John Lincoln Clem: Civil War Drummer Boy	Abbott	8+	1861-1865
Mary Bowser and the Civil War Spy Ring	Alberti	8+	1861-1865
My Brother's Keeper	Osborne	7+	1861-1865
O Captain, My Captain	Burleigh	10+	1861-1865
One Real American	Bruchac	10+	1861-1865
Rifles for Waite	Keith	13+	1861-1865
Soldier Song	Levy	8+	1861-1865
Spies in the Civil War	Lewer	8+	1861-1865
The Eternal Soldier	Kimmel	6+	1861-1865

The Flag Never Touched the Ground	Magoon	8+	1861-1865
The Last Brother: A Civil War Tale	Noble	6+	1861-1865
The Silent Witness	Friedman	4+	1861-1865
To the Front!	Friddell	7+	1861-1865
Two Miserable Presidents	Sheinkein	10+	1861-1865
What Was the Battle of Gettysburg?	O'Connor	8+	1861-1865
Who Was Robert E. Lee?	Bader	8+	1861-1865
What Was Reconstruction?	Smith	8+	1865-1877
Aftermath of the War: Reconstruction 1865-1877	Baby Professor	8+	1865-1877
Reconstruction: The Rebuilding of the United States after the Civil War	Rauch	12+	1865-1877
Opposing Viewpoints in American History: Reconstruction to the Present	Dudley	12+	1865-1877

Terms to Know

1. antebellum: occurring or existing before a particular war, especially the American Civil War.

2. assassination: the action of assassinating someone; murdering an important person for political or religious reasons

3. border states: a state bordering on an antislavery state and favoring slavery before the Civil War[81] (Maryland, Delaware, West Virginia, Kentucky, and Missouri)

4. brogan: a coarse stout leather shoe reaching to the ankle (worn by soldiers in the Civil War)

5. carpetbagger: (in the US) a person from the northern states who went to the South after the Civil War to profit from the Reconstruction.

---

[81] Merriam-Webster

6. casualty: a person killed or injured in a war or accident.

7. commutation: the legal option for an American man during the Civil War era to pay a fee of $300 to be excused from the draft (he could also hire someone to be a soldier-substitute for him)

8. confederacy: (in this instance) the Confederate States of America; the southern states which fought against the Union in the Civil War (Texas, Arkansas, Louisiana, Tennessee, Mississippi, Alabama, Georgia, Florida, South Carolina, North Carolina, and Virginia)

9. copperhead: "Peace Democrats" from the Union who opposed the American Civil War (can also mean a northerner who sympathized with the South)

10. dixie: also "Dixie Land", an informal name for the states in the US South (particularly those which formed the Confederacy)

11. Eastern theater (of the Civil War): battles from southern Pennsylvania to Virginia's North Carolina border, and from the Chesapeake Bay to the mountains west of the Shenandoah Valley

12. Western theater (of the Civil War): Appalachian Mountains in the east of the Mississippi River in the west, and from the Ohio River to the north of the Gulf of Mexico in the South[82]

13. Yankee: a person who lives in, or is from, the US; a Union soldier in the Civil War.

14. Emancipation Proclamation: President Abraham Lincoln issued the Emancipation Proclamation on January 1, 1863, announcing, "that all persons held as slaves" within the rebellious areas "are, and henceforward shall be free."[83]

15. Federal: having or relating to a system of government in which several states form a unity but remain independent in internal affairs; soldiers in the federal army

---

[82] https://history.army.mil/html/books/075/75-7/cmhPub_75-7.pdf
[83] https://www.archives.gov/milestone-documents/emancipation-proclamation

16. Greenback: a dollar bill, or, a form of legal tender paper money created by the Union government to help finance the Civil War.[84]

17. rebel: a person who rises in opposition or armed resistance against an established government or ruler.

18. secede: withdraw formally from membership of a federal union, an alliance, or a political or religious organization.

19. sectionalism: restriction of interest to a narrow sphere; undue concern with local interests or petty distinctions at the expense of general well-being.

20. scalawag: a white Southerner who collaborated with northern Republicans during Reconstruction, often for personal profit. The term was used derisively by white Southern Democrats who opposed Reconstruction legislation.

Areas to Know

- The Defining Moments and Historic Places of the Civil War
  https://www.doi.gov/blog/defining-moments-and-historic-places-civil-war

- Areas on this interactive map
  https://www.battlefields.org/learn/maps/civil-war-animated-map

People to Know

- Ulysses S. Grant
- William Tecumseh Sherman
- Winfield Scott
- George B. McClellan
- Ambrose Burnside
- Winfield Scott Hancock
- George Meade
- Joshua Chamberlain

---

[84] https://www.moaf.org/exhibits/checks_balances/abraham-lincoln/greenback

- Philip Sheridan
- Abraham Lincoln
- Frederick Douglass
- Jefferson Davis
- Robert E. Lee
- Thomas 'Stonewall' Jackson
- Clara Barton

Enrichment Activities

General Enrichment Ideas:

- Letters from the Past: write a letter during each lesson from the perspective of a person living during that time period. Be sure to include the date, mention anything historically relevant, and try to understand the perspective of the person in which you're writing. Keep the letters in a folder or binder.
- Book of Eras: Create a timeline for each lesson, illustrating key people and events, and writing the dates chronologically. When the year is over, you have a whole history book you created yourself!
- Book of Bios: Focus specifically on the people you've learned about this year. Create a bio for one or more important people from each lesson and think of creative ways to document their lives and roles in the past. (Ex: create a social media "profile" for each person, or a text/conversation between two or more people.)
- A Taste of History: For each lesson or time period, research a recipe from that era and write it on a notecard. Save your recipes in a recipe box and cook your way through the past. Another idea is to keep a blog or YouTube channel documenting each recipe, how it was typically prepared (comparing/contrasting it to modern day methods), and any other historical tidbit you find interesting.
- Travel Thru History: For each lesson, create a travel brochure depicting important areas of interest in the area. (It can be funny or serious.)
- Diorama: Choose one (or more) period to illustrate with a diorama.
- Fashion through the Ages: Design a fashion magazine using what you've learned about each era's dress and style.

Specific to this lesson:

- Download and print this short unit study on the Civil War: https://www.123homeschool4me.com/free-civil-war-worksheets-for-kids/

- Use this website (and five printable maps) to view where the battles of the Civil War took place: https://www.thecleverteacher.com/civil-war-map-worksheets/
  Then, choose one battle to research.
  Write a 1-page essay on the battle using this resource: https://education.nationalgeographic.org/resource/defining-battles-civil-war/

- Check out the book *The Civil War for Kids* (Herbert) and choose one activity from the book to complete.

- Watch the movie "Lincoln" (2012, PG-13). Write an essay explaining who Abraham Lincoln was, his role in the Civil War, his personal beliefs (about slavery, state's rights, etc.), and his legacy.

- Read the following website article on the Civil War: https://www.ducksters.com/history/civil_war.php
  Then, **answer** the following: Which states fought for the Union (northern states) and which fought for the Confederation (southern states)? Why did the south want to leave the Union? Why did Lincoln's election trigger the Civil War?

- Download this free lesson plan, "10 Interesting Facts": https://bookunitsteacher.com/civil_war/blog/TenInterestingFactsCivilWar.pdf

- View and download these free lessons and resources about Clara Barton, Civil War nurse and founder of the American Red Cross: https://heritageletter.com/blogs/lessonplans/clara-barton

Making Connections

The immediate effect of the removal of federal troops from the south was that Reconstruction (and especially Radical Reconstruction) was over. African Americans who stayed in the south were in some instances back in the same system of forced labor through black codes, Jim Crow laws, and the sharecropping system. Some, however, began migrating to the north in what would become known as the Great Migration. This occurred before the 20th Century but began in earnest around 1910, during the Second (American) Industrial Revolution.[85] Six million African Americans moved from the south to places like New York, Chicago, Detroit, and Pittsburgh. During the first World War (1917) many industrial jobs were vacant, leaving openings for the newcomers. This growth in urban population (along with the millions of immigrants arriving to the United States) caused a period of economic success for industries, and a period of poverty and dangerous working conditions for the labor population.

---

[85] https://www.archives.gov/research/african-americans/migrations/great-migration

Lesson 18: The American Industrial Revolution (1876-1900) and Gilded Era (1877-1896)

Lesson 18: The American Industrial Revolution (1876-1903) and Gilded Era (1877-1896)

Introduction

The period of American history following the end of the Civil War through the early 20th Century saw major developments. The United States, through the Industrial Revolution, evolved from a more agrarian nation into an industrialized one. Technological and industrial advancements made production more efficient, and a weak federal government (particularly the office of President) made it possible for tycoons and robber barons to rise to an unprecedented status (both in terms of financial and political power). Powerful men like Rockefeller, Carnegie, Morgan, and Vanderbilt made millions while the working class struggled under unfair working conditions. This dichotomy between the appearance of lavish wealth and the grisly reality for industrial laborers beneath the opulence earned this period the title, the Gilded Era.

Questions to Ask

1. How did the Industrial Revolution fuel the Gilded Era?
2. What was life like in the cities during this period?
3. Who were the major businesses and tycoons during this era?
4. How did the actions of the US presidents impact the Gilded Era?
5. What were working conditions like for American laborers?

US Presidents between 1876-1900

President	Vice President	Years
Ulysses S. Grant	Office vacant	1875-1877
Rutherford B. Hayes	William Wheeler	1877-1881
James A. Garfield	Chester Arthur	1881
Chester Arthur	Office vacant	1881-1884
Grover Cleveland	Thomas Hendricks/vacant	1885-1889
Benjamin Harrison	Levi Morton	1889-1893
Grover Cleveland	Adlai Stevenson	1893-1897
William McKinley	Garret Hobart	1897-1901
William McKinley	Theodore Roosevelt	1901
Theodore Roosevelt	Vacant	1901-1904

States Admitted to the Union

Nebraska	1867
Colorado	1876
North Dakota	1889
South Dakota	1889
Montana	1889
Washington	1889
Idaho	1890
Wyoming	1890
Utah	1896

Primary Sources

- Industrial Revolution (Library of Congress): https://www.loc.gov/classroom-materials/industrial-revolution-in-the-united-states/

- The Development of the Industrial United States: https://www.archives.gov/education/lessons/industrial-us.html

- Gilded Age/Progressive Era (Lone Star College): https://kwlibguides.lonestar.edu/PrimarySources-History/gildedage

- Statue of Liberty, 1884 (Gilder Lehrman Institute): https://www.gilderlehrman.org/history-resources/spotlight-primary-source/statue-liberty-1884

- Pacific Railway Act (Library of Congress): https://www.loc.gov/rr/program/bib//ourdocs/pacificrail.html

- Thomas Edison (Christopher Newport University): https://cnu.libguides.com/psenergy/thomasedison

General Spines, Series, and Reference Books

Inventions that Shaped America (Children's Inventory Books)
The Gilded Age: A Tale of Today (Mark Twain)[86]

---

[86] This book may not be completely suitable for children, but adults should read it to understand the term "Gilded Age" by the person who coined it: read selections to your child from this book if suitable.

Web resources

- History:
  https://www.history.com/topics/19th-century/gilded-age
  https://www.history.com/topics/industrial-revolution/industrial-revolution
  https://www.history.com/topics/inventions/wright-brothers

- Library of Congress: Rise of Industrial America:
  https://loc.gov/classroom-materials/united-states-history-primary-source-timeline/rise-of-industrial-america-1876-1900/overview

- Gilder Lehrman: AP US History Study Guide (1865-1898):
  https://ap.gilderlehrman.org/period/6

- Khan Academy: Introduction to the Gilded Age:
  https://www.khanacademy.org/humanities/us-history/the-gilded-age#gilded-age

Suggested movies/documentaries

The Men Who Built America series (History Channel)

Youtube videos

Elementary

- Industrial Revolution for Kids: A Simple Yet Comprehensive Overview (Learn Bright)

- What was the Industrial Revolution? (Pursuit of History)

- The Gilded Age: When America Became a Superpower (Untold History)

Middle

- Chapter 1 | The Gilded Age | American Experience (PBS)

- Mark Twain: His Amazing Adventures (Biography)

- The Gilded Age History (The Daily Bellringer)

History:
- The Transcontinental Railroad Unites | America: The Story of Us (S1, E6)

- Skyscrapers & Steel Forge the Modern City | America: The Story of Us (S1, E7)

- The Industrial Revolution | Mankind: The Story of All of Us (S1, E11)

High

Professor Dave Explains:
- Rutherford B. Hayes: His Fraudulency (1877 - 1881)

- James Garfield: What Could Have Been? (1881)

- Chester A. Arthur: Turning Tables (1881 - 1885)

- Grover Cleveland: White House Wedding (1885 - 1889)

- Benjamin Harrison: Make Grandpa Proud (1889 - 1893)

- Grover Cleveland Part 2: The Grovering (1893 - 1897)

- William McKinley: Annex Like the Dickens (1897 - 1901)

Tom Richey:
- APUSH Unit 6 Review (Industrial America / Gilded Age)

- The Gilded Age (APUSH Corona Class)

- The Second Industrial Revolution

Crash Course:

- Gilded Age Politics: Crash Course US History #26

- Ford, Cars, and a New Revolution: Crash Course History of Science #28

Fiction & Nonfiction Books

Title	Author	Age	Period
Who Was Mark Twain?	Prince	8+	1835-1910
R is for Railway: An Industrial Revolution Alphabet	Paprocki	0+	1830-
Full Steam Ahead	Blumberg	10+	1830-
Iron Horses	Kay	4+	1830-
The Railroad Grows into an Industry	Tracy	9+	
A Picture Book of Thomas Alva Edison	Adler	4+	1847-1931
Who Was Thomas Alva Edison?	Frith	7+	1847-1931
The Transcontinental Railroad	Perritano	10+	1863-1869
The Great Railroad Race: The Diary of Libby West	Gregory	9+	1863-1869
Ten Mile Day	Fraser	8+	1863-1869
Coolies	Soenpiet	7+	1863-1869
The Journal of Sean Sullivan: Transcontinental Railroad Worker	Durbin	9+	1863-1869
Industrial Revolution for Kids	Mullenbach	9+	1876-1900
The Industrial Revolution	Mooney	9+	1876-1900
What Was it Like to Work in a Factory in the 1880s	Baby Professor	8+	1876-1900
Children in the Industrial Revolution	Roberts	9+	1876-1900
The Industrial Revolution	Helfand	12+	1876-1900
How Machines Changed Cultures	Baby Professor	8+	NA
Horrible Jobs of the Industrial Revolution	Gray	10+	1876-1900

The Industrial Era: 1865-1915	Saddleback Educational Publishing	10+	1876-1900
The Gilded Age	Henderson	12+	1877-1896
The Story of the Statue of Liberty	Maestro	5+	1886
What is the Statue of Liberty?	Holub	8+	1886
Who Were the Wright Brothers?	Buckley	7+	1903
We Were There at the First Airplane Flight	Sutton	7+	1903

Terms to Know

1. industrialist: a person involved in the ownership and management of industry.

2. tycoon: a wealthy, powerful person in business or industry.

3. porter: a person employed to carry luggage and other loads, especially in a railroad station, airport, or hotel.

4. robber barons: a person who has become rich through ruthless and unscrupulous business practices (originally with reference to prominent US businessmen in the late 19th century).

5. entrepreneur: a person who organizes and operates a business or businesses, taking on greater than normal financial risks in order to do so.

6. mogul: an important or powerful person, especially in the motion picture or media industry.

Areas to Know

- Location of the Transcontinental Railroad:
  https://exhibits.stanford.edu/rr/feature/maps-of-the-railroads

- Location of the Wright's original flight (now a National Memorial): https://www.nps.gov/wrbr/index.htm

People to Know

- Cornelius Vanderbilt
- Jay Gould
- Andrew Carnegie
- John D. Rockefeller
- Henry Frick
- Mark Twain
- Leland Stanford
- J.P. Morgan
- George Westinghouse
- Thomas Edison
- Henry Bessemer
- Alexander Graham Bell
- Nikola Tesla
- William Burton
- Christopher Latham Sholes
- John Froelich
- King Gillette
- Guglielmo Marconi

Enrichment Activities

General Enrichment Ideas:

- Letters from the Past: write a letter during each lesson from the perspective of a person living during that time period. Be sure to include the date, mention anything historically relevant, and try to understand the perspective of the person in which you're writing. Keep the letters in a folder or binder.
- Book of Eras: Create a timeline for each lesson, illustrating key people and events, and writing the dates chronologically. When the year is over, you have a whole history book you created yourself!
- Book of Bios: Focus specifically on the people you've learned about this year. Create a bio for one or more important people from each lesson and

think of creative ways to document their lives and roles in the past. (Ex: create a social media "profile" for each person, or a text/conversation between two or more people.)

- A Taste of History: For each lesson or time period, research a recipe from that era and write it on a notecard. Save your recipes in a recipe box and cook your way through the past. Another idea is to keep a blog or YouTube channel documenting each recipe, how it was typically prepared (comparing/contrasting it to modern day methods), and any other historical tidbit you find interesting.
- Travel Thru History: For each lesson, create a travel brochure depicting important areas of interest in the area. (It can be funny or serious.)
- Diorama: Choose one (or more) period to illustrate with a diorama.
- Fashion through the Ages: Design a fashion magazine using what you've learned about each era's dress and style.

Specific to this lesson:

- Watch the YouTube video, Industrial Revolution for Kids (Learn Bright) **Answer**: Describe the difference between life before and after the Industrial Revolution. What kinds of developments happened during this time? Was the Industrial Revolution a good thing? (Why/why not.)

- Read about the inventions of the Industrial Revolution here: https://www.ducksters.com/history/us_1800s/inventions_technology_industrial_revolution.php Then, choose one invention to research using Kiddle.co. **Answer** the question: How did this invention change life as we know it?

- Read about the Transcontinental Railroad here: https://kids.britannica.com/students/article/transcontinental-railroad/629320 **Answer**: Which Native American tribes met the workers on the railroad with resistance? Describe the minorities who worked on the railroad during this time. What were the consequences for the Native American tribes during this period?

- Create this free Industrial Revolution lap book: *thehermitcrabshomeschool.blogspot.com/2017/04/industrial-revolution-lap-book.html?m=1*

- Gather free resources (Free Science Studies: Orville & Wilbur Wright) from this blog: https://diyhomeschooler.com/2015/04/21/free-science-studies-orville-wilbur-wright/

- Choose a lesson from this list by The Homeschool Mom: https://www.thehomeschoolmom.com/homeschool-lesson-plans/statue-of-liberty/

Making Connections

It's important to note that even though this guide treats these subjects separately (for the purpose of giving them enough attention), Reconstruction, Westward Expansion, the Industrial Revolution, the Gilded Age, and the American frontier were all happening around the same time:

- The beginning of the Industrial Revolution helped enable the north (who was industrializing) to beat the south (who had much less industry, fewer railroads, and adopted the telegraph later than the Union army).
- The end of Reconstruction led to an increased number of southern blacks into northern cities.
- Northern cities (having begun the process of industrialization) already had a large number of immigrants living and working in squalid conditions; the cities didn't have the infrastructure to deal with so many people.
- Families and individuals left the cities to pursue the opportunities, land, and the potential for gold available in the West (this had been happening since the 1820s, actually, but not to the same degree).
- Industry owners like Carnegie, Ford, Rockefeller, and Vanderbilt grew rich and powerful, playing a larger role in shaping the US than the Presidents during the same era. [87]

---

[87] https://online.maryville.edu/business-degrees/americas-gilded-age

Lesson 19: The American Frontier (1804-1912)

Lesson 19: The American Frontier (1804-1912)

Introduction

The American frontier is defined as the border between the developed land inhabited by whites, and land which Native Americans lived. Beginning as early as the colonial period, the border of the frontier moved further and further west as the US acquired more territory from the French (in 1803) and the native population. White encroachment of the frontier garnered hostility in the form of attacks and open war. The Indian Wars, beginning in 1622 and ending in the early 20th Century, made relationships between Native Americans and United States settlers tumultuous. Life on the frontier was also dangerous for other reasons, including the risk of accidental death on the roads, wild animals, harsh weather, and isolation. This period saw the rise of the cowboy, the gold rush, the Oregon Trail, and many other important events.

A Special Note

Westward Expansion, the Wild West, and the American Frontier can be sensitive subjects because while it meant lands acquired for some, it also meant displacement for others. Please read and utilize the following National Archives' DocsTeach lesson plan if/when appropriate for your student(s):

- The Impact of Westward Expansion on Native American Communities: https://www.docsteach.org/activities/teacher/the-impact-of-westward-expansion-on-native-american-communities

Questions to Ask

1. The American Frontier spanned the historical periods from the first settlers in Eastern colonies to the settling of the Far West in the 19th Century. Why, then, do most people tend to think only of the Oregon Trail or the Wild West as the frontier?

2. Does Westward Expansion (the movement of settlements into western territories) symbolize something about America or Americans?

3. How did the First Americans (indigenous tribes) react and respond to "white encroachment"? Did their reactions alter over time?

4. What kinds of people decided to move West? Did these people have anything in common?

5. What was life like on the American frontier and how did it change over time?

US Presidents between 1904-1914

President	Vice President	Years
Theodore Roosevelt	Charles W. Fairbanks	1905-1909
William H. Taft	James Sherman	1909-1912
William H. Taft	Office vacant	1912-1913
Woodrow Wilson	Thomas R. Marshall	1913-1921

States Admitted to the Union between 1904-1914

Oklahoma	1907
New Mexico	1912
Arizona	1912

Primary Sources

- Frontier and the American West: Primary Sources (Furman University): https://libguides.furman.edu/frontier/primary

- -Exploring the Western Frontier with the Records of Congress (National Archives): https://www.archives.gov/legislative/resources/education/frontier

- The American West: Primary Sources (Christopher Newport University): https://cnu.libguides.com/c.php?g=23306&p=136967

General Spines, Series, and Reference Books

The World of Laura Ingalls Wilder: The Frontier Landscapes that Inspired the Little House Books (McDowell)
The Split History of the Westward Expansion in the United States (Musolf)

The Wild West in Color (Guntzelman)

Web resources

- The Significance of the Frontier in American Society (American Historical Association, 1893): https://www.historians.org/about-aha-and-membership/aha-history-and-archives/historical-archives/the-significance-of-the-frontier-in-american-history-(1893)

- The American West: 1865-1900 (Library of Congress): https://loc.gov/classroom-materials/united-states-history-primary-source-timeline/rise-of-industrial-america-1876-1900/american-west-1865-1900/

- Western Frontier Life in America (University of North Carolina): https://faculty.chass.ncsu.edu/slatta/cowboys/essays/front_life2.htm

- Conquering the West (Georgia Highlands College): https://getlibraryhelp.highlands.edu/c.php?g=768076&p=5508089

- The Westward Movement (maps): https://www.loc.gov/resource/g3701sm.gct00483/?sp=45&r=-0.053,-0.006,1.134,0.807,0

Suggested movies/documentaries

The West (Ken Burns)

Youtube videos

Elementary

- Into the Frontier: US History for Kids (Miacademy Learning Channel)

- The American Frontier series (Townsends)

- How to Survive in the Wild West (1800) (Simple History)

- Oregon Trails: History of American Westward Explained on Maps (History on Maps)

Middle

- History of the Oregon Trail and the Pony Express (Great Documentaries)

- Oregon Trails: History of American Westward Explained on Maps (History on Maps)

- The Klondike Gold Rush (Buffalo Toronto Public Media)

- What Was Life like for People in the Wild West? (Captivating History)

History:

- America's Westward Expansion | America: The Story of Us (S1, E3)

- The War for California | America: The Story of Us (S1, E4)

- Cowboys and Outlaws series

High

- AP US History Study Guide: Period 7-1890 to 1945 (Gilderlehrman)

Professor Dave Explains:

- Theodore Roosevelt: The Rough Rider (1901-1909)

- William Howard Taft: The Plus-Sized President (1909-1913)

- Woodrow Wilson: A World War and a League of Nations (1913-1921)

Tom Richey:

- Developing the American West

Crash Course:

- Westward Expansion: Crash Course US History #24

Fiction & Nonfiction Books

Title	Author	Age	Period
A Pioneer Sampler	Greenwood	10+	1840

Across the Wide and Lonesome Prairie	Dear America	9+	1847
All the Stars in the Sky	Dear America	7+	1848
Josephina	American Girl (Tripp)	8+	1824
Kirsten	American Girl (Shaw)	8+	1854
Apples to Oregon	Hopkinson	4+	1830-1910
B is for Buckaroo	Whitney	1+	1865-1900
Boss of the Plains	Carlson	6+	1865-1900
Caddie Woodlawn	Brink	9+	1860s
Children of the Wild West	Freedman	10+	1865-1900
Covered Wagons, Bumpy Trails	Schindler	4+	1830-1910
Cowboys	Penner	2+	1865-1900
Cowboys and Cowgirls: Yippee Yay!	Gibbons	6+	1865-1900
Daily Life in a Covered Wagon	Erickson	5+	1853
Dandelions	Bunting	4+	1830-1910
Explore the Wild West!	Yasuda	6+	1830-1910
Fearless Mary	Charles	5+	1895
Hattie Big Sky	Larson	10+	1830-1910
Horse Diaries: Penny	Sanderson	8+	1848-1855
If You Were a Kid on the Oregon Trail	Gregory	7+	1840-1860
Into the West	Collins	8+	1830-1910
Joshua's Oregon Trail Diary	Hermes	7+	1848
Land of the Buffalo Bones	Dear America	9+	1873
Little House on the Prairie	Laura Ingalls-Wilder	6+	1870-1894
Meg's Prairie Diary	McMullan	7+	1856
Mr. Tucket	Paulsen	9+	1840-1860
My Face to the Wind	Dear America	9+	1881
Our Only May Amelia	Holm	8+	1899
Rough, Tough Charlie	Kay	7+	1860-1890
Sarah Plain and Tall	MacLachlan	8+	1890s
The Cowboy ABCs	Demarest	5+	1860-1890
The Great Railroad Race	Dear America	9+	1868
The Journal of Douglas Allen Deeds (Donner Party)	My Name is America	8+	1846
The Journal of Jedidiah Barstow	My Name is America	8+	1840-1860
The Long Way Westward	Sandin	4+	1860s
The Wild West: 1840-1890	Kunstler	9+	1840-1890

They're Off!: The Story of the Pony Express	Harness	7+	1860-1861
Top Secret Files: The Wild West: Secrets, Strange Tales, and Hidden Facts about the Wild West	Bearce	9+	1830-1910
True Tales of the Wild West	Walker	7+	1830-1910
West to a Land of Plenty	Dear America	9+	1883
Westward Ho! The Story of the Pioneers	Penner	6+	1830-1910
Westward Movement (curriculum workbook)	Spotlight on America	1+	1830-1910
What Was the Wild West?	Pascal	8+	1865-1895
Which Way to the Wild West?	Sheinkin	10+	1830-1910

Terms to Know

1. Manifest Destiny: the 19th-century doctrine or belief that the expansion of the US throughout the American continents was both justified and inevitable.

2. Mexican American War: a conflict between the US and Mexico, 1846-1848, which ended with the Treaty of Guadalupe Hidalgo.

3. Battle at the Alamo: The Battle of the Alamo was a pivotal event and military engagement in the Texas Revolution. Following a 13-day siege, Mexican troops under President General Antonio López de Santa Anna reclaimed the Alamo Mission near San Antonio de Béxar, killing most of the occupants.

4. Trail of Tears: the removal and relocation of the Cherokee nation from their lands east of the Mississippi to Oklahoma between 1838-1839.

5. Forty-niners: people that migrated to California from 1848-1849 in search of gold

6. Transcontinental telegraph: the completion of the link between eastern and western telegraph networks which allowed for instant communication between Washington, D.C., and San Francisco.

7. <u>Gold rush:</u> rapid movement of people to a newly discovered goldfield. The first major gold rush, to California in 1848–49, was followed by others in the US, Australia (1851–53), South Africa (1884), and Canada (Klondike, 1897–98)

8. <u>Oregon trail:</u> a 2,000-mile route from Independence, Missouri, to Oregon City, Oregon, that was used by thousands of Americans during the era of Westward Expansion

9. <u>Homestead Act:</u> the federal allowance of American adults (who "never borne arms against the US government) to claim 160 acres of government land to cultivate and improve[88]

10. <u>Battle of Little Bighorn:</u> also known as Custer's Last Stand, marked the most decisive Native American victory and the worst U.S. Army defeat in the long Plains Indian War[89]

11. <u>Pacific Railroad Act:</u>[90] an act which offered government incentives to help "men of talent, men of character, men who are willing to invest" in developing the first transcontinental rail line

Areas to Know

- Yellowstone National Park
- Oregon territory
- Salt Lake City Utah
- Black hills (South Dakota)
- the routes west as depicted here: https://mrnussbaum.com/westward-trails-interactive-map

People to Know

- John Deere
- Annie Oakley
- James K Polk
- Wild Bill Hickok

---

[88] https://www.archives.gov/milestone-documents/homestead-act
[89] https://www.nps.gov/libi/learn/historyculture/battle-story.htm
[90] https://www.senate.gov/artandhistory/history/common/generic/PacificRailwayActof1862.htm

- Billy the Kid
- Jesse James
- Wyatt Earp
- Brigham Young
- The Wild Bunch: Sundance Kid, Butch Cassidy, Kid Curry, Belle Star

Enrichment Activities

General Enrichment Ideas:

- <u>Letters from the Past</u>: write a letter during each lesson from the perspective of a person living during that time period. Be sure to include the date, mention anything historically relevant, and try to understand the perspective of the person in which you're writing. Keep the letters in a folder or binder.
- <u>Book of Eras</u>: Create a timeline for each lesson, illustrating key people and events, and writing the dates chronologically. When the year is over, you have a whole history book you created yourself!
- <u>Book of Bios</u>: Focus specifically on the people you've learned about this year. Create a bio for one or more important people from each lesson and think of creative ways to document their lives and roles in the past. (Ex: create a social media "profile" for each person, or a text/conversation between two or more people.)
- <u>A Taste of History</u>: For each lesson or time period, research a recipe from that era and write it on a notecard. Save your recipes in a recipe box and cook your way through the past. Another idea is to keep a blog or YouTube channel documenting each recipe, how it was typically prepared (comparing/contrasting it to modern day methods), and any other historical tidbit you find interesting.
- <u>Travel Thru History</u>: For each lesson, create a travel brochure depicting important areas of interest in the area. (It can be funny or serious.)
- <u>Diorama</u>: Choose one (or more) period to illustrate with a diorama.
- <u>Fashion through the Ages</u>: Design a fashion magazine using what you've learned about each era's dress and style.

Specific to this lesson:

- Watch the <u>Youtube series "The American Frontier" by Townsends.</u> Illustrate a wilderness guide from what you learned in the short survival videos.

- Choose one of the ten hands-on activities here:
  https://tinasdynamichomeschoolplus.com/westward-expansion/

- Create a salt dough map of the United States and paint it. Then, trace the Oregon Trail onto the map:
  https://www.123homeschool4me.com/the-oregon-trail-for-kids_23/

- Complete this panning for gold activity
  learningthroughliterature.com/panning-for-gold-kids-activity/

- Learn about the Pony Express here:
  https://homeschoolgiveaways.com/2021/02/free-printables-and-unit-studies-about-the-pony-express/
  Then, choose one of the free lessons posted in the article.

- Who were the cowboys? Visit the following link and then answer the questions below:
  https://www.ducksters.com/history/westward_expansion/cowboys.php
  Answer: What was the job of a cowboy? What was the most important possession to a cowboy? What happens at a rodeo? How much money did a cowboy make during this period?

- Learn about the Mexican-American War here:
  https://www.legendsofamerica.com/ah-mexicanamericanwar/
  Answer: What was the end result of the Treaty of Guadalupe Hidalgo? Write an essay explaining what you think might have happened if the treaty did not demand that Mexico give up its right to those territories. Use this website and interactive map to help:
  https://illinois.pbslearningmedia.org/resource/akh10.socst.ush.now.westexpans/westward-expansion-18601890/

- Learn about the Battle of the Alamo here:
  https://www.history.com/topics/latin-america/alamo
  Then, recreate the Alamo with this eHow tutorial:
  https://www.ehow.com/how_5795778_build-alamo-school-project.html

- Visit the following link to learn about the cultural experiences and conflicts in Westward Expansion, including interactions with the indigenous population. Use the teacher guide for enrichment suggestion: https://www.loc.gov/classroom-materials/westward-expansion-encounters-at-a-cultural-crossroads/

Making Connections

The American Frontier (the area of land which separates developed settlements from wild or Indian territory) has existed since the earliest American colonies, and continued to move further and further west until it was "conquered" by the 1890 census. The "conquering" of the West officially ended the American Frontier period, but some historians argue that the American spirit to conquer led us to become successful in space exploration. (More on that in a later lesson.)

By this point, several Indian reservations existed (largely in Oklahoma). For more information on federally recognized tribes and reservations, visit:

www.bia.gov/sites/default/files/dup/assets/bia/ots/webteam/pdf/idc1-028635.pdf

Lesson 20: The Immigration Age (1830-1920)

Lesson 20: The Immigration Age (1830-1920)

Introduction

As in previous places in Chronos, it's important to note that the Immigration Age chronologically overlapped with the Industrial Revolution, the Gilded Era, WWI, and the Progressive Era. It also occurred at the same time as the American frontier period (the Wild West, etc.).

As immigrants flooded to northern American cities (which had no infrastructure to support them), industrial companies saw the opportunity for cheap labor. Immigrant families worked long days for little pay, living in cramped tenements in dangerous and unclean areas of the cities. The 1840s saw a large boom of German and Irish immigrants, followed by a larger boom in the 1880s and 1890s of non-English speaking Europeans and Asians. Ellis Island in the East and Angel Island in the West welcomed some (and resisted others) in a process tempered by periods of immigration restrictions. By 1910, 3/4 New Yorkers were immigrants or first-generation Americans.

Questions to Ask

1. What was happening around the world during this time which would cause such a huge number of immigrants to the US?
2. What role did immigration play in American culture?
3. How were immigrants treated by nativists (people born and raised in the US), and did this treatment depend upon the nationality or region of the immigrant? (For example, German immigrants were looked upon with suspicion in the US during the first World War.)
4. Is the United States truly a "nation of immigrants"? In what way?

Primary Sources

- Primary Source: Immigration (Lonestar College):
  https://kwlibguides.lonestar.edu/PrimarySources-History/immigration

- Immigration and Americanization, 1880-1930:
  https://dp.la/primary-source-sets/immigration-and-americanization-1880-1930

- US History: Primary Sources: Immigration (Southern Connecticut State University: https://libguides.southernct.edu/ushistoryprimary/immigration

General Spines, Series, and Reference Books

Images of America: Ellis Island's Famous Immigrants (Moreno)
Images of America: Angel Island (Fanning/Wong)

Web resources

- Urbanization and Its Challenges (Lumen Learning): https://courses.lumenlearning.com/suny-ushistory2os2xmaster/chapter/urbanization-and-its-challenges/

- Immigration to the United States, 1851-1900 (Library of Congress): https://www.loc.gov/classroom-materials/united-states-history-primary-source-timeline/rise-of-industrial-america-1876-1900/immigration-to-united-states-1851-1900/

- Immigration and the American Industrial Revolution From 1880 to 1920: https://www.ncbi.nlm.nih.gov/pmc/articles/PMC2760060/

- The Rush of Immigrants (Independence Hall Association): https://www.ushistory.org/us/38c.asp

Suggested movies/documentaries

An American Tail (1986)

Youtube videos

Elementary

- Ellis Island (Brain Pop)

- History Brief: The Great Migration (Reading Through History)[91]

Middle

- The New Immigrants (Mr. Bett's Class)

- Animated Map Shows History of Immigration to the US (Insider Business)

- The European Wave-America's Immigration Story (TDC)

- Ellis Island - History of Immigration to the United States | 1890-1920 | Award Winning Documentary (The Best Films Archive)

History:

- America's Westward Expansion | America: The Story of Us (S1, E3)

- Immigration at Ellis Island

High

- "New Immigrants" and Migration (APUSH Unit 6) (Marco Learning)

- APUSH Review-Immigration (Kevin Irvin)

- Immigration and Urbanization in the Industrial Age (Robert Chodola)

Khan Academy:

- Immigration and Migration in the Gilded Age (1865-1898) (Khan Academy)

- 1920s Urbanization and Immigration (1890-1945)

Adam Norris:

- APUSH Review: "Old" Immigration and Nativism (Adam Norris)

---

[91] Although the Great Migration was a domestic relocation of people from the south to the north, it needs to be considered when we're talking about the Immigration Age: the surplus of people who moved to the north during this era impacted the already weak urban infrastructures which eventually led to the Progressive Era.

- APUSH Review: Video #24 Immigration and Native Americans (Adam Norris)

- APUSH Review: Nativism in the 1920s

Crash Course:
- Growth, Cities, and Immigration: Crash Course #25

Fiction & Nonfiction Books

Title	Author	Age	Period
Turning Points in U.S. History: Immigration Through Ellis Island	Forest	8+	1830-1920
House of Tailors	Giff	8+	1870s
Angel Island	Britton	8+	1910-1940
Angel Island	Flanagan	7+	1910-1940
At Ellis Island: A History in Many Voices	Peacock	7+	1892-1954
Bridge to America	Glaser	10+	1920
Coming to America	Maestro	4+	1830-1920
Dreams in Golden Country	Lasky	9+	1903
In the Shadow of Lady Liberty	Kravitz	8+	1892-1954
Letters from Rifka	Hesse	9+	1919
Li on Angel Island	Bybee	8+	1910-1940
Maggie's Door	Giff	8+	1845
Meet Rebecca	American Girls	8+	1914
National Geographic Readers: Ellis Island	Carney	5+	1892-1954
Peppe the Lamplighter	Bartone	4+	1890
Pick and Shovel Poet: The Journeys of Pascal D'Angelo	Murphy	10+	1910
The Girl in the Torch	Sharenow	8+	1900
The Journal of Otto Peltonen	My Name is America (Durbin)	9+	1900
The Orphan of Ellis Island	Woodruff	9+	1892-1954
When Jessie Came Across the Sea	Hest	6+	1900

Terms to Know

1. <u>emigrate</u>: leave one's own country in order to settle permanently in another

2. <u>immigration</u>: the action of coming to live permanently in a foreign country

3. <u>Chinese Exclusion Act of 1882</u>: an act passed by Congress and signed by President Arthur which banned Chinese laborers from entering the country for ten years

4. <u>"America's Golden Door"</u>: a nickname for Jersey City where Ellis Island was

5. <u>migration</u>: movement of people to a new area or country in order to find work or better living conditions

6. <u>ethnicity</u>: the quality or fact of belonging to a population group or subgroup made up of people who share a common cultural background or descent

7. <u>nativist</u>: relating to or supporting the policy of protecting the interests of native-born or established inhabitants against those of immigrants

Areas to Know

- Chicago
- New York City
- Pittsburgh
- Detroit
- Cleveland
- Boston
- San Francisco
- Los Angeles

People to Know

NA

Enrichment Activities

General Enrichment Ideas:

- Letters from the Past: write a letter during each lesson from the perspective of a person living during that time period. Be sure to include the date, mention anything historically relevant, and try to understand the perspective of the person in which you're writing. Keep the letters in a folder or binder.
- Book of Eras: Create a timeline for each lesson, illustrating key people and events, and writing the dates chronologically. When the year is over, you have a whole history book you created yourself!
- Book of Bios: Focus specifically on the people you've learned about this year. Create a bio for one or more important people from each lesson and think of creative ways to document their lives and roles in the past. (Ex: create a social media "profile" for each person, or a text/conversation between two or more people.)
- A Taste of History: For each lesson or time period, research a recipe from that era and write it on a notecard. Save your recipes in a recipe box and cook your way through the past. Another idea is to keep a blog or YouTube channel documenting each recipe, how it was typically prepared (comparing/contrasting it to modern day methods), and any other historical tidbit you find interesting.
- Travel Thru History: For each lesson, create a travel brochure depicting important areas of interest in the area. (It can be funny or serious.)
- Diorama: Choose one (or more) period to illustrate with a diorama.
- Fashion through the Ages: Design a fashion magazine using what you've learned about each era's dress and style.

Specific to this lesson:

- Read the article, *The Rush of Immigrants*:
  https://www.commonlit.org/en/texts/the-rush-of-immigrants
  Answer: What's the difference between "Old Immigration" versus "New Immigration"? Make a Venn diagram to compare and contrast these people groups. Include: nationality/country of origin, reasons for coming to the US, the way in which they were received by American citizens when they arrived, and whether or not they intended to stay (i.e., "Birds of passage"). Lastly, explain whether there were any acts of Congress which barred these groups from entering the US.

- According to the National Park Service, it's believed that 40% of Americans today can trace their ancestry to Ellis Island. Read more about Ellis Island here: https://www.nps.gov/npnh/learn/news/fact-sheet-elis.htm
Using the following link, join FamilySearch.org and begin developing your family tree: https://www.familysearch.org/en/wiki/How_to_Start_Your_Family_History

- Using this following web article, create a poster inviting immigrants to the US: http://crfimmigrationed.org/index.php/lessons-for-teachers/71-immigrant-article-1
Answer: What would have been appealing about the United States for potential immigrants? What did the US have to offer?

- Read the book, *We Came Through Ellis Island* (Thompson). Write a letter to Emma Markowitz as if you are a friend left behind in Russia. Ask about her experience as an immigrant, what it was like to enter the US through Ellis Island, and what it was like to start a new life in New York.

- When immigrants arrive in the United States, they often move to areas in which their family members, friends, or people of common national origins have established. Chicago, for example, has "Little Italy" and China Town. Use this map to help locate historical areas in your state or city where immigrants have typically gathered: https://www.migrationpolicy.org/programs/data-hub/maps-foreign-born-united-states **Answer**: What legacy did the immigrants in your areas leave behind? Did their presence make an impact on the food, music, religious heritage, or cultural environment of their town or city? Are there any special events (parades, festivals) which can be traced back to their influences?

- Read the following article about famous Americans who immigrated to the US through Ellis Island. Choose one in which to write an essay, report, or presentation: https://www.statueofliberty.org/discover/famous-passengers/

- (Note: This article is for older students due to sensitive material. Parents, please review the website first.) The KKK had its largest members to date in the 1920s, largely due to the influx of immigrants to American shores. Read this article about the relationship between the Immigration Age and the KKK.

  https://billofrightsinstitute.org/essays/the-ku-klux-klan-in-the-1920s

Answer the following:

1. Explain the differences between the behaviors and beliefs of the KKK in the post-Civil War South versus those of the North and Midwest.
2. What influence did the movie, *Birth of a Nation*, have on Americans during this period?
3. What did the Klan believe about labor unions, immigration, big business, and chain stores?
4. What is "vocational Klannishness"?
5. What were the Klan members most concerned with in regard to immigration?
6. What contributed to the growth of the KKK between 1915-1925?
7. What factors caused the collapse of the KKK (before its resurgence in the 1950s)?

Making Connections

The increase in immigrant population corresponded to the rise of industrialism in the United States. Immigrants provided cheap labor for growing industries but had virtually no rights, especially those who spoke little to no English. Working conditions were often cramped, dangerous, dirty, and offered no legal protection from exploitation. American cities didn't have the infrastructure to support thousands of new immigrants, so tenements sometimes housed a dozen people living in squalid conditions. As conditions worsened, a new group of activists and reformers rose to sway popular opinion and enact political action: the Progressives.

Lesson 21: The Progressive Era (1900-1929)

Lesson 21: The Progressive Era (1900-1929)

Introduction

Overcrowded cities, filthy slums, unfair and dangerous working conditions, and political corruption caused a massive movement of reform known as the Progressive Era. Journalists known as "muckrakers" infiltrated labor houses and slums to shed light on corruption and poverty: this led to federal involvement by Progressive presidents like Theodore Roosevelt. Progressive-Era policies helped working conditions, gave rights to women and the poor, and also contributed to environmental protections which led to the National Parks.

Questions to Ask

1. What was the ultimate goal of the Progressives?
2. Did the Progressive movement succeed in their mission?
3. What were the lasting political, cultural, conservational impacts of this time period?

Primary Sources

- Gilded Age and Progressive Era, 1878-1920:
  loc.gov/rr/program/bib/ourdocs/gilded.html

- Gilded Age & Progressive Era, 1877-1917:
  https://libguides.wustl.edu/gilded-progressive

- UVA Miller Center: Progressive Era:
  https://millercenter.org/the-presidency/teacher-resources/primary-resources/progressive-era

General Spines, Series, and Reference Books

The Progressive Era: A Reference Guide (Sicius)

Web resources

- Progressive Era to New Era, 1900-1929 (Library of Congress): https://loc.gov/classroom-materials/united-states-history-primary-source-timeline/progressive-era-to-new-era-1900-1929/

- The Progressive Era (Khan Academy): https://www.khanacademy.org/humanities/us-history/rise-to-world-power/age-of-empire/a/the-progressive-era

- The Progressives and Direct Democracy (Constitutional Rights Foundation): https://www.crf-usa.org/election-central/the-progressives.html

- Cities During the Progressive Era: https://www.loc.gov/classroom-materials/united-states-history-primary-source-timeline/progressive-era-to-new-era-1900-1929/cities-during-progressive-era/

Suggested movies/documentaries

NA

Youtube videos

Elementary

(There are no recommended Youtube videos for this subject for these grades. Consider one of the Middle school options or find a video on your own ancestral history: What was the nationality of your ancestors? When did they come to America? Etc.)

Middle

The Progressive Movement (Jorge Aguilar)

The Progressive Era (M.D. Jones)

Reform in the Progressive Era, USH13 (GeorgiaStandards.org)

History:
- Skyscrapers and Steel Forge the Modern City | America: The Story of Us
- The US Strikes Oil | America: The Story of Us (S1, E8)

High
- AP US History Prep with Tom Richey #6: The Gilded Age and the Progressive Era (1860-1920) (Bill of Rights Institute)
- APUSH Review: The Progressive Era (Adam Norris)
- The Progressive Movement and American Society (1890-1920) (Kevin Irvin)

Crash Course Black American History (WARNING: Sensitive material)
- Ida B. Wells: Crash Course Black American History #20
- Plessy V Ferguson and Segregation: Crash Course Black American History #21
- Booker T. Washington and W.E.B. DuBois: Crash Course Black American History #22
- The Black Women's Club Movement: Crash Course Black American History #23
- The Great Migration: Crash Course Black American History #24
- The Red Summer of 1919: Crash Course Black American History #25

Khan Academy:
- The Progressives/Period 7/1890-1945/AP History
- The 19th Amendment and Citizenship (High School)

Tom Richey:

- The Progressive Era (APUSH Corona Class)

- Gilded Age and Progressive Era Compared (APUSH Review)

Crash Course:

- The Progressive Era: Crash Course US History #27

- Progressive Presidents: Crash Course US History #29

- Women's Suffrage: Crash Course US History #31

Fiction & Nonfiction Books

Title	Author	Age	Period
The Progressive Era	Hillstom	12+	1900-1929
The Gilded Age & Progressive Era: A Student Companion	Student Companions to American History	12+	1865-1929
Jacob Rii's Camera	O'Neill	7+	1900-1929
The Only Woman in the Photo	Krull	4+	1900-1929
Mother Jones and Her Army of Mill Children	Winter	4+	1900-1929
Dangerous Jane	Slade	6+	1900-1929
The Child Labor Reform Movement	Otcinowski	8+	1900-1929
Kids at Work	Hine	10+	1900-1929
Breaker Boys	Burgan	10+	1900-1929
Rightfully Ours: How Women Won the Vote	Hollihan	9+	1900-1929
Bold and Brave	Gillibrand	6+	1900-1929
Marching with Aunt Susan	Murphy	6+	1900-1929
Elizabeth Leads the Way	Stone	6+	1900-1929
You Want Women to Vote, Lizzie Stanton	Fritz	8+	1900-1929
Muckrakers: How Ida Tarbell, Upton Sinclair, and	Bausum	10+	1900-1929

Lincoln Steffens Helped Expose Scandal, Inspire Reform, and Invent Investigative Journalism			
Ida B. Well: Let the Truth be Told	Myers	4+	1900-1929

Terms to Know

1. <u>activism:</u> the policy or action of using vigorous campaigning to bring about political or social change

2. <u>child labor</u>: the use of children in industry or business, especially when illegal or considered inhumane

3. <u>suffrage</u>: the right to vote in political elections

4. <u>Prohibition</u>: the action of forbidding something, especially by law

5. <u>social welfare</u>: organized public or private social services for the assistance of disadvantaged groups; specifically: social work.[92]

6. <u>Bull Moose party</u>: Another term for the Progressive Party, borrowed from Roosevelt's comment that he felt "Strong as a bull moose" when he lost the Republican nomination in 1912

7. <u>graduated rate income tax</u>: consists of tax brackets where tax rates increase as income increases.[93]

Areas to Know

- Chicago
- New York City
- Pittsburgh
- Detroit

---

[92] Merriam-Webster
[93] www.thetaxFoundation.org

- Cleveland
- Boston
- San Francisco
- Los Angeles

People to Know

- Theodore Roosevelt
- William Jennings Bryant
- Woodrow Wilson
- Jane Addams
- Grace Abbott
- Nellie Bly
- Ida B. Wells-Barnett
- Mary McLeod
- Lincoln Steffens
- Ray Stannard Baker
- Ida M. Tarbell

Enrichment Activities

General Enrichment Ideas:

- Letters from the Past: write a letter during each lesson from the perspective of a person living during that time period. Be sure to include the date, mention anything historically relevant, and try to understand the perspective of the person in which you're writing. Keep the letters in a folder or binder.
- Book of Eras: Create a timeline for each lesson, illustrating key people and events, and writing the dates chronologically. When the year is over, you have a whole history book you created yourself!
- Book of Bios: Focus specifically on the people you've learned about this year. Create a bio for one or more important people from each lesson and think of creative ways to document their lives and roles in the past. (Ex: create a social media "profile" for each person, or a text/conversation between two or more people.)
- A Taste of History: For each lesson or time period, research a recipe from that era and write it on a notecard. Save your recipes in a recipe box and cook your way through the past. Another idea is to keep a blog or YouTube

channel documenting each recipe, how it was typically prepared (comparing/contrasting it to modern day methods), and any other historical tidbit you find interesting.

- Travel Thru History: For each lesson, create a travel brochure depicting important areas of interest in the area. (It can be funny or serious.)
- Diorama: Choose one (or more) period to illustrate with a diorama.
- Fashion through the Ages: Design a fashion magazine using what you've learned about each era's dress and style.

Specific to this lesson:

- Read the book *The House That Jane Built* (Stone). Then watching the Youtube video on Jane Addams and Hull House, Jane Addams, Neighboring with the Poor (NBC News Learn).

- Read this article *The Progressive Era Key Facts*:
https://www.britannica.com/summary/The-Progressive-Era-Key-Facts
Then, using the dates and facts from the article, create a history web: begin with writing the word "Progressive era" in the middle in a bubble. Then, draw a line from it to another bubble and write one aspect of the Progressive era (ex: immigration, urbanization, labor rights, women's rights, muckrakers, conservation, etc.). Write any important facts underneath each bubble. See how many bubbles connect together.

  Visit this website to learn about Jacob Riis:
https://www.icp.org/browse/archive/constituents/jacob-riis?all/all/all/all/0
Then, study the included photos. Write a 1-page essay on what you believe was moving about Riis' photography. How did Riis contribute to the Progressive Era?

- Research immigration history in your state: first, contact your local historical society and ask if there are any books, museum exhibits, or re-enactments which demonstrate the role of immigration in your community. Then, search online to find out the following:
  1. Which immigrant groups settled in your state/town, and if these groups came for a specific reason (i.e.. The potato famine in Ireland brought thousands of Irish to the US)

2. How the nativist Americans reacted to these groups, and if the immigrants created any cultural centers or areas in your community (i.e.. "Little Italy" is an area of Chicago which drew Italian immigrants and continues to be a cultural center)
   Check out this website for help:
   https://depts.washington.edu/moving1/migrationhistory-states.shtml

- Read this article by Khan Academy and answer the questions beneath the "What do you think?" subtitle: https://www.khanacademy.org/humanities/us-history/rise-to-world-power/age-of-empire/a/the-progressive-era

Making Connections

The Progressive Era founded investigative journalism, the birth of modern social work, labor law (including children labor laws), and many other reforms. It also grew the power of the federal government thanks to a string of Progressive presidents. It's possible the growing strength of the presidency helped the American image during its launch into WWI (this is speculation, but it's compelling nonetheless).

For an extensive list of Progressive-era Reforms, read:
personal.umd.umich.edu/~ppennock/Progressive%20Reforms.htm

Lesson 22: World War 1
(1914-1918)

Lesson 22: World War 1 (1914-1918)

Introduction

World War 1 was the world's first truly global war, involving over thirty countries, several continents, and eventually the deaths of 17 million people (including 100,000 Americans). Upon the assassination of the Archduke of Austria-Hungary by a Serbian nationalist group, a series of treaties and defense agreements pulled various nations into what otherwise would have been a smaller, European conflict. As a result, two main war zones developed: the Eastern and Western fronts (the Eastern front being known especially for its use of trench warfare). The United States didn't enter the war until 1917, due to a series of events which can be studied here: https://www.in.gov/doe/files/guide.pdf

Questions to Ask

1. What events caused WWI?

2. Why was it called "the war to end all wars"? Why was it unique compared to previous military conflicts?

3. What was the role of the US in the war?

4. Did Americans generally agree with the decision to send troops to Europe?

5. Did WWI cause any social or cultural changes in the US during and after this period?

Primary Sources

- World War 1 (University of San Diego):
  https://ucsd.libguides.com/primarysources/ww1

- World War 1: (Oklahoma State University):
  https://info.library.okstate.edu/warprimarysources/wwi

- World War 1 Primary & Secondary Sources (University of Pennsylvania):
  https://guides.library.upenn.edu/WorldWarI

General Spines, Series, and Reference Books

World War 1: The Essential Reference Guide (Tucker)

Web resources

- History: https://www.history.com/topics/world-war-i/world-war-i-history

- World War 1, 1914-1921 (Library of Congress): https://www.loc.gov/collections/stars-and-stripes/articles-and-essays/a-world-at-war/timeline-1914-1921/

- U.S. Participation in the Great War (Library of Congress): https://www.loc.gov/classroom-materials/united-states-history-primary-source-timeline/progressive-era-to-new-era-1900-1929/united-states-participation-in-world-war-i/

- World War 1 Centennial (National Archives): *archives.gov/topics/wwi*

- WWI: Building the American Military (US Army):

  https://www.army.mil/article/185229/world_war_i_building_the_american_military

Suggested movies/documentaries

1917 (Note: This is rated R for violence, but an *incredible* picture of trench warfare. It's one of the best movies I've seen for WWI history. I recommend finding a clip from the movie for middle school students and consider the maturity level of high school students in showing them larger clips.)

The First World War (13+)
All is Quiet on the Western Front (1979) (14+)

Youtube videos

Elementary

- What Caused the First World War? (Simple History)

- Life Inside a WWI A7V Tank (Cross Section) (Simple History)

- Let's Explore World War 1 (parts 1 and 2) (Miacademy Learning Channel)

Middle

- World War One (ALL PARTS) (Epic History TV)

- The True Cost of Peace After WWI (Timeline-World History Documentaries)

- How the First World War Changed the World Forever: Great War in Numbers (War Stories)

- How Did World War 1 Start? (Infographics Show)

- Life in a Trench (History)

High

- Woodrow Wilson: A World War and a League of Nations (Professor Dave Explains)

- WWI: How Tension Between Imperial Powers Started a War (Timeline-World History Documentaries)

Crash Course:

- How WW1 Started (Crash Course History World History 209)

- America in WWI (Crash Course US history #30)

Khan Academy:

- Empires before World War 1

- German and Italian Empires in 1914

- Alliances leading to World War 1

- Assassination of Franz Ferdinand

- The Great War begins

- Blockades, U-boats, and the sinking of the Lusitania

- United States enters World War 1

- Comparing the Eastern and Western fronts in WWI

- Battles of Verdun, Somme and the Hindenburg Line

- Closing stages of World War 1

- Woodrow Wilson's Fourteen Points

- Paris Peace Conference and the Treaty of Versailles

- Technology in World War 1

Tom Richey:

- The Imperial Presidents: Roosevelt, Taft, and Wilson

- The United States in World War 1

Fiction & Nonfiction Books

Title	Author	Age	Period
A Brave Soldier	Debon	6+	1914-1918
A Song for Will	Robinson	8+	1914-1918
Archie's War	Williams	8+	1914-1918

Best Little Stories from World War 1	Kelly	NA	1914-1918
Charlie's War	Manning	5+	1914-1918
Charlotte Sometimes	Nicholls	9+	1914-1918
Dear Jelly	Ridley	8+	1914-1918
DK Eyewitness World War 1	DK	9+	1914-1918
Flo of the Somme	Robinson	5+	1914-1918
Grace Banker and her Hello Girls Answer the Call	Friddell	7+	1914-1918
In Flanders Fields	Granfield	10+	1914-1918
Knit Your Bit: A World War 1 Story	Hopkinson	5+	1914-1918
Line of Fire: Diary of an Unknown Soldier	Morpurgo	10+	1914-1918
National Geographic: Everything World War 1	Kenney	8+	1914-1918
Only Remembered	Beck	12+	1914-1918
Rags: Hero Dog of WWI	Raven	7+	1914-1918
Remembrance	Breslin	12+	1914-1918
See Inside the First World War	Usborne	9+	1914-1918
Sergeant Billy	Messier	4+	1914-1918
Shooting Stars	Hendrix	8+	1914-1918
Simple History: A Simple Guide to World War 1	Turner	9+	1914-1918
Stories of World War 1	Bradman	NA	1914-1918
Stubby: the Dog Soldier World War 1 Hero	Hoena	5+	1914-1918
The Amazing Tale of Ali Pasha	Foreman	8+	1914-1918
The Christmas Truce	Robinson	5+	1914-1918
The Foreshadowing	Sedgwick	12+	1914-1918
The Poppy Lady	Michael	7+	1914-1918
The Singing Tree	Seredy	8+	1914-1918
The Story of the First World War for Children	IWM	8+	1914-1918
The Story of World War 1	Brassey	5+	1914-1918
Truce: The Day Soldiers Stopped Fighting	Murphy	9+	1914-1918
War Game: Village Green to No-Man's-Land	Ridley	9+	1914-1918
What Was World War 1?	Medina	8+	1914-1918

When Christmas Comes Again: The World War 1 Diary of Simone Spencer (Dear America)	Levine	9+	1914-1918
Where the Poppies Now Grow	Robinson	5+	1914-1918
Winnie	Walkers	5+	1914-1918
Winnie's Great War	Mattick	8+	1914-1918
World War 1	Eyewitness Books	8+	1914-1918

Terms to Know

1. activism: the policy or action of using vigorous campaigning to bring about political or social change.

2. Nationalism: identification with one's own nation and support for its interests, especially to the exclusion or detriment of the interests of other nations.

3. Militarism: the belief or desire of a government or people that a country should maintain a strong military capability and be prepared to use it aggressively to defend or promote national interests.

4. Red Scare: The rounding up and deportation of several hundred immigrants of radical political views by the federal government in 1919 and 1920[94]

5. Treaty of Versailles: outlined the conditions of peace between Germany and the victorious Allies on June 28, 1919

6. League of Nations: The League of Nations (1920 – 1946) was the first intergovernmental organization established "to promote international cooperation and to achieve international peace and security". It is often referred to as the "predecessor" of the United Nations.[95]

---

[94] Dictionary.com
[95] https://www.ungeneva.org/en/library-archives/league-of-nations

7. Trench warfare: warfare in which opposing armed forces attack, counterattack, and defend from relatively permanent systems of trenches dug[96]

8. Lusitania: British ocean liner, the sinking of which by a German U-boat on May 7, 1915, contributed indirectly to the entry of the United States[97]

9. Propaganda: information, especially of a biased or misleading nature, used to promote or publicize a particular political cause or point of view.

10. Reparation: the making of amends for a wrong one has done, by paying money to or otherwise helping those who have been wronged.

11. Neutral: an impartial or unbiased country or person; not helping or supporting either side in a conflict, disagreement, etc.; impartial.

12. 14 Points: declaration by U.S. Pres. Woodrow Wilson during World War I outlining his proposals for a postwar peace settlement.[98]

13. Socialism: a political and economic theory of social organization which advocates that the means of production, distribution, and exchange should be owned or regulated by the community as a whole.

14. Capitalism: an economic and political system in which a country's trade and industry are controlled by private owners for profit.

15. Western front: refers to the western side of territory under the control of Germany, which was also fighting on its eastern flank for most of the conflict. The struggle between the Allied and Central armies at the Western Front largely determined the course of the war.[99]

16. Selective Service Act: passed by Congress on May 18, 1917, in which authorized the Federal Government to temporarily expand the military through conscription.

---

[96] Encyclopedia Britannica
[97] Ibid.
[98] Ibid.
[99] Ibid.

17. <u>Espionage Act of 1917</u>: prohibited obtaining information, recording pictures, or copying descriptions of any information relating to the national defense with intent or reason to believe that the information may be used for the injury of the United States or to the advantage of any foreign nation.[100]

18. <u>Dogfight</u>: a close combat between military aircraft.

19. <u>Doughboys</u>: nickname given to US soldiers during WWI

20. <u>No-man's land</u>: the narrow, muddy, treeless stretch of land, characterized by numerous shell holes, that separated German and Allied trenches during the First World War[101]

21. <u>Spanish Flu Epidemic</u>: a severe influenza pandemic in 1918 caused by an H121 virus; infected 500 million people globally

Areas to Know
- The Western front battlefields:
  cwgc.org/our-work/blog/best-ww1-battlefields-to-visit-a-guide/

- The Eastern Front: (National Archives)
  nationalarchives.gov.uk/pathways/firstworldwar/document_packs/eastern.htm

People to Know

- Vladimir Lenin
- Mustafasa Kemal Ataturk
- Woodrow Wilson
- Nicholas II of Russia
- Franz Ferdinand
- Franz Joseph 1 of Austria
- Bernard Baruch
- George Creel
- King George V of the United Kingdom

---

[100] https://www.mtsu.edu/first-amendment/article/1045/espionage-act-of-1917
[101] https://www.warmuseum.ca/overthetop/glossary/no-mans-land

- Gen. John J. Pershing
- King Albert 1
- Constantine I
- David Lloyd George

Enrichment Activities

General Enrichment Ideas:

- <u>Letters from the Past</u>: write a letter during each lesson from the perspective of a person living during that time period. Be sure to include the date, mention anything historically relevant, and try to understand the perspective of the person in which you're writing. Keep the letters in a folder or binder.
- <u>Book of Eras</u>: Create a timeline for each lesson, illustrating key people and events, and writing the dates chronologically. When the year is over, you have a whole history book you created yourself!
- <u>Book of Bios</u>: Focus specifically on the people you've learned about this year. Create a bio for one or more important people from each lesson and think of creative ways to document their lives and roles in the past. (Ex: create a social media "profile" for each person, or a text/conversation between two or more people.)
- <u>A Taste of History</u>: For each lesson or time period, research a recipe from that era and write it on a notecard. Save your recipes in a recipe box and cook your way through the past. Another idea is to keep a blog or YouTube channel documenting each recipe, how it was typically prepared (comparing/contrasting it to modern day methods), and any other historical tidbit you find interesting.
- <u>Travel Thru History</u>: For each lesson, create a travel brochure depicting important areas of interest in the area. (It can be funny or serious.)
- <u>Diorama</u>: Choose one (or more) period to illustrate with a diorama.
- <u>Fashion through the Ages</u>: Design a fashion magazine using what you've learned about each era's dress and style.

Specific to this lesson:

- Read the book, *Nathan Hale's Hazardous Tales: Treaties, Trenches, Mud and Blood.* Then, create this WWI helmet:
  adventuresinmommydom.org/how-to-make-a-world-war-1-helmet

- Download the *World War 1 History for Kids* app (by Abecedaire). At the time of this publication, the app is $4.99, and well worth the money.

- Explore this article called *Life in the Trenches*:
  bbc.co.uk/bitesize/topics/zqhyb9q/articles/z8sssbk
  Then, similar to this blogpost by Over the Crescent Moon, create a diorama depicting WWI trench warfare (free download of 1918 paper dolls included):
  overthecrescentmoon.blogspot.com/2014/03/world-war-1-history-unit.html

- Watch the Youtube video, World War 1: Summary on a Map (Geo History). Then, visit this interactive WW1 map by the National Archives:
  nationalarchives.gov.uk/first-world-war/a-global-view/
  Select each region to read a small overview of its role in the Great War.

- Learn about Flanders' Field and WWI Remembrance Day:
  britishlegion.org.uk/get-involved/remembrance/about-remembrance/in-flanders-field
- Then, create this Remembrance Day mason jar lantern:
  teachstarter.com/gb/blog/remembrance-day-classroom-activities-2/

Making Connections

World War I made enormous changes to the United States, the most important being that it greatly increased the power and size of the federal government. Mobilizing men for war also meant mobilizing resources they would require in order to win: the federal government nationalized the shipping, telegraph, railroad, and telephone industries and increased the role of the Federal Reserve.[102]

Two acts, the Espionage Act of 1917, and the Sedition Act of 1918, made criticism of the government or its mobilization essentially an act of treason. The war altered the roles of African Americans (who experienced a more progressive level of equality in the armed forces) and women (who went to work while the men were at war), increasing interest in both suffrage and early civil rights.[103]

Men came back from war maimed and many with PTSD (then, called "shell shock"), and those disenchanted by war (and the simultaneous Spanish flu

---

[102] https://fee.org/articles/how-war-amplified-federal-power-in-the-twentieth-century
[103] www.sites.si.edu/s/topic/0TO36000000acs4GAA/world-war-i-lessons-and-legacies#media-1

epidemic) caused waves in the literary world, as writers like Hemingway and Dos Passos. It also set a precedent for future American involvement in international matters which would continue through the 20th and 21st Centuries.

Lesson 23: The Roaring Twenties (1920-1929)

Lesson 23: The Roaring Twenties (1920-1929)

Introduction

The decade of the 1920s represents a huge shift in American culture. Republican Presidents (Harding, Coolidge, and Hoover) believed in "laisez faire" capitalism, which greatly decreased the economic restrictions on businesses and helped the American economy thrive. This era is marked by a rapid increase in the use of credit rather than cash, an explosion of new technology and inventions, and a growing divide between progressive secularism in the cities and traditional conservatism in towns and rural communities. The Spanish Flu ravaged the US. Many American soldiers returned home from WWI maimed by war and carrying a newly defined mental illness: PTSD. Post-war Disenchantment influenced an "Age of Anxiety" among young people which resulted in darker themes in literature and poetry. Books like *The Waste Land* (T. S. Eliot), *The Great Gatsby* (F. Scott Fitzgerald), and *The Sun Also Rises* (Ernest Hemingway) represent this era of disillusionment.

The massive migration of black Americans to northern cities from the south helped to create the Harlem Renaissance and the birth of jazz. Meanwhile, Prohibition (the criminalization of alcohol sales through the passing of the 18th amendment) enabled "speakeasies" and organized crime to flourish. The Mafia—particularly mob bosses like Al Capone—become more powerful and richer during this period.

Lastly, its important to note that the 1920s began the Fundamentalist movement in the United States—a conservative, Christian-based pushback to progressivism, especially in education. This can be seen during the Scope's Trial of 1925 The following two sources (with opposing views) demonstrate the division between fundamentalist-modernist debate:

- The Modernist-Fundamentalist Controversy and its Impact on Liberal Religion (by Daniel Ross Chandler): https://huumanists.org/publications/journal/modernist-fundamentalist-controversy-and-its-impact-liberal-religion

- Fundamentalists, Modernists, and Evolution in the 1920's (Ted David): https://biologos.org/series/should-christians-take-the-vaccine/articles/fundamentalists-modernists-and-evolution
- Dr. Rob Kajiwara, a PhD graduate from Liberty University, shares a detailed account of the Fundamentalist-Modernist Controversy in the Youtube video, J.Gersham Machen & Fundamentalist-Modernist Controversy (Rob Kajiwara)

Questions to Ask

1. Which areas did the "roaring 20s" affect? Did this culture shift happen everywhere?

2. What did "becoming modern" mean? How did this differ depending on gender?

3. To what extent did women's suffrage affect this era?

4. What was American culture generally like during this decade?

5. How did the Fundamentalist-Modernist Controversy impact American society?

US Presidents between 1920-1929

President	Vice President	Years
Woodrow Wilson	Thomas R. Marshall	1913-1921
Warren Harding	Calvin Coolidge	1921-1923
Calvin Coolidge	Office vacant	1923-1925
Calvin Coolidge	Charles G. Dawes	1925-1929

Primary Sources

- The 1920's (Christopher Newport University):
  https://cnu.libguides.com/1920s/general

- Becoming Modern: America in the 1920's (National Humanities Center):
  https://americainclass.org/sources/becomingmodern/index.htm

- Roaring Twenties (Queens University of Charlotte):
  https://library.queens.edu/prohibition/resources

- The Roaring 1920's (University of Virginia): https://millercenter.org/the-presidency/teacher-resources/primary-resources/roaring-1920s

General Spines, Series, and Reference Books

The Boxcar Children (Warner)

Web resources

- History: https://www.history.com/topics/roaring-twenties

- The Roaring Twenties (Gilder Lehrman Institute of American History): AP US History Study Guide: https://ap.gilderlehrman.org/essays/roaring-twenties

- Overview of the 1920s (University of Houston): https://www.digitalhistory.uh.edu/era.cfm?eraid=13&smtid=1

Suggested movies/documentaries

Bugsy Malone (1976) (G)

Citizen Cane (1941) (PG

Thoroughly Modern Millie (1967) (G)

The Great Gatsby (1974) (PG)

(Note: The following two movies, while good examples of life in the 1920s, contain subjects and scenes not always suited for children. VidAngel would be the best way to watch this with your family):

    The Great Gatsby (2013) (13+)

    Chicago (2002) (13+)

Youtube videos

Elementary

- History Brief: Daily Life in the 1920s (Reading Through History)
- The Roaring Twenties Explained in 11 Minutes (Captivating History)
- Objective 4.8: Roaring Twenties Culture (You Will Love History)

Middle

- What Was Life Like in 1920s America? (AJ Merrick)
- The Roaring Twenties in 2 Minutes (History Skills)

High

- APUSH Review: The 1920s (Adam Norris)
- Origins of the Sicilian Mafia (Kings and Generals)

Crash Course:
- The Roaring 20s: Crash Course US History #32

Tom Richey:
- The Roaring Twenties: Part 1 (US History EOC Review-USHC 6.1)
- The 1920s (USVID-01)-APUSH

Fiction & Nonfiction Books

Title	Author	Age	Period
America in the 1920s	Oneal	10+	1920-1929
Celeste's Harlem Renaissance	Tate	8+	1920-1929
Harlem Stomp!	Hill	12+	1920-1929
Mama and Me and the Model-T	Gibbons	4+	1920-1929
The Roaring Twenties: Discover the Era of Prohibition, Flappers, and Jazz	Lusted	12+	1920-1929
What Were the Roaring Twenties?	Mortlock	8+	1920-1929
Ella's Big Chance	Hughes	4+	1920-1929
Snow White in New York	French	5+	1920-1929
Unspeakable: The Tulsa Race Massacre	Weatherford	6+	1920-1929
Lord of the Mountain	Kidd	9+	1920-1929

Terms to Know

1. Harlem Renaissance: a period of rich cross-disciplinary artistic and cultural activity among African Americans between the end of World War I (1917)

and the onset of the Great Depression and lead up to World War II (the 1930s).[104]

2. 18th Amendment: Prohibition: An amendment to the US Constitution which prohibited the "the manufacture, sale, or transportation of intoxicating liquours" but not the consumption, private possession, or production for one's own consumption.

3. 19th Amendment: An amendment to the US Constitution which granted women the right to vote

4. Teapot Dome Scandal: a government scandal involving a former United States Navy oil reserve in Wyoming that was secretly leased to a private oil company in 1921[105]

5. flapper: (in the 1920s) a fashionable young woman intent on enjoying herself and flouting conventional standards of behavior.

6. Lost Generation: the generation reaching maturity during and just after World War I, a high proportion of whose men were killed during those years: an unfulfilled generation coming to maturity during a period of instability.

7. Tin Pan Alley: the district of a city, especially New York City, where most of the popular music is published.[106]

8. jazz: a type of music of African American origin characterized by improvisation, syncopation, and usually a regular or forceful rhythm, emerging at the beginning of the 20th century. Brass and woodwind instruments and piano are particularly associated with jazz, although guitar and occasionally violin are also used; styles include Dixieland, swing, bebop, and free jazz.

9. "Return to Normalcy": President Warren Harding popularized the word normalcy with his slogan, "Return to normalcy." Harding was referring getting back to normal life after World War I[107]

10. speakeasies: (during Prohibition) an illicit liquor store or nightclub

---

[104] https://www.nga.gov/learn/teachers/lessons-activities/uncovering-america/harlem-renaissance.html
[105] Vocabulary.com
[106] Dictionary.com
[107] Vocabulary.com

11. <u>bootleggers</u>: a person who makes, distributes, or sells goods illegally

12. <u>gangster</u>: Although the term "gangster" is used for any criminal from the 1920s or 30s that operated in a group, it refers to two different breeds. Mobsters belonged to organized crime rings. They generally lived in large cities, and most were immigrants, or children of immigrants.[108]

Areas to Know

- Harlem, New York City

People to Know

- Henry Ford
- Louis Armstrong
- Albert Einstein
- Coco Chanel
- Charlie Chaplin
- Al Capone
- Babe Ruth
- F. Scott Fitzgerald
- Charles Lindbergh
- Rudolph Valentino
- Louise Brooks (famous flapper)
- Anna May Wong
- Josephine Baker
- Pablo Picasso
- Henry Hoover
- Duke Ellington
- Greta Garbo
- Georgia O'Keeffe
- Jack Dempsey
- Clarence Darrow
- William Jennings Bryan

---

[108] https://www.pbs.org/wgbh/americanexperience/features/dillinger-gangsters-during-depression

Enrichment Activities

General Enrichment Ideas:

- <u>Letters from the Past</u>: write a letter during each lesson from the perspective of a person living during that time period. Be sure to include the date, mention anything historically relevant, and try to understand the perspective of the person in which you're writing. Keep the letters in a folder or binder.
- <u>Book of Eras</u>: Create a timeline for each lesson, illustrating key people and events, and writing the dates chronologically. When the year is over, you have a whole history book you created yourself!
- <u>Book of Bios</u>: Focus specifically on the people you've learned about this year. Create a bio for one or more important people from each lesson and think of creative ways to document their lives and roles in the past. (Ex: create a social media "profile" for each person, or a text/conversation between two or more people.)
- <u>A Taste of History</u>: For each lesson or time period, research a recipe from that era and write it on a notecard. Save your recipes in a recipe box and cook your way through the past. Another idea is to keep a blog or YouTube channel documenting each recipe, how it was typically prepared (comparing/contrasting it to modern day methods), and any other historical tidbit you find interesting.
- <u>Travel Thru History</u>: For each lesson, create a travel brochure depicting important areas of interest in the area. (It can be funny or serious.)
- <u>Diorama</u>: Choose one (or more) period to illustrate with a diorama.
- <u>Fashion through the Ages</u>: Design a fashion magazine using what you've learned about each era's dress and style.

Specific to this lesson:

- Read this article about the 1920s:
  https://www.ducksters.com/history/us_1900s/roaring_twenties.php
  Then, **answer**:
    1. What was the general feeling of the 1920s?
    2. What was the economy like for most people?
    3. What was being mass produced at this time, and how did those items change lives?
    4. Sometimes the Roaring Twenties is also called the Age of _____.
    5. Which amendment was ratified in 1920, and what did it do?

6. Explain what "mass culture" means.
7. How much was a Model T Ford car in 1925? What did this mean for Americans?

- Watch the Youtube video, *The Great Migration and the Harlem Renaissance* (The 1920s Channel).
  Then create a Venn diagram, anchor chart, or "doodle notes" explaining how the Great Migration and Harlem Renaissance impacted each other.

- Watch the Youtube video, *1920s Dances Featuring the Charleston, the Peabody, Turkey Trot, and more* (Savoy Hop). Compare that style of dance with the three below (which were common in the 1900-1910 period.
  1. Cake Walk (Library of Congress)
  2. Stanford at Spoleto Festival: Winner's Redowa (Jason Anderson)
  3. Quadrille Club dancing the Beseda Quadrille (Ellis Rogers)

Answer: Do you think parents of young people in the 1920s might have been concerned about dances like the Charleston? Why/why not? What might the changes in dance style reflect about American society?

Making Connections

The 1920s were a period of remarkable social, technological, and cultural changes. The horrors of World War 1 impacted the way younger Americans viewed their world, and this shift was reflected in music, literature, and poetry of the day. Cinema saw a boom during this era as they transitioned from silent films to "talkies" (movies with sound), and Americans flocked to movies all around the country. This shared experience created a "mass culture", along with the spread of new music and dances.

The 1920s also reflects a growing cultural division which persists to this day: city culture became more modern and progressive, while rural areas generally remained traditional. Affordability caused by mass production (in terms of everything from vehicles to home appliances) helped increase personal wealth of Americans, but racial disparities still existed. The lavishness and excess of the American economy (and spending habits) helped to create the Great Depression, which would begin following the Stock Market Crash in 1929.

Lesson 24: The Great Depression (1930-1940)

Lesson 24: The Great Depression (1930-1940)

Introduction

One of the most devastating events in recent American history was the Great Depression. Beginning with (but not because of) the Stock Market Crash in 1929, the US would enter a decades-long period of economic struggle. The causes of the Great Depression are a combination of factors, including a series of bank failures, bank rushes (people rushing to withdrawal their money all at once), the federal government's decision to increase tariffs on international trade, failures in the stock market and the over-abundant use of credit. The beginning of the decade saw a string of droughts which created the Dust Bowl, which had its own causes and effects. This era demonstrated the differences between a weak, generally hands-off Executive branch (Hoover) and a strong, involved one (FDR). The policies enacted by FDR are debated to this day as they relate to the role of the federal government in the national economy.

Questions to Ask

1. What were the events leading to the Great Depression?

2. What caused the stock market to crash?

3. How did the Great Depression affect the lives of everyday Americans?

4. What policies were put in place to help pull the nation out of this economic depression?

5. What are the various views of FDR's "New Deal"?

6. Are there any lasting impacts today from this period?

7. Can the Great Depression happen again?

US Presidents between 1929-1941

President	Vice President	Years
Herbert Hoover	Charles Curtis	1929-1933
Franklin D. Roosevelt	John N. Garner	1933-1941

Primary Sources

- Great Depression Primary Sources (National Archives):
  https://education.blogs.archives.gov/2021/02/18/great-depression-2/

- Great Depression Era (Lone Star College):
  https://kwlibguides.lonestar.edu/PrimarySources-History/depressionera

- The Great Depression and the 1930s (Christopher Newport University):
  https://cnu.libguides.com/psthegreatdepression

General Spines, Series, and Reference Books

NA

Web resources

- History: https://www.history.com/topics/great-depression

- Federal Reserve History: https://www.federalreservehistory.org/essays/great-depression

- Great Depression (EconLib):
  https://www.econlib.org/library/Enc/GreatDepression.html

- The Great Depression (Khan Academy):
  https://www.khanacademy.org/humanities/us-history/rise-to-world-power/great-depression/a/the-great-depression

- Americans React to the Great Depression (Library of Congress):
  https://loc.gov/classroom-materials/united-states-history-primary-source-timeline/great-depression-and-world-war-ii-1929-1945/americans-react-to-great-depression/

- The Great Depression (essay by David Wheelock):
  https://www.stlouisfed.org/-/media/project/frbstl/stlouisfed/files/pdfs/great-depression/the-great-depression-wheelock-overview.pdf

- The Great Depression (Ducksters):
  https://www.ducksters.com/history/us_1900s/causes_of_the_great_depression.php

- African Americans and the New Deal:
  digitalhistory.uh.edu/disp_textbook.cfm?smtID=2&psid=3447

- African American Life During the Great Depression and the New Deal: https://www.britannica.com/topic/African-American/African-American-life-during-the-Great-Depression-and-the-New-Deal

- Depression and World War II (1929-1945) Ken Burns in the Classroom: https://pbslearningmedia.org/collection/kenburnsclassroom/era/depression-and-world-war-ii-1929-1945/

Suggested movies/documentaries

Cinderella Man
The Dust Bowl (Ken Burns)
The Grapes of Wrath (1940)
O Brother, Where Art Thou? (2000) (13+)[109]
Of Mice and Men (1992) (13+)
Race (2016) (13+)

Youtube videos

Elementary

- The Great Depression for Kids (Learn Bright)

- History Brief: Daily Life in the 1930s (Reading Through History)

- Great Depression, What Was Life Actually Like (The Infographics Show)

- The Great Depression: 5th Grade Social Studies (Courtney Larson)

- The Great Depression (FDR Library)

- Great Depression Cooking series

---

[109] This can also be watched when you're learning about the Odyssey.

Middle

- The Great Depression Explained in One Minute (One Minute Economics)

- The Great Depression and FDRs New Deal: America, the Story of Us (S1:E9)

- Black Tuesday: The People Who Lived Through the Great Depression (Timeline: World History Documentaries)

- Life on the Plains: Remembering the Dust Bowl and the Great Depression (Mark Albertins Time Capsule)

High

- The Dust Bowl Explained (Hip Hughes)

Crash Course:
- The Great Depression: Crash Course US History #33

Tom Richey:
- The Great Depression (1929-1933): APUSH Topic 7.9

- AP US History Prep with Tom Richey #8: The Great Depression and World War II (1929-1945) (Bill of Rights Institute)

Professor Dave Explains:
- Calvin Coolidge: Silent Cal (1923-1929)

- Herbert Hoover: The Great Depression Begins (1929-1933)

Fiction & Nonfiction Books

Title	Author	Age	Period
A Long Way From Chicago	Peck	9+	1930-1940
Born and Bred in the Great Depression	Winter	5+	1930-1940

Children of the Great Depression	Freedman	10+	1930-1940
Christmas After All (Dear American series)	Lasky	8+	1930-1940
Crash	Favreau	10+	1930-1940
Daily Life in the United States, 1920-1940: How Americans Lived Through the Roaring Twenties and the Great Depression	Kyvig	12+	1930-1940
Dorathea's Eyes	Rosenstock	7+	1930-1940
Dust for Dinner	Barrett	4+	1930-1940
Lucky Beans	Birtha	4+	1930-1940
Moon Over Manifest	Vanderpool	10+	1930-1940
My Heart Will Not Sit Down	Rockliff	5+	1930-1940
Nice Work, Franklin!	Jurmain	5+	1930-1940
No Promises in the Wind	Hunt	12+	1930-1940
Nothing to Fear	Koller	10+	1930-1940
Out of the Dust	Hesse	10+	1930-1940
Potato: A Tale from the Great Depression	Lied	6+	1930-1940
Roll of Thunder, Hear My Cry	Taylor	10+	1930-1940
Rose's Journal: The Story of a Girl of the Great Depression	Moss	8+	1930-1940
Rudy Rides the Rails	Mackall	6+	1930-1940
Six Days in October	Blumenthal	12+	1930-1940
Sky Boys	Hopkinson	4+	1930-1940
The Dust Bowl	Reczuch	5+	1930-1940
The Gardener	Stewart	3+	1930-1940
The Great Depression: A History Just for Kids	KidCaps	9+	1930-1940
The Lucky Star	Young	6+	1930-1940
The Truth About Sparrows	Hale	12+	1930-1940
Voices of the Dust Bowl	Garland	8+	1930-1940
We Had Everything but Money	Mulvey	13+	1930-1940
What Was the Great Depression?	Pascal	8+	1930-1940
The Miner's Daughter	Laskas	13+	1930-1940

Terms to Know

1. Agricultural Adjustment Act: The Agricultural Adjustment Act (AAA) was a federal law passed in 1933 as part of U.S. president Franklin D. Roosevelt's New Deal. The law offered farmers subsidies in exchange for limiting their production of certain crops. The subsidies were meant to limit overproduction so that crop prices could increase.[110]

2. Bank holiday: After a month-long run on American banks, Franklin Delano Roosevelt proclaimed a Bank Holiday, beginning March 6, 1933, that shut down the banking system. When the banks reopened on March 13, depositors stood in line to return their hoarded cash.[111]

3. Black Tuesday: October 29, 1929. On this date, share prices on the New York Stock Exchange completely collapsed, becoming a pivotal factor in the emergence of the Great Depression.

4. Black Sunday: April 14th, 1935, when a dust storm (dubbed the worst dust storm in the Dust Bowl) covered the Great Plains

5. Civilian Conservation Corp: a federal program enacted by FDR's New Deal which allowed single men between the ages of 18 and 25 to enlist in work programs to improve America's public lands, forests, and parks

6. Bonus Army: a group of 12,000 World War I veterans who massed in Washington, D.C., the summer of 1932 to induce Congress to appropriate moneys for the payment of bonus certificates granted in 1924.[112]

7. Dust Bowl: an area of Oklahoma, Kansas, and northern Texas affected by severe soil erosion (caused by windstorms) in the early 1930s, which obliged many people to move.

8. Great Depression: the financial and industrial slump of 1929 and subsequent years; a long and severe recession in an economy or market.

---

[110] Georgia Encyclopia.org
[111] www.newyorkfed.org/research/epr/09v15n1/0907silb.html
[112] Dictionary.com

9. <u>Fireside chats</u>: Roosevelt called his radio talks about issues of public concern "Fireside Chats." Informal and relaxed, the talks made Americans feel as if President Roosevelt was talking directly to them.[113]

10. <u>Gold standard</u>: the system by which the value of a currency was defined in terms of gold, for which the currency could be exchanged. The gold standard was generally abandoned in the Depression of the 1930s.

11. <u>New Deal</u>: a series of programs and projects instituted during the Great Depression by President Franklin D. Roosevelt that aimed to restore prosperity to Americans.[114]

12. <u>Inflation</u>: a general increase in prices and fall in the purchasing value of money.

13. <u>Recession</u>: a period of temporary economic decline during which trade and industrial activity are reduced, generally identified by a fall in GDP in two successive quarters.

14. <u>Works Process Administration</u>: a program created by then-President Franklin Delano Roosevelt in 1935 to boost employment and the purchasing power Americans by placing millions of skilled and unskilled workers in a broad range of jobs covering everything from the construction of infrastructure and public structures to the arts and manufacturing.[115]

15. <u>Hoovervilles</u>: a shantytown built by unemployed and destitute people during the Depression of the early 1930s.

Areas to Know

- The areas on this Great Depression atlas map:
https://wps.pearsoncustom.com/wps/media/objects/2428/2487068/atlas/atl_ah5_m005.html

---

[113] https://www.archives.gov/education/lessons/fdr-fireside
[114] https://www.history.com/topics/great-depression/new-deal
[115] https://www.investopedia.com/works-progress-administration-wpa-definition-5204419

People to Know

- Franklin Delano Roosevelt
- Herbert Hoover
- Huey Long
- Father Coughlin

Enrichment Activities

General Enrichment Ideas:

- Letters from the Past: write a letter during each lesson from the perspective of a person living during that time period. Be sure to include the date, mention anything historically relevant, and try to understand the perspective of the person in which you're writing. Keep the letters in a folder or binder.
- Book of Eras: Create a timeline for each lesson, illustrating key people and events, and writing the dates chronologically. When the year is over, you have a whole history book you created yourself!
- Book of Bios: Focus specifically on the people you've learned about this year. Create a bio for one or more important people from each lesson and think of creative ways to document their lives and roles in the past. (Ex: create a social media "profile" for each person, or a text/conversation between two or more people.)
- A Taste of History: For each lesson or time period, research a recipe from that era and write it on a notecard. Save your recipes in a recipe box and cook your way through the past. Another idea is to keep a blog or YouTube channel documenting each recipe, how it was typically prepared (comparing/contrasting it to modern day methods), and any other historical tidbit you find interesting.
- Travel Thru History: For each lesson, create a travel brochure depicting important areas of interest in the area. (It can be funny or serious.)
- Diorama: Choose one (or more) period to illustrate with a diorama.
- Fashion through the Ages: Design a fashion magazine using what you've learned about each era's dress and style.

Specific to this lesson:

- Read this article about the Great Depression:
  https://kids.britannica.com/students/article/Great-Depression/274639
  Then, create a brief timeline to show import events which led to the
  Great Depression, and what occurs during it, including the terms:
  Stock Market Crash, bank failures, manufacturing company closures,
  drought, Dust Bowl, collapse in international trade, Hoovervilles, FDR
  election, the New Deal, WWII

- Download this free elementary-age unit study:
  https://homeschoolgiveaways.com/2019/08/free-great-depression-unit-
  study/

- Choose a game to play from this list:
  https://greatdepression.mrdonn.org/games.html

- Choose a recipe to make from this collection of Great Depression
  recipes: https://www.tasteofhome.com/collection/depression-era-recipes/

- Watch Great Depression Cooking videos on YouTube from Clara, a
  woman who lived through the depression. Great Depression Cooking
  series

- Read this article about the music written during the 1930s:
  https://www.loc.gov/item/ihas.200197402/
  Answer: How did the music of this era reflect the views of everyday
  Americans? What did the WPA accomplish during this era which is of
  particular use to historians today? What did the Federal Theatre
  Project and the Federal Music Project do for musicians? List and listen
  to a few of the songs written about in this article.

Making Connections

The actions of FDR further expanded the role of the federal government, to the
cheer of some and the protest of others. While the New Deal helped Americans find
gainful employment, banks were restored with new federal restrictions, and the
droughts in the plains ended, many historians agree that what truly pulled America

out of a decade-long depression was the development of the war-time economy. Mobilizing the economy for war[116] put Americans to work, especially women, who would fill a large role on the home front. The impact of Great Depression policies is something which is still debated by economists, politicians, and historians in present day.

---

[116] www.loc.gov/classroom-materials/united-states-history-primary-source-timeline/great-depression-and-world-war-ii-1929-1945/

Lesson 25: World War II
(1939-1945)

Lesson 25: World War II (1939-1945)

Introduction

World War II began with Germany invading Poland in 1939 and ended with Japan signing the Instrument of Surrender on an American battleship off the coast of Tokyo in 1945. What happened in the middle was the deadliest world conflict in history, with a casualty of an estimated 56.4 million.[117] Many historians believe it was the treatment of Germany after WWI which enabled Hitler to take power and wage war in Europe. His "final solution" included both work and death camps for Jews: The Holocaust killed 6 million Jews by the time the Allies were able to liberate them.

The United States began offering military supplies and other help to the Allies in 1940, but under FDR determined to stay neutral in the war. Then, on December 7, 1941, Japan bombed the US navy base at Pearl Harbor, Hawaii, catapulting America into WWII.[118] Average Americans went to war on the home front, rationing food, digging "victory gardens", organizing scrap metal drives, and buying war bonds. American factories were adapted to build tanks, Jeeps, bombs, planes, and other military supplies. World War II was the final event which brought America out of the Great Depression and on its way to becoming a world superpower.

Questions to Ask

1. What conditions led to World War 2?

2. How could Hitler have been so successful?

3. Why were Jews and others (including the disabled, Roma people, and political opponents) targeted by the Nazi party?

4. Which countries were involved in World War 2, and what was the nature of their involvement?

5. In what ways did the wartime economy pull the US out of their Great Depression?

---

[117] www.guinnessworldrecords.com/world-records/highest-death-toll-from-wars
[118] www.history.state.gov/milestones/1937-1945/lend-lease

6. What lasting impact does WWII have upon world political, social, and cultural relationships?

7. What was the role of nuclear power in WWII?

US Presidents between 1939-1945

President	Vice President	Years
Franklin D. Roosevelt	Henry Wallace	1941-1945
Franklin D. Roosevelt	Harry S. Truman	1945
Harry S. Truman	Office vacant	1945-1949

Primary Sources

- World War II (University of Washington): https://guides.lib.uw.edu/research/history-military/wwii

- WWII (Docs Teach): https://docsteach.org/topics/wwii

- World War II: A Resource Guide (Library of Congress): https://guides.loc.gov/ww2/library-of-congress-resources

General Spines, Series, and Reference Books

The Chronicles of Narnia (Lewis)

Web resources

- History: https://www.history.com/topics/world-war-ii/world-war-ii-history https://www.history.com/topics/world-war-ii/us-home-front-during-world-war-ii

- Britannica: https://www.britannica.com/event/World-War-II

- Significant Events in WWII (US Department of Defense): https://www.defense.gov/News/Feature-Stories/story/article/2293108/

Suggested movies/documentaries

A Call to Spy (PG13)
Ann Frank: Parallel Stories (14+)
As it Happened: Tarawa (13+)
Attack on Pearl Harbor: Minute by Minute (14+)
Berlin 1945 (16+)
Bonhoeffer: Agent of Grace (13+)
Churchills Secret Agents (MA)
Darkest Hour (PG13)
D-Day: The Price of Freedom (7+)
Greatest Tank Battles (13+)
Last Secrets of the 3rd Reich (13+))
Omaha Beach: Honor and Sacrifice (13+)
Operation Mincemeat (PG13)
Prisoner Number A26188: Surviving Auschwitz (13+)
Storming Juno (7+)
The Complete Story of Hitler and the Nazis (13+)
The Forgotten Battle (18+)
The Hiding Place (13+)
The Liberator (18+)
The Real Inglorious Bastards (13+)
The Zookeeper's Wife (PG13)
War in the Pacific (13+)
World War 2-The Call of Duty: A Complete Timeline (13+)
World War II: Total War (13+)
WWII in Color (18+)
WWII in HD (13+)

Youtube videos

Elementary

- World War II for Kids (Learn Bright)
- A Brief Overview of World War II (Simple History)
- World War II (short version) (Geo History)

Middle

- World War II Casualties by Country (World Data 3D)
- World War II: Summary on a Map (Geo History)

History:

- The US Enters WWII: America: The Story of Us (S1, E10)

High School

Crash Course:
- WWII: Crash Course World History #38
- WWII Part 1: Crash Course US History #35
- WWII Part 2: Crash Course US History #36

Timeline (History Hits Channel):
- The American Workers that helped the US dominate WW2 (Timeline-World History Documentaries)
- Behind the scenes of the WWII German war machine
- Hitlers End: the final months of WW2 in Europe

Professor Dave Explains:
- Franklin Delano Roosevelt: Four-Term Phenomenon (1933-1945)
- Harry Truman: Dropping Bombs (1945-1953)

Fiction & Nonfiction Books

Title	Author	Age	Period
What Was Pearl Harbor Day?	Demuth	8+	1941
What Was D-Day?	Demuth	8+	1944
What Was the Holocaust?	Herman	8+	1939-1945
Who Was Anne Frank?	Abramson	8+	1939-1945
Allies	Gratz	10+	1939-1945
Always Remember Me	Russo	6+	1939-1945
America in the 1940s	Wills	8+	1939-1945
Anne Frank: Diary of a Young Girl	Frank	9+	1939-1945
Bomb	Sheinkin	10+	1939-1945
Carrie's War	Bawden	8+	1939-1945
Children of the WWII Homefront	Whitman	7+	1939-1945
Codename Celine	Eldridge	14+	1939-1945
Courage Has No Color	Stone	10+	1939-1945
Goodnight, Mr. Tom	Magorian	9+	1939-1945
Growing Up in World War II: 1941-1945	Josephson	9+	1939-1945
Letters from the Lighthouse	Carroll	9+	1939-1945

My Secret War Diary	Williams	8+	1939-1945
Nim and the War Effort	Lee	6+	1939-1945
No Better Friend	Weintraub	10+	1939-1945
Number the Stars	Lowry	9+	1939-1945
Passage to Freedom: The Sugihara Story	Mochizuki	6+	1939-1945
Rose Blanch	McEwan	10+	1939-1945
See Inside the Second World War	Usborne	9+	1939-1945
Simple History: A Simple Guide to World War II	Turner	4+	1939-1945
The Emergency Zoo	Halahmy	9+	1939-1945
The Faithful Spy: Dietrich Bonhoeffer and the Plot to Kill Hitler	Hendrix	10+	1939-1945
The Lion and the Unicorn	Hughes	5+	1939-1945
The Lion, the Witch, and the Wardrobe	Lewis	5+	1939-1945
The Little Ships: The Heroic Rescue at Dunkirk		9+	1939-1945
We Had to be Brave	Hopkinson	8+	1939-1945
What Was the Bombing of Hiroshima?	Brallier	8+	1945
When Hitler Stole Pink Rabbit	Kerr	9+	1939-1945
Who Were the Navajo Code Talkers?	Buckley	8+	1939-1945
Who Were the Tuskegee Airmen?	Smith	6+	1939-1945
World War II for Kids	Panchyk	8+	1939-1945
World War II Visual Encyclopedia	DK	8+	1939-1945
You Wouldn't Want to Be a Secret Agent in World War II	Malaam	8+	1939-1945
You Wouldn't Want to be a World War II Pilot	Graham	8+	1939-1945

Terms to Know

1. <u>imperialism</u>: a policy of extending a country's power and influence through diplomacy or military force.

2. <u>appeasement</u>: Foreign policy of pacifying an aggrieved country through negotiation in order to prevent war

3. <u>World War II</u>: the war that was fought mainly in Europe and Asia from 1939 to 1945.

4. <u>Allies</u>: during World War II, the group of nations including the United States, Britain, the Soviet Union, and the Free French, who joined in the war against Germany and other Axis countries[119]

5. <u>Axis Powers</u>: (Germany, Italy, Japan) were opposed by the Allied Powers (led by Great Britain, the United States, and the Soviet Union). 2. Five other nations joined the Axis during World War II: Hungary, Romania, Bulgaria, Slovakia, and Croatia. 3. The decline and fall of the Axis alliance began in 1943[120]

6. <u>Pearl Harbor</u>: a harbor near Honolulu, on S Oahu, in Hawaii: surprise attack by Japan on the U.S. naval base and other military installations December 7, 1941.

7. <u>Iwo Jima</u>: An island in the Pacific Ocean, taken from the Japanese by United States Marines near the end of World War II after a furious battle

8. <u>D-Day</u>: the day (June 6, 1944) in World War II on which Allied forces invaded northern France by means of beach landings in Normandy.

9. <u>VE Day</u>: the day (May 8) marking the Allied victory in Europe in 1945.

10. <u>VJ Day</u>: the day (August 15) in 1945 on which Japan ceased fighting in World War II, or the day (September 2) when Japan formally surrendered.

---

[119] www.fcit.usf.edu/holocaust/DEFN/allies.htm#
[120] https://encyclopedia.ushmm.org/content/en/article/axis-powers-in-world-war-ii

11. Holocaust: destruction or slaughter on a mass scale, especially caused by fire or nuclear war.

12. concentration camp: internment centre for political prisoners and members of national or minority groups

13. atomic bomb: a bomb that derives its destructive power from the rapid release of nuclear energy by fission of heavy atomic nuclei, causing damage through heat, blast, and radioactivity

14. United Nations: an international organization founded in 1945 after the Second World War by 51 countries committed to maintaining international peace and security, developing friendly relations among nations and promoting social progress, better living standards and human rights.[121]

15. UN Security Council: The Security Council has primary responsibility for the maintenance of international peace and security. It has 15 Members, and each Member has one vote. Under the Charter of the United Nations, all Member States are obligated to comply with Council decisions.[122]

16. internment camps: Executive Order 9066 that resulted in the internment of Japanese Americans. The order authorized the Secretary of War and military commanders to evacuate all persons deemed a threat from the West Coast to internment camps, that the government called "relocation centers," further inland[123]

17. antisemitism: hostility to or prejudice against Jewish people

18. fascism: a political philosophy, movement, or regime (such as that of the Fascisti) that exalts nation and often race above the individual and that stands for a centralized autocratic government headed by a dictatorial leader, severe economic and social regimentation, and forcible suppression of opposition[124]

---

[121] https://www.un.org/un70/en/content/history/index.html
[122] https://www.un.org/securitycouncil/
[123123] https://www.archives.gov/education/lessons/japanese-relocation
[124] https://www.merriam-webster.com/dictionary/fascism

19. dictator: a ruler with total power over a country, typically one who has obtained control by force

20. genocide: the deliberate killing of a large number of people from a particular nation or ethnic group with the aim of destroying that nation or group

21. blitzkrieg: an intense military campaign intended to bring about a swift victory

22. Manhattan Project: U.S. government research project (1942–45) that produced the first atomic bombs[125]

23. Third Reich: often used to describe the Nazi regime in Germany from January 30, 1933, to May 8, 1945[126]

24. eugenics: the study of how to arrange reproduction within a human population to increase the occurrence of heritable characteristics regarded as desirable. Developed largely by Sir Francis Galton as a method of improving the human race, eugenics was increasingly discredited as unscientific and racially biased during the 20th century, especially after the adoption of its doctrines by the Nazis in order to justify their treatment of Jews, disabled people, and other minority groups.

25. kamikaze: (in World War II) a Japanese aircraft loaded with explosives and making a deliberate suicidal crash on an enemy target.

26. Navajo Codetalkers: the name given to American Indians who used their tribal language to send secret communications on the battlefield

27. totalitarianism: a system of government that is centralized and dictatorial and requires complete subservience to the state

28. ration: ration books contained removable stamps good for certain rationed items, like sugar, meat, cooking oil, and canned goods

---

[125] https://www.britannica.com/event/Manhattan-Project
[126] https://encyclopedia.ushmm.org/content/en/article/third-reich

29. socialism: a political and economic theory of social organization which advocates that the means of production, distribution, and exchange should be owned or regulated by the community as a whole

Areas to Know

- Watch World War II Unfold Day by Day: An Animated Map
  https://www.openculture.com/2022/11/watch-world-war-ii-unfold-day-by-day-an-animated-map.html

People to Know

- Franklin Delano Roosevelt
- Joseph Stalin
- Harry Truman
- Benito Mussolini
- Winston Churchill
- Emperor Hirohito
- Adolf Hitler
- Rosie the Riveter
- Dwight D. Eisenhower

Enrichment Activities

General Enrichment Ideas:

- Letters from the Past: write a letter during each lesson from the perspective of a person living during that time period. Be sure to include the date, mention anything historically relevant, and try to understand the perspective of the person in which you're writing. Keep the letters in a folder or binder.
- Book of Eras: Create a timeline for each lesson, illustrating key people and events, and writing the dates chronologically. When the year is over, you have a whole history book you created yourself!
- Book of Bios: Focus specifically on the people you've learned about this year. Create a bio for one or more important people from each lesson and

think of creative ways to document their lives and roles in the past. (Ex: create a social media "profile" for each person, or a text/conversation between two or more people.)

- A Taste of History: For each lesson or time period, research a recipe from that era and write it on a notecard. Save your recipes in a recipe box and cook your way through the past. Another idea is to keep a blog or YouTube channel documenting each recipe, how it was typically prepared (comparing/contrasting it to modern day methods), and any other historical tidbit you find interesting.
- Travel Thru History: For each lesson, create a travel brochure depicting important areas of interest in the area. (It can be funny or serious.)
- Diorama: Choose one (or more) period to illustrate with a diorama.
- Fashion through the Ages: Design a fashion magazine using what you've learned about each era's dress and style.

Specific to this lesson:

- Download this free lesson on the rise of dictators by Students of History: https://www.studentsofhistory.com/rise-of-dictators

- Make these WW2 ration cakes: https://tinasdynamichomeschoolplus.com/world-war-ii-hands-history-2/

- Learn about WWII aircraft and make your own planes here: https://layers-of-learning.com/world-war-ii-printable-planes-battle-britain/

- Buy this WW2 replica memorabilia pack: https://www.amazon.com/Childrens-Replica-Memorabilia-Contains-Period/dp/B0025BEPUI

- Visit Nat Geo Kids to learn more about WWII: https://www.natgeokids.com/uk/discover/history/general-history/world-war-two/
  Then, explain the causes of WWII and its effects by creating an informative poster.

- Explore the DK findout! website: https://www.dkfindout.com/us/history/world-war-ii/
  Then, write an essay about one aspect of the war as listed on each drop-down. For a longer project, write a summary paragraph on each link.

- Watch the YouTube video, World War 2 - Explained in 5 Minutes (VidyPedia).
  Then, download and print this free map activity:
  https://standrewsprimarybath.com/wp-content/uploads/2013/07/WW2-Map-of-Europe-1.pdf

- Explore this interactive WWII website!
  https://www.abmc.gov/sites/default/files/interactive/interactive_files/WW2/index.html

Making Connections

Although the United States originally sought to stay out of WWII, the attack at Pearl Harbor changed everything. The wartime economy finished the intention of the New Deal by mobilizing Americans: production of weapons, tanks, Jeeps, and other war-related products helped America grow wealthy. By the time the war ended, the United States emerged a stronger superpower than before...along with the Soviet Union. The relationship between the Soviet Union and the United States grew more hostile as they each fought to be the dominating world power. This tension launched the US into another "war"—the Cold War.

Lesson 26: Post-War Period
(1945-1964)

Lesson 26: Post-War Period (1945-1968)

Introduction

At the end of World War II, American soldiers returned home to a thriving economy. Technological advancements were booming and so was the population: 4.24 million babies were added to the US population every year between 1946-1964.[127] Soldiers received the new GI Bill which helped them buy homes, and the suburbs were born. Thanks to President Truman, 41,000 miles of national interstates and highways connected Americans like never before. The economy soared as 60% of Americans were considered middle class. Higher incomes meant more money to pay for extras like new cars, vacations, and items which made life easier. A car culture emerged, which took advantage of the high way system: this creation a travel industry which included the growth of hotels, motels, and fast-food chains. Although it was an easier time for almost everyone, racial inequality existed in the form of segregation: the Civil Rights movement targeted segregation in schools, restaurants, and transportation. For the first time, the television (in 90% of homes by 1960) was able to show the violence endured by black Americans in the South. The 1950s also saw the launch of the Cold War, a political rivalry between the Soviet Union and the United States. This geopolitical struggle for supremacy caused fear of communism and nuclear war, leading to an Arms Race and the race to conquer the final frontier: space. In the attempt to control the Communism, the US fought in two wars: the Korean War (1950-1953) and the Vietnam War (1955-1975).

Questions to Ask

1. What caused the US to become a superpower following World War II?
2. How did technology change American culture during this time?
3. What impact did the Baby Boom make on the economy?
4. Why did America feel compelled to compete with the Soviet Union?
5. How did Americans feel about entering two new wars right after WWII?

---

[127] https://www.khanacademy.org/humanities/us-history/postwarera/postwar-era/a/the-baby-boom

US Presidents between 1945-1968

President	Vice President	Years
Harry S. Truman	Office vacant	1945-1949
Harry S. Truman	Alben Barkley	1949-1953
Dwight D. Eisenhower	Richard M Nixon	1953-1961
John F. Kennedy	Lyndon B. Johnson	1961-1963
Lyndon B. Johnson	Office vacant	1963-1965
Lyndon B. Johnson	Hubert Humphrey	1965-1969

States added to the Union between 1945-1964

Alaska	1959
Hawaii	1959

Primary Sources

- The Post War United States, 1945-1968: https://loc.gov/classroom-materials/united-states-history-primary-source-timeline/post-war-united-states-1945-1968

- Post War America 1945-1974: https://cnu.libguides.com/pspostwaramerica

- HIST 674: Seminar Recent US History: https://libguides.csun.edu/hist674/coldwarsources

- Lessons: 1945-1970 https://www.archives.gov/education/lessons/postwar-us.html

- US History, 1945-1960: Post-War America Primary Sources: https://libguides.exeter.edu/c.php?g=465071&p=3179188

General Spines, Series, and Reference Books

The 1950s (American Popular Culture Through History) (Young)

This collection of children's books between 1950-1959: https://www.biblio.com/book-collecting/by-year/childrens-books/1950-1959

This collection of children's books between 1960-1969: https://www.biblio.com/book-collecting/by-year/childrens-books/1960-1969

Web resources

- US History Primary Source Timeline: Overview: https://loc.gov/classroom-materials/united-states-history-primary-source-timeline/post-war-united-states-1945-1968/overview

- Overview of the Post-War Era (University of Houston): https://www.digitalhistory.uh.edu/era.cfm?eraid=16&smtid=1

- Post War United States (1945-1970s) (Smithsonian American Art Museum): https://americanexperience.si.edu/historical-eras/post-war-united-states/

- History:
  https://www.history.com/topics/cold-war/cold-war-history
  https://www.history.com/topics/us-presidents/harry-truman

- The Postwar Era (1945-1980) (Khan Academy):
  https://www.khanacademy.org/humanities/us-history/postwarera

- The Civil Rights Act of 1964: A Long Struggle for Freedom:
  https://www.loc.gov/exhibits/civil-rights-act/civil-rights-era.html

- Life of John F. Kennedy: https://www.jfklibrary.org/learn/about-jfk/life-of-john-f-kennedy

- Overview of the Vietnam War (University of Houston):
  https://www.digitalhistory.uh.edu/era.cfm?eraid=18&smtid=1

- Popular culture and mass media in the 1950s:
  https://www.khanacademy.org/humanities/us-history/postwarera/1950s-america/a/popular-culture-and-mass-media-cnx

Suggested movies/documentaries

Hidden Figures (PG)

The Battle of Chosin (13+)

The Courier (true story: movie) (13+)

Counter Histories: Rock Hill (13+)

Vietnam in HD (14+)

Medal of Honor (E4, E6): Korea

Medal of Honor (E7): Vietnam

Youtube videos

Elementary

- How Did the Cold War Happen? (The Infographics Show)

- Civil Rights Act of 1964 (Kids Academy)

- Civil Rights Heroes for Kids (Homeschool Pop)

Middle

- The Cold War-Summary on a Map (Geo History)

- The Cold War in 7 Minutes (Visual Academy)

- The US Becomes a Global Superpower: America: The Story of Us (S1, E11) (History)

- The Civil Rights Movement and the Civil Rights Act of 1964 (Florida PASS Program)

High

- Prof. Brian Domitrovic: Post-WWII Boom-Transition to a Consumer Economy (Learn Liberty)

- The Cold War Explained from Beginning to End in One Minute (One Minute Economics)

Crash Course:
(Note: Some subjects in the following videos are sensitive. Please watch before showing to children.)

- Civil Rights and the 1950s: Crash Course US History #39

- The Cold War: Crash Course US History #37

- The Cold War in Asia: Crash Course US History #38

- The 1960s in America: Crash Course US History #40 (This video includes the Women's Movement, LGBT history, etc.)

- USA vs USSR Fight! The Cold War: Crash Course World History #39

Tom Richey:
- The Cold War (APUSH) Review Unit 8 Topic 2 (Heimler's History)

- AP Euro Post-WWII Stuff (Cold War, Feminism, European Integration, etc)

Khan Academy:
- Origin of the Cold War (Kim Kutz Elliott)

- Korean War Overview

- Communism

- Cuban Missile Crisis

- Bay of Pigs Invasion

- Vietnam War

Professor Dave Explains:
- Dwight Eisenhower: I Like Ike (1953-1961)

- John F. Kennedy: The New Frontier (1961-1963)

- <u>Lyndon B. Johnson: A Tragic Figure (1963-1969)</u>

Fiction & Nonfiction Books

Title	Author	Age	Period
Postwar United States	Combs	9+	1945-1970
The Journal of Biddy Owens	My Name is America	9+	1948
The Other Side	Woodson	5+	1950s
Ruth and the Green Book	Ramsey	6+	1950s
A is for Atom	Paprocki	1+	1950s
America in the 1950s	Wills	10+	1950s
As Seen on TV	Marling	10+	1950s
The Korean War	Streissguth	10+	1950-1953
The Korean War: An Interactive Modern History Adventure	Burgan	8+	1950-1953
The Borrowers	Norton	6+	1950s
Breaking Stalin's Nose	Yelchin	9+	1953
Charlotte's Web	White	5+	1930s-1950s
Nobody Gonna Turn Me 'Round	Rappaport	9+	1955
Freedom Walkers: The Story of the Montgomery Bus Boycott	Freedman	10+	1955
Boycott Blues: How Rosa Parks Inspired a Nation	Pinkney	4+	1955
Miracles on Maple Hill	Sorenson	8+	1957
The Family Under the Bridge	Carlson	7+	1958
Where Wizards Stay Up Late	Hafner	16+	1960s
Freedom Summer	Wiles	4+	1960
The Story of Ruby Bridges	Coles	6+	1960
New Shoes	Meyer	6+	1960s
Hidden Figures: The True Story of Four Black Women and the Space Race	Shetterfly	6+	1961
A Night Divided	Nielson	10+	1961
A Picture Book of John F. Kennedy	Adler	4+	1961-1963
Countdown	Wiles	9+	1962

Fallout	Strasser	10+	1962
A Ride to Remember	Langley	6+	1963
Lillian's Right to Vote	Winter	5+	1965
(Vietnam War)			
The Wall	Bunting	7+	1955-1975
Patrol: An American Soldier in Vietnam	Myers	6+	1955-1975
Suspect Red	Elliot	10+	1955-1975
10,000 Days of Thunder	Caputo	9+	1955-1975
Vietnam War	DK Eyewitness Books	8+	1955-1975
Boots on the Ground: America's War in Vietnam	Partridge	12+	1955-1975
Cracker! The Best Dog in Vietnam	Kadohata	12+	1955-1975
(Berlin Wall)			
What Was the Berlin Wall?	Medina	8+	1961-1989
The Berlin Wall	Doedon	8+	1961-1989
The Race to Space	Gifford	7+	1957-1969

Terms to Know

1. <u>suburb</u>: an outlying district of a city, especially a residential one.

2. "<u>Golden Age of American Capitalism</u>": the period between 1945-1959 in which the majority of Americans were classified as middle class, and per capita income increased.

3. <u>G.I. Bill</u>: provided World War II veterans with funds for college education, unemployment insurance, and housing. It put higher education within the reach of millions of veterans of WWII and later military conflicts.[128]

4. <u>Brown v. Board of Education</u>: the name given to five separate cases that were heard by the U.S. Supreme Court concerning the issue of segregation in public schools[129]

---

[128] https://www.archives.gov/milestone-documents/servicemens-readjustment-act
[129] https://www.uscourts.gov/educational-resources/educational-activities/history-brown-v-board-education-re-enactment

5. <u>imperialism</u>: a policy of extending a country's power and influence through diplomacy or military force

6. <u>counterculture</u>: a way of life and set of attitudes opposed to or at variance with the prevailing social norm.

7. <u>generation gap</u>: the difference in values and opinions between older and younger people.[130]

8. <u>NASA</u>: the National Aeronautics and Space Administration; created by the National Aeronautics and Space Act of 1958

9. <u>Apollo 8</u>: the first manned spacecraft to reach orbit and first human spaceflight to reach the Moon

10. <u>Birmingham church bombing</u>: the bombing of Baptist church by the KKK in 1963 in which four African American girls died

11. <u>"Great Society"</u>: President Johnson's program to address problems in education, disease, conservation, poverty, and crime control

12. <u>Tet Offensive</u>: a major military operation which marked the peak involvement of the US in the Vietnam War, and the decline of American public support[131]

13. <u>Black Panthers</u>: a militant Marxist-Leninist organization set up in the US in 1966

Areas to Know

- Cape Canaveral, Florida (Kennedy Space Center)
- Vietnam
- Korea

---

[130] https://study.com/learn/lesson/generation-gap-causes-effects.html
[131] https://www.defense.gov/News/Feature-Stories/story/Article/3291950/highlighting-history-how-tet-began-the-end-of-vietnam

People to Know

- Martin Luther King, Jr.
- Richard Nixon
- Barry Goldwater
- Lyndon B. Johnson
- John Kennedy
- John Wayne
- James Stuart
- Charlton Heston
- Dean Martin
- Grace Kelly
- Marilyn Monroe
- Elvis Presley
- Johnny Cash
- Buddy Holly

Enrichment Activities

General Enrichment Ideas:

- Letters from the Past: write a letter during each lesson from the perspective of a person living during that time period. Be sure to include the date, mention anything historically relevant, and try to understand the perspective of the person in which you're writing. Keep the letters in a folder or binder.
- Book of Eras: Create a timeline for each lesson, illustrating key people and events, and writing the dates chronologically. When the year is over, you have a whole history book you created yourself!
- Book of Bios: Focus specifically on the people you've learned about this year. Create a bio for one or more important people from each lesson and think of creative ways to document their lives and roles in the past. (Ex: create a social media "profile" for each person, or a text/conversation between two or more people.)
- A Taste of History: For each lesson or time period, research a recipe from that era and write it on a notecard. Save your recipes in a recipe box and cook your way through the past. Another idea is to keep a blog or YouTube channel documenting each recipe, how it was typically prepared

(comparing/contrasting it to modern day methods), and any other historical tidbit you find interesting.

- Travel Thru History: For each lesson, create a travel brochure depicting important areas of interest in the area. (It can be funny or serious.)
- Diorama: Choose one (or more) period to illustrate with a diorama.
- Fashion through the Ages: Design a fashion magazine using what you've learned about each era's dress and style.

Specific to this lesson:

- Download this free 1950s flip book activity: https://simplelivingcreativelearning.com/1950-research-flip-book

- Read about the Cold War here: https://www.ducksters.com/history/cold_war/summary.php Then, illustrate a timeline with important events from the Cold War.

- Watch the Youtube video, *How Did the Cold War Happen?* (Infographics Show) explaining the Cold War. **Answer**: Why did the USSR and the USA have mistrust? Define the term "the Cold War" in your own words. What is "the iron curtain"? Explain the Berlin blockade and the Berlin airlift. What two other wars were a side effect of the idea of "containment"?

- Learn about Civil Rights here: https://kids.britannica.com/kids/article/civil-rights-movement/403522 Then, create a protest poster expressing your views on civil rights. (Note: the poster can be political, social, religious, or a combination of the three.)

- The 1950s were the first time that music was catered to young people, creating a new youth culture. Listen to the songs in the Youtube video, *Back To The 50s & 60s | 50s & 60s Greatest Music Playlist | Best Old School Music Hits* (Music Express). How does this music differ from what people listen to today?

- The 1950s and 1960s produced many popular TV shows for families, including:
  Bonanza
  Adventures of Ozzie and Harriet
  Father Knows Best
  Gunsmoke
  Have Gun-Will Travel
  The Honeymooners

I Love Lucy
Leave it to Beaver
The Lone Ranger
For this assignment, choose a show to watch. (You can use this: https://www.classic-tv.com/watch) Then, write your own episode for your chosen show using the main characters. Keep in mind the beliefs, music, clothing, and behavior of the people during this time period.

- Interview a person alive during the 1950s and 1960s and record your interview (with their permission) either in a video or voice recorder. Ask the following questions:
  1. Please state your name and birthdate.
  2. What was your childhood like growing up? (What did kids do for fun? What kinds of things did you learn at school? How did kids treat their parents or other adults? What differences can you tell me about children then and now?)
  3. Can you tell me about (*anything listed in this lesson*)? What was your experience when _____ (President Kennedy was assassinated, etc.)?
  4. What do you think American society felt about _____?
  5. What was it like for you when _____?
  6. Can you explain what changes you've experienced in your life (politics, technology, gender roles, family, etc) since the 1950s and 1960s?
  7. If you had advice for American students today, what would it be?
  8. What lessons do you think American kids today could learn from your experiences and those in your age group?
     (If the person is a veteran)
  9. What did you do in the _____ War? What was a normal day like for you while you were serving in the Armed Forces?
  10. Can you tell me about any combat experiences you might have? (*Don't press for details: let him/her respond in their own way and if they seem uncomfortable, change the subject. Be sure to thank them for their service at the end of the interview or whenever appropriate.*)

Making Connections

Post-War Americans faced many rapid changes. Fear of Communism impacted foreign policies and thrust the US into the Korean War and the Vietnam War, drawing criticism from antiwar protestors especially in the 1960s. The threat of nuclear war developed into a Cold War with the Soviet Union and led to many technological advancements (such as NASA). Youth culture was shaped by popular music, while television saw a boom with shows like *I Love Lucy* and *The*

Honeymooners. Television brought news of racial violence and inequality and the Vietnam War into American living rooms; the Civil Rights movement worked towards desegregation while Marxist groups like the Black Panthers took a militant approach. Cultural divisions continued to deepen despite the economic growth and prosperity which existed during this period.

Lesson 27: Contemporary America
(1968-present day)

Lesson 27: Contemporary America (1968 – Modern Day)

Introduction & Conclusion of Modern America

While it may seem that 1968 through modern day covers a lot of time, it's important to note that historians are still collecting information in the years since the turn of the 21st Century. Enough time hasn't passed for there to be established "movements" and eras", so modern day is (for now) lumped in with what's happened since 1968. The 1960s and 1970s saw more Civil Rights protests and marches, along with the development of fourth-wave feminism and concerns for rights of marginalized people. Liberalism and conservatism continued to battle (much as they do today) over important social, educational, and political issues. This period also saw the first man walk on the moon, the end of the Cold War, and major progress for minorities. The 1980s and 1990s continued to see technological advancements. Military operations in the Middle East (through the War on Terror and others) continued to increase the role of the US in foreign affairs in the past twenty years, and only time will tell what lasting impact this involvement will have for Americans and the world.

Meanwhile, Americans today experience faster and more complicated technology which seems to rapidly progress and improve every year (causing some concerns with where all this technology is leading us as a nation). Social issues have caused deeper divisions within the already aggressive culture wars, and very real concerns about the role and power of the federal government continue to divide Americans, particularly in the wake of Covid-19 restrictions and mandates, national debt, and gun violence in schools. Many speculate where our nation is heading, but the only people who will know for sure will be those historians who write our story.

Questions to Ask

1. How did American culture and society changed between 1968 and present day?
2. What major events have transpired?
3. What role does the US have in the world today, and how has this changed since WWII?
4. What struggles do Americans currently face and why?

US Presidents between 1968-2023

President	Vice President	Years
Lyndon B. Johnson	Hubert H. Humphrey	1965-1969
Richard M. Nixon	Spiro Agnew	1969-1973
Richard M. Nixon	Gerald R. Ford	1973-1974
Gerald R. Ford	Nelson Rockefeller	1974-1977
Jimmy Carter	Walter F. Mondale	1977-1981
Ronald Reagan	George Bush	1981-1989
George Bush	Dan Quayle	1989-1993
Bill Clinton	Al Gore	1993-2001
George W. Bush	Richard Cheney	2001-2009
Barack Obama	Joseph Biden	2009-2017
Donald Trump	Mike Pence	2017-2021
Joseph Biden	Kamala Harris	2021-

Primary Sources

- Elon University (United States History 1970s Resource Guide): https://elon.libguides.com/US_history_1970s/Primary_Sources

- University of Northern Iowa (Primary Sources-Advanced Methods 1980-2000): https://guides.lib.uni.edu/primary-sources-advanced-methods/American-History-1980-2000

- US Military History: Middle East Wars (Grove City College): https://hbl.gcc.libguides.com/c.php?g=339608&p=2285680

General Spines, Series, and Reference Books

The Oxford History of the Twentieth Century (Howard)
Twentieth-Century America: A Brief History (Reeves)
American Decades: Primary Sources (Rose)
Terrorism: Essential Primary Sources (Lerner)

Web resources

- 1945 to the Present (Gilder Lerhman Institute of American History):
  https://ap.gilderlehrman.org/history-by-era/essays/1945-present?period=9

- The Age of Reagan (Gilder Lerhman Institute of American History):
  https://ap.gilderlehrman.org/history-by-era/essays/age-reagan

- A More Perfect Union? Barack Obama and the Politics of Unity ((Gilder
  Lerhman Institute of American History):
  https://ap.gilderlehrman.org/history-by-era/facing-new-
  millennium/essays/more-perfect-union-barack-obama-and-politics-
  unity?period=9

- Disasters and the Politics of Memory (Gilder Lerhman Institute of American
  History): https://ap.gilderlehrman.org/history-by-era/facing-new-
  millennium/essays/disasters-and-politics-memory?period=9

- Securities and Exchange Commission:
  https://www.sechistorical.org/museum/timeline/2000-timeline.php

- 1970-2000 Timeline (University of Houston):
  1970s: https://www.nixonlibrary.gov/news/1970s-america

- Census.gov
  census.gov/history/www/through_the_decades/fast_facts/1980_new.html
  census.gov/history/www/through_the_decades/fast_facts/1990_new.html
  census.gov/history/www/through_the_decades/fast_facts/2000_new.html
  census.gov/history/www/through_the_decades/fast_facts/2010_fast_facts.html
  census.gov/history/www/through_the_decades/fast_facts/2020_fast_facts.html

Suggested movies/documentaries

The Warfighters series (History) (2016) (Unknown rating: I would guess 13+)

The Toys That Made Us (Netflix) (**Note**: Some episodes have language, so please
watch first).

Youtube videos

Elementary

- Daily Life and Popular Culture in the 1970s (Reading Through History)
- Daily Life and Popular Culture in the 1980s (Reading Through History)
- Daily Life and Popular Culture in the 1990s (Reading Through History)
- Daily Life and Popular Culture in the 2000s (Reading Through History)
- Richard Nixon: 60-Second Presidents (PBS Presidents)
- Gerald Ford: 60-Second Presidents (PBS Presidents)
- Jimmy Carter: 60-Second Presidents (PBS Presidents)
- Ronald Reagan: 60-Second Presidents (PBS Presidents)
- George Bush: 60-Second Presidents (PBS Presidents)
- Bill Clinton: 60-Second Presidents (PBS Presidents)
- George W. Bush: 60-Second Presidents (PBS Presidents)
- Barack Obama: 60-Second Presidents (PBS Presidents)

Middle

- What is Reaganomics? (Investors Trading Academy)
- How did Reagan's policies affect the economy? | US Government and Civics | (Khan Academy)

Rhetty for History:
- 1980s Things Found In Every Home
- Back To School In The 1980s
- Classic Foods Of The 1980s!
- Most Popular Toys of the 1990s!

National Geographic: **(Sensitive material for younger students)**
- First Response (Full Episode) | 9/11: One Day in America

High

- AP US History Study Guide: Period 9 - 1945 to the present day (Gilderlehrman)

Crash Course:
(NOTE: Some subjects in the following videos are sensitive. Please watch before showing to children.)

- The Rise of Conservatism: Crash Course US History #41

- Ford, Carter, and the Economic Malaise: Crash Course US History #42

- The Reagan Revolution: Crash Course US History #43

- George HW Bush and the End of the Cold War: Crash Course US History #44

- The Clinton Years, or the 1990s: Crash Course US History #45

- Terrorism, War, and Bush 43: Crash Course US History #46

- Obamanation: Crash Course US History #47

Professor Dave Explains:
- Richard Nixon: I Am Not a Crook (1969-1974)

- Gerald Ford: Taking Tumbles (1974-1977)

- Jimmy Carter: Successes and Failures Abroad (1977-1981)

- Ronald Reagan: The End of the Cold War (1981-1989)

(Note: Due to the clearly political biases which abound in the media about presidents Clinton through Biden, I'm unable to officially recommend any current YouTube videos fairly describing their presidencies. Good history is question-driven, not philosophy or bias-driven, and I have yet to find a fair video source for these Presidents.)

Fiction & Nonfiction Books

Title	Author	Age	Period
A Computer Called Katherine	Slade	4+	1969
Grace Hopper: Queen of Computer Code	Wallmark	7+	1943-1986

First Man on the Moon	Hubbard	8+	1969
One Giant Leap	Burleigh	6+	1969
America in the 1970s	Burns	10+	1970s
America in the 1970s for Kids	Goodman	7+	1970s
Border Breakdown: The Fall of the Berlin Wall	Smith	7+	1989
How the Internet Happened: From Netscape to the iPhone	McCullough	16+	1990
Inside the Internet	Pai	5+	1990s
The 1990s	Kallen	14+	1990s
The Magic School Bus Gets Programmed	Cole	4+	1990s
Cloud and Wallfish	Nesbet	10+	1989

Terms to Know

1. <u>Watergate Scandal</u>: interlocking political scandals of the administration of U.S. Pres. Richard M. Nixon that were revealed following the arrest of five burglars at Democratic National Committee (DNC) headquarters in the Watergate office-apartment-hotel complex in Washington, D.C., on June 17, 1972.[132]

2. <u>"New Right"</u>: grassroots coalition of American conservatives that collectively led what scholars often refer to as the "conservative ascendancy" or "Republican ascendancy" of the late 20th century.[133]

3. <u>Populism</u>: a term in political science which describes the idea that society is separated into groups which are at odds with each other

4. <u>"Silent majority"</u>: An expression coined by President Nixon in 1969 in reference to the fact that "most Americans" agreed with him; sometimes the expression is used to describe the idea that Americans are mostly conservative but are silent about their beliefs

---

[132] https://www.britannica.com/event/Watergate-Scandal
[133] https://www.britannica.com/topic/New-Right

5. <u>Welfare state</u>: a system whereby the government undertakes to protect the health and well-being of its citizens, especially those in financial or social need, by means of grants, pensions, and other benefits. The foundations for the modern welfare state in the US were laid by the New Deal programs of President Franklin D. Roosevelt.

6. <u>Affirmative action</u>: (in the context of the allocation of resources or employment) the practice or policy of favoring individuals belonging to groups regarded as disadvantaged or subject to discrimination.

7. <u>Environmentalism</u>: concern about and action aimed at protecting the environment.

8. <u>Equal Rights Amendment (ERA)</u>: a proposed 28th amendment to the US Constitution (passed by Congress in 1972)

9. <u>"Yuppie"</u>: a young person with a well-paid job and a fashionable lifestyle.

10. <u>AIDS crisis</u>: a period between 1981 and the early 1990s in which the AIDS epidemic gained international attention

11. <u>Reaganomics</u>: a term referring to the economic policies of President Ronald Reagan that impacted government spending, regulation, and taxes.[134]

12. <u>Industrial deregulation</u>: the removal of regulations or restrictions, especially in a particular industry.

13. <u>Tax cuts</u>: a reduction made by the government in the amount of tax that people pay[135]

14. <u>Supply-side economics</u>: a theory that maintains that increasing the supply of goods and services is the engine for economic growth[136]

15. <u>Reagan doctrine</u>: used to characterize the Reagan administration's (1981-1988) policy of supporting anti-Communist insurgents wherever they might

---

[134] www.Investopedia.com
[135] www.Collinsdictionary.com
[136] www.Investopedia.com

be. In his 1985 State of the Union address, President Ronald Reagan called upon Congress and the American people to stand up to the Soviet Union, what he had previously called the "Evil Empire".[137]

16. Iran-Contra Affair: a U.S. political scandal in which the National Security Council (NSC) became involved in secret weapons transactions and other activities that were either prohibited by the U.S. Congress or violated the stated public policy of the government[138]

17. European Union: intergovernmental and supranational organization of 27 countries across Europe[139]

18. Gulf War: 1990-1991; a war initiated by the invasion of Iraq into Kuwait, in which 35 countries were involved[140]

19. Y2K: referred to potential computer problems which might have resulted when dates used in computer systems moved from the year 1999 to the year 2000.[141]

20. Occupy Wallstreet: a sociopolitical movement which was created in response to the global financial crisis of 2008[142]

21. Black Lives Matter: an international activist movement, originating in the African American community, that campaigns against violence and systemic racism toward black people.[143] It is a highly debated and controversial group and subject for many Americans.

22. "Make America Great Again": the slogan for Donald Trump's 2016 presidential campaign, sometimes shortened to MAGA

23. Brexit: an abbreviation of "Britain" and "exit" created to define the withdrawal process of the United Kingdom from the European Union.[144]

---

[137] https://2001-2009.state.gov/r/pa/ho/time/rd/17741.htm
[138] https://www.britannica.com/event/Iran-Contra-Affair
[139] https://www.cia.gov/the-world-factbook/countries/european-union/
[140] https://history.state.gov/milestones/1989-1992/gulf-war
[141] https://americanhistory.si.edu/collections/object-groups/y2k
[142] https://www.hbs.edu/faculty/Pages/item.aspx?num=43632
[143] https://www.loc.gov/item/lcwaN0016241/
[144] https://www.lamoncloa.gob.es/lang/en/brexit/AboutBrexit/Paginas/index.aspx

24. <u>Covid-19 pandemic:</u> a worldwide pandemic caused by an infectious SARS-CoV-2 virus[145]

People to Know

- Lyndon B. Johnson
- Richard Nixon
- Gerald Ford
- Jimmy Carter
- Ronal Reagan
- George Bush
- Bill Clinton
- George W. Bush
- Barack Obama
- Donald Trump
- Joseph Biden
- People listed on the Time's 100 Persons of the (20th) Century: https://content.time.com/time/magazine/article/0,9171,26473,00.html

Enrichment Activities

General Enrichment Ideas:

- <u>Letters from the Past:</u> write a letter during each lesson from the perspective of a person living during that time period. Be sure to include the date, mention anything historically relevant, and try to understand the perspective of the person in which you're writing. Keep the letters in a folder or binder.
- <u>Book of Eras:</u> Create a timeline for each lesson, illustrating key people and events, and writing the dates chronologically. When the year is over, you have a whole history book you created yourself!
- <u>Book of Bios:</u> Focus specifically on the people you've learned about this year. Create a bio for one or more important people from each lesson and think of creative ways to document their lives and roles in the past. (Ex: create a social media "profile" for each person, or a text/conversation between two or more people.)

---

[145] https://www.who.int/health-topics/coronavirus

- <u>A Taste of History</u>: For each lesson or time period, research a recipe from that era and write it on a notecard. Save your recipes in a recipe box and cook your way through the past. Another idea is to keep a blog or YouTube channel documenting each recipe, how it was typically prepared (comparing/contrasting it to modern day methods), and any other historical tidbit you find interesting.
- <u>Travel Thru History</u>: For each lesson, create a travel brochure depicting important areas of interest in the area. (It can be funny or serious.)
- <u>Diorama</u>: Choose one (or more) period to illustrate with a diorama.
- <u>Fashion through the Ages</u>: Design a fashion magazine using what you've learned about each era's dress and style.

Specific to this lesson:

- Explore this website for lessons about the Korean War: koreanwarlegacy.org/teaching-tools/korean-war-legacy/

- Visit and select any of these Vietnam War lessons from TheHomeschoolMom: https://www.thehomeschoolmom.com/homeschool-lesson-plans/vietnam-conflict/

- Download this free unit study about the 1970s: https://homeschoolgiveaways.com/2020/05/free-modern-history-activities-notebooking-1970s/

- Before the advent of video games, kids played all kinds of outdoor and indoor games. Select a game (or more) from the following list and try it:
    1. Red Rover
    2. Freeze Tag
    3. Red Light Green Light
    4. Ghost in the Graveyard
    5. Sardines
    6. Mother, May I?
    7. Marbles
    8. Hopscotch

- Choose one of these vintage 1960s recipes to make: https://humbly-homemade.com/cooking-vintage-recipes-from-the-1960s/

- Visit this website to learn more about the period of 1980-present: https://ap.gilderlehrman.org/period/9

- Although there were video games in the 1970s, the 1980s is when they became a staple of most childhoods. Watch the Youtube video, Modern Marvels: Gadgets of the 1980s (S12, E15) from the History channel. Then, try some of the vintage video games for free here: https://www.free80sarcade.com/

- Download this free unit study about the 1990s: https://homeschoolgiveaways.com/2020/06/free-modern-history-activities-notebooking-1990s/

- Have a "90's Kid Day": ask a parent (or someone who was a child in the 1990s) to describe what their childhood was like. Try to replicate some of those activities. Some examples include:
  1. Drink from the hose
  2. Wear a 90's outfit/hairstyle for the day
  3. Watch "old school" (appropriate) MTV videos
  4. Watch a classic 90s movie
  5. Find and listen to a 90s music playlist
  6. Buy, use, and develop a disposable camera
  7. Listen to the boy bands of the era (then choose a favorite…#teamNSYNC)
  8. Go an entire day with a smart phone (no social media either)
  9. Watch TV shows from the TGIF programming block (Boy Meets World, Hangin' with Mr. Cooper, Step by Step, Sabrina the Teenage Witch, Full House, Family Matters, etc.)
  10. Use Sun-in hair lightener (maybe just on a strip of hair)

A Final Note

The most difficult thing about finding sources for this final lesson is the fact that all the historians who have written about the past 40 years are all *living in the period they're writing about.* This personal experience with recent history makes it challenging (maybe impossible) to analyze and interpret current events fairly and objectively. Almost every source I have found from the 1980s onward have been painfully biased. Historians don't even try to hide it. This is a perfect example of how historians are lumped into historiographic "schools" and interpret the past from their specific lenses. In my unwillingness to make this curriculum guide a "written history" (i.e. me explaining the past rather than offering resources to learn about it yourselves), I can't offer any more commentary about these issues. Just, please, review this article by *AllSides: How to Spot 16 Types of Media Bias.* This will help you decipher information through a critical lens, empowering you to not be swayed by propaganda. Like I tell my kids: don't be a pawn, don't be a chump.

allsides.com/media-bias/how-to-spot-types-of-media-bias

The next several lessons will target civics and government—ideas and terms which were touched upon in previous lessons but deserve their own explanations.

Part 2: Civics & Government 101

Terms to Know for this Section [146]

1. Amendment - an addition or change to the U.S. Constitution. It must be ratified by three-fourths of the U.S. States. There are currently twenty-seven amendments to the Constitution.

2. Articles of Confederation - A document that served as the first Constitution of the United States. It was ratified by the thirteen original states in 1781.

3. Bill - A law that has been proposed to Congress but has not yet been passed.

4. Bill of Rights - The first ten amendments to the Constitution which guarantee a number of personal freedoms.

5. Bipartisanship - This is when two opposing political parties (Ex. Democrats and Republicans) work together to find common ground and a compromise.

6. Bureaucracy - The various divisions and departments that actually run a large government.

7. Cabinet - A group of people that work for and advise the president. The members include the vice president and the heads of the 15 executive departments (for example the Secretary of State, the Secretary of Defense, and the Secretary of the Treasury).

8. Capitalism - An economic system where trade and industry are owned and controlled by private citizens for profit.

9. Citizen - A recognized legal member of a country.

10. Civil Rights - Rights guaranteed to all citizens of a country without discrimination.

11. Checks and Balances - A system of government that keeps any one branch of government from becoming too powerful.

12. Congress - The Legislative Branch of the U.S. Government which includes the Senate and the House of Representatives.

---

[146] https://www.ducksters.com/history/us_government/glossary_and_terms.php

13. Constitution - A document that is the highest law in the land and defines the U.S. federal government. It includes seven articles and twenty-seven amendments.

14. Delegate - A person who is designated to represent a group of people.

15. Democracy - A system of government where the power rests with the people. The people either rule directly or through representatives who are elected by the people.

16. Electoral College - The institution that elects the President of the United States. Each state gets a certain number of electoral votes based on the population of the state.

17. Executive Branch - The branch of government headed up by the president. It includes the president, vice-president, and 15 main executive departments.

18. House of Representatives - A group of elected officials that makes up half of the Legislative Branch of government. The number of representatives from each state is determined by population. There are 435 total members.

19. Impeachment - The formal process of removing someone from political office.

20. Judicial Branch - The branch of government that includes the courts and judges. The highest court in the Judicial Branch is the Supreme Court.

21. Jury - A group of people who hear a court case and determine the verdict.

22. Law - A rule that is enforced by the government.

23. Legislative Branch - The branch of government that includes the Senate and the House of Representatives.

24. Lobbyist - A person who tries to influence the government on behalf of a special interest group.

25. Political Party - An organization of people with similar political goals and beliefs.

26. President - The head of the Executive Branch of government. The primary leader of the U.S. government.

27. Senate - A group of elected officials that makes up half of the Legislative Branch of government. There are two Senators per state for a total of 100 Senators.

28. Supreme Court - The highest court in the Judicial Branch. There are currently 9 Supreme Court justices.

29. Tax - A fee charged by the government on citizens and businesses.

30. Term Limits - A legal limit on how long an elected official may serve in an office. For example, the president can only serve two terms of four years each.

31. Veto - The power of the president to reject a bill. The veto may be overridden by a two-thirds vote in both the House and the Senate.

Lesson 28:
Branches of Government

Lesson 28: Branches of Government

Introduction

The US government is organized through a balance of power between the Legislative, Executive, and Judicial branches. Knowing how each branch works (and how they work together) is crucial for good citizenship.

Web Sources

- How the US Government is Organized (USA.gov): https://www.usa.gov/branches-of-government

- Executive Branch (Whitehouse.gov): https://www.whitehouse.gov/about-the-white-house/our-government/the-executive-branch/

- Legislative Branch (Whitehouse.gov): https://www.whitehouse.gov/about-the-white-house/our-government/the-legislative-branch/

- Judicial Branch (Whitehouse.gov): https://www.whitehouse.gov/about-the-white-house/our-government/the-judicial-branch/

Web Sources especially for kids

- Ben's Guide: https://bensguide.gpo.gov/a-what-are-branches
- Kids in the House: https://kids-clerk.house.gov/grade-school/

Youtube videos (12+)

- How is Power Divided in the US Government (TED ED)
- Separation of Powers and Checks and Balances (Crash Course Government and Politics)
- The Senate and the House of Representatives Explained (Tom Richey)
- The Presidency: AP Review (Tom Richey)
- Bicameral Congress (Crash Course Government and Politics #2)
- Presidential Power (Crash Course Government and Politics #11)

Youtube videos especially for kids (under 12)

- What are the three branches of United States government? (Miacademy Learning Channel)

Fiction & Nonfiction Books

Title	Author	Age
Checks and Balances	Kenney	7+
Government for Kids: Citizenship to Governance	Baby Professor	8+
House Mouse, Senate Mouse	Barnes	6+
How Does the US Government Work?	Universal Politics	8+
If I Were President	Stier	5+
National Government (Kids Guide to Government)	Giesecke	9+
Our Government: Three Branches	Buchanan	6+
The Adventures of Chloe and Chris: The Three Branches of Government	Goins	4+
The Everything US Government Book	Ragone	NA
The US Congress for Kids	Reis	10+
Usborne Understanding Politics and Government	Usborne	10+
What Are the Three Branches of Government? and other questions about the Constitution	Richmond	7+
What is the President's Job?	Singer	5+

Enrichment Activities

- Choose an activity from We Are Teachers: https://www.weareteachers.com/teach-kids-branches-of-government/

- Complete the lesson in this free download from Education.com: https://bpb-us-w2.wpmucdn.com/wpstudents.towson.edu/dist/3/3348/files/2021/06/the-branches-of-government.pdf

- Visit this website from the US.gov. Then, create an infographic using the content from this article: https://www.usa.gov/branches-of-government
    1. Make a set of flash cards using 3x5 note cards. Include terms you find on the website.
    2. Visit an agency listed under the "Executive Branch Agencies, Commissions, and Committees" header: select one. Then create a tri-fold pamphlet explaining what the agency does and its usefulness in the US government.

Lesson 29:
The Election Process

Lesson 29: The Election Process

Introduction

In US elections, candidates are chosen directly by popular vote. In presidential elections, however, the election process uses a process called the Electoral College. Learn more about the election process and voting in the US in this lesson.

Web Sources

- Presidential Election Process:
  https://www.usa.gov/election

- Electoral College Fast Facts:
  https://history.house.gov/Institution/Electoral-College/Electoral-College/

- Presidential Elections:
  https://www.history.com/topics/us-presidents/presidential-elections-1

- The Presidential Elections Process (Library of Congress):
  https://loc.gov/classroom-materials/elections/presidential-election-process/

Web Sources especially for kids

- How Voting Works (Ducksters):
  https://www.ducksters.com/history/us_government_voting.php

- How Voting Works: Lesson for Kids:
  https://study.com/academy/lesson/how-voting-works-lesson-for-kids.html

Youtube videos (12+)

- US Presidential Election explained (explainity explainer video)
- Understanding the Voting Process (Short version) (BCTV)
- Scholar Exchange: Voting Rights Amendments Session (National Constitutional Center)

Youtube videos especially for kids (Under 12)

- Presidential Elections-U.S. Government for Kids! (Miacademy)
- Voting for Kids: Why Voting is Important?-Election Day (Kids Academy)

Fiction & Nonfiction Books

Title	Author	Age
Elections and Voting for Kids! A Guided Coloring and Activity Book About the Election and Voting Process	Bond	NA
One Vote, Two Votes, I Vote, You Vote	Worth	4+
See How They Run	Goodman	8+
So You Want to be President?	St. George	6+
The Election Activity Book	Baicker	6+
The Electoral College: A Kid's Guide	Meister	8+
The Kids' Complete Guide to the Elections	Carlson	8+
The Night Before Election Day	Wing	3+
The President of the Jungle	Rodrigues	5+
Vote!	Christelow	6+
What's the Big Deal About Elections?	Shamir	4+

Enrichment Activities

- Download and print this free US Presidential Election Lap Book: https://researchparent.com/united-states-presidential-election-lap-book/?ssp_iabi=1677686682318

- Read this article by US.gov: Overview of the Presidential Election Process. https://www.usa.gov/presidential-election-process Then, create a board game using the steps listed (and any other fun/silly/creative elements you want): (This infographic might help: th.usembassy.gov/summary-of-the-u-s-presidential-election-process/)

- Read about Election Administration at State and Local Levels: https://www.ncsl.org/elections-and-campaigns/election-administration-at-state-and-local-levels

Then, write an essay about the process covering the following subjects:
1. the history of the state election process
2. the two Acts which added more responsibilities to the state
3. the role of the chief election official or election board
4. any information within the article which pertains to your state

- Read about how voting works. Then, create a video in which you are running for President or another official office.
https://www.ducksters.com/history/us_government_voting.php
Tell the viewers why they should vote for you and what you will do for the country.

- Download this free electoral college vote unit: https://fittedto4th.com/election-2020/?ssp_iabi=1677798358926

Lesson 30:
How Laws Are Made

Lesson 30: How Laws Are Made

Introduction

In the United States, Congress (which includes the House of Representatives and the Senate) creates and passes bills. These bills may or may not be signed into law by the sitting president. If the law is considered unconstitutional, it can be rejected by federal courts.

Web Sources

- How Laws Are Made and How to Research Them: https://www.usa.gov/how-laws-are-made

- The Legislative Process: https://www.house.gov/the-house-explained/the-legislative-process

Web Sources especially for kids

- How Laws Are Made: https://bensguide.gpo.gov/a-how-made

- How a Bill Becomes a Law: https://kids-clerk.house.gov/grade-school/lesson.html?intID=17

- US Government: How Laws Are Made: https://www.ducksters.com/history/us_government/how_laws_are_made.php

Youtube videos (12+)

- How a Bill Becomes a Law (Crash Course Government and Politics #9)
- How a Bill Becomes a Law (Khan Academy)
- Diagramming How a Bill Becomes a Law (Khan Academy)

Youtube videos especially for kids (Under 12)

- Schoolhouse Rock: How a Bill Becomes a Law (Jack Italix)

Fiction & Nonfiction Books

Title	Author	Age
Understanding How Laws Are Made	Bowers	7+
Travels with Max: How a Bill Becomes a Law	Wie	5+
How a Bill Becomes a Law	Steinkraus	8+
The Lobster Bill: How a Bill Becomes a Law	MacInness	8+
Easy Simulations: How a Bill Becomes a Law: A Complete Tool Kit With Background Information, Primary Sources, and More to Help Students Build Reading	Luce	10+
A Bill's Journey into Law	Slade	6+
Making Laws: A Look at How a Bill Becomes a Law	Donovan	10+

Enrichment Activities

- Read "How Laws are Made" (Ducksters): https://www.ducksters.com/history/us_government/how_laws_are_made.php Then, complete the free activity from Education.com https://www.education.com/worksheet/article/bills-path/?ssp_iabi=1677799703150

- Watch the YouTube video (How a Bill Becomes a Law: Crash Course Government and Politics #9). Then, use this link to create an infographic explaining how laws are made: https://www.usa.gov/how-laws-are-made

- Visit the Library of Congress' search engine, Historic American Law. https://guides.loc.gov/historic-american-law
    1. Scroll down to the "Guide to Law Online: _____" and find your state.
    2. Then, click "Legislation", and then any option in your state in which you can look up bill-tracking or any interesting laws in your state.
    3. Write a 1-page essay about the bill/law, why it was introduced, and what impact it made in your state.

Lesson 31:
Historical Documents

Lesson 31: Historical Documents

Introduction

The United States has several historical documents archived in the National Archives Building in Washington, D.C. Three of the most famous and important documents are known as the Charters of Freedom: these include the Declaration of Independence, the Constitution, and the Bill of Rights.[147] There are also documents called Milestone Documents, which represent key moments in American history. These include: https://www.archives.gov/milestone-documents/list

Web Sources

- Charters of Freedom: America's Founding Documents: https://www.archives.gov/founding-docs

- Milestone Documents: https://www.archives.gov/milestone-documents/list

- 10 Important Documents of American History (Norwich University Online): https://online.norwich.edu/academic-programs/resources/10-important-documents-of-american-history

Web Sources especially for kids

- The United States Government for Kids: The Constitution: https://www.ducksters.com/history/us_constitution.php

- The United States Government for Kids: The Bill of Rights: https://www.ducksters.com/history/us_bill_of_rights.php

- The United States Government for Kids: US Constitutional Amendments: https://www.ducksters.com/history/us_constitution_amendments.php

Youtube videos (12+)

- Declaring America's Independence: The Revolution (episode 3) (History)
- The Declaration of Independence (Tom Richey)

---

[147] https://www.archives.gov/founding-docs

- The Constitution, the Articles, and Federalism (Crash Course US History #8)
- The United States Constitution and Bill of Rights (Ryan Hill)
- The US Constitution: Period 3: 1754-1800 (Khan Academy)

Youtube videos especially for kids (Under 12)

- Bill of Rights for Kids (Learn Bright)
- The Bill of Rights (Mr. Raymond's Social Studies Academy)
- Charters of Freedom: Building a More Perfect Union (Presidential Primary Sources Project)

Fiction & Nonfiction Books

Title	Author	Age
A Kids Guide to America's Bill of Rights	Krull	8+
A More Perfect Union	Maestro	7+
A New Kind of Government: Articles of Confederation to Constitution	Baby Professor	8+
Constitution: Translated for Kids	Travis	10+
Give Me Liberty!	Freedman	
If You Were There When They Signed the Constitution	Levy	8+
In Defense of Liberty	Freedman	10+
Our Nation's Documents	Time for Kids	
Shh! We're Writing the Constitution	Fritz	8+
The Constitution Decoded: A Guide to the Document that Shaped Our Nation	Kennedy	8+
The Declaration of Independence from A-Z	Osornio	7+
The Declaration of Independence: The Words that Made America	Fink	1+
The Journey of the One and Only Declaration of Independence	St. George	8+
The United States Constitution	Hennessey	11+
United States Civics: Articles of Confederation for Kids	Baby Professor	8+
We the Kids	Catrow	5+
We the People: The Constitution of the United States	Spier	5+

What Does the Constitution Say? A Kid's Guide to How Our Democracy Works	Sheehan	8+

Enrichment Activities

- Read about the Charters of Freedom, the collection of the three most important historical documents in the US: https://museum.archives.gov/founding-documents Read a transcript of each item. Write a paragraph about the importance of each document.

- Review the list of foundational American documents here: https://www.archives.gov/historical-docs Then, create an illustrated timeline of when these documents were written.

- Choose a historical document from the link above. Write a newspaper article information the public about the document. Include the date, authors, immediate significance, any relevant details, and long-term significance.

- Download this free lesson about the parts of the Constitution: https://www.thecleverteacher.com/parts-of-the-us-constitution-lesson/?ssp_iabi=1677801895948

- Download this free lesson about the Bill of Rights: https://www.thecleverteacher.com/us-constitution-primary-sources/?ssp_iabi=1677801973654

- Download this free lesson about the Declaration of Independence timeline: https://www.thecleverteacher.com/declaration-of-independence-free-lesson/?ssp_iabi=1677802070314

Lesson 32:
American Symbols & Landmarks

Lesson 32: American Symbols & Landmarks

Introduction

Millions of tourists travel to see American landmarks every year, but many Americans don't know the location (or significance) of these national landmarks. This lesson reviews major American landmarks and symbols which the rest of the world identifies with the United States.

Web Sources

- Symbols of the United States: https://loc.gov/classroom-materials/symbols-of-the-united-states/

- 25 Most Famous Landmarks in the USA: https://www.attractionsofamerica.com/thingstodo/most-famous-landmarks-usa.php

Web Sources especially for kids

- US Landmarks for Kids: https://homeschoolgiveaways.com/2019/09/free-unit-studies-and-printables-for-landmarks-in-the-usa/

- The United States Government for Kids: The Bill of Rights: https://www.ducksters.com/history/us_bill_of_rights.php

- US National Landmarks Facts: https://softschools.com/facts/us_national_landmarks/

Youtube videos (all videos G/PG)

- History of the US Flag, in paper (Vexillographer)
- A Moment in History: The Liberty Bell (FISM TV)
- Great Seal of the United States: Americas Emblem (National Museum of American Diplomacy)
- The Battle of Fort McHenry, through Francis Scott Key's Eyes (Smithsonian Channel)
- Who is Uncle Sam? (The Casual Historian)
- Why is the Bald Eagle a Symbol of America? (The Daily Bellringer)

- The Statue of Liberty (Liberty Treehouse)
- The Statue of Liberty History (The Daily Bellringer)

Fiction & Nonfiction Books

Title	Author	Age
A Kids Guide to America's Bill of Rights	Krull	8+
A More Perfect Union	Maestro	7+
A New Kind of Government: Articles of Confederation to Constitution	Baby Professor	8+
Constitution: Translated for Kids	Travis	10+
Give Me Liberty!	Freedman	
If You Were There When They Signed the Constitution	Levy	8+
In Defense of Liberty	Freedman	10+
Our Nation's Documents	Time for Kids	
Shh! We're Writing the Constitution	Fritz	8+
The Constitution Decoded: A Guide to the Document that Shaped Our Nation	Kennedy	8+
The Declaration of Independence from A-Z	Osornio	7+
The Declaration of Independence: The Words that Made America	Fink	1+
The Journey of the One and Only Declaration of Independence	St. George	8+
The United States Constitution	Hennessey	11+
United States Civics: Articles of Confederation for Kids	Baby Professor	8+
We the Kids	Catrow	5+
We the People: The Constitution of the United States	Spier	5+
What Does the Constitution Say? A Kid's Guide to How Our Democracy Works	Sheehan	8+

Enrichment Activities

- Read about the Charters of Freedom, the collection of the three most important historical documents in the US: https://museum.archives.gov/founding-documents Read a transcript of each item. Write a paragraph about the importance of each document.

- Review the list of foundational American documents here: https://www.archives.gov/historical-docs Then, create an illustrated timeline of when these documents were written.

- Choose a historical document from the link above. Write a newspaper article information the public about the document. Include the date, authors, immediate significance, any relevant details, and long-term significance.

- Download this free lesson about the parts of the Constitution: https://www.thecleverteacher.com/parts-of-the-us-constitution-lesson/?ssp_iabi=1677801895948

- Download this free lesson about the Bill of Rights: https://www.thecleverteacher.com/us-constitution-primary-sources/?ssp_iabi=1677801973654

- Download this free lesson about the Declaration of Independence timeline: https://www.thecleverteacher.com/declaration-of-independence-free-lesson/?ssp_iabi=1677802070314

Sources

Bibliography

"The Late Middle Ages: Crisis and Recovery, 1300-1450." The Late Middle Ages. Accessed April 4, 2023. http://facstaff.bloomu.edu/mhickey/late_middle_ages.htm.

"The 1920s." General - Primary Sources: The 1920s - LibGuides at Christopher Newport University, n.d. https://cnu.libguides.com/1920s/general.

1945 to the Present | AP US History Study Guide from The Gilder Lehrman Institute of American History, December 1, 2011. https://ap.gilderlehrman.org/history-by-era/essays/1945-present?period=9.

"1945-1968" The Library of Congress, n.d. https://www.loc.gov/classroom-materials/united-states-history-primary-source-timeline/post-war-united-states-1945-1968/overview/.

1970s America | Richard Nixon Museum and Library, July 6, 2021. https://www.nixonlibrary.gov/news/1970s-america.

3, March, and February 28. "Exploring the Unparalleled Significance of the Civil War." American Civil War Museum, April 4, 2023. https://acwm.org/.

"5 Fun Ways to Teach Cause and Effect in Reading and Writing." Literacy Ideas, March 24, 2023. https://literacyideas.com/teaching-cause-effect-in-english/.

"Abolitionism Timeline." The Gilder Lehrman Center for the Study of Slavery, Resistance, and Abolition, April 27, 2015. https://glc.yale.edu/abolitionism-timeline.

"About This Collection: Abraham Lincoln Papers at the Library of Congress : Digital Collections : Library of Congress." The Library of Congress. https://www.loc.gov/collections/abraham-lincoln-papers/about-this-collection/.

"About This Collection: Andrew Johnson Papers : Digital Collections : Library of Congress." The Library of Congress. https://www.loc.gov/collections/andrew-johnson-papers/about-this-collection/?loclr=blogmss.

"About This Collection : Civil War Maps : Digital Collections : Library of Congress." The Library of Congress. Accessed April 5, 2023. https://www.loc.gov/collections/civil-war-maps/about-this-collection/?loclr=blogmap.

"The Account given by Wulfstan." Anglo. http://anglo-saxon.archeurope.com/literature/ohthere-and-wulfstan-at-the-court-of-king-alfred/the-account-given-by-wulfstan/.

The Age of Reagan | AP US History Study Guide from The Gilder Lehrman Institute of American History, January 29, 2012. https://ap.gilderlehrman.org/history-by-era/essays/age-reagan.

"Almanacs, Transcripts, and Maps." Encyclopedia.com.
    https://www.encyclopedia.com/history/encyclopedias-almanacs-transcripts-and-
    maps/timeline-events-middle-ages.

America in the 1920s, Primary Sources for Teachers, America in Class, National Humanities
    Center, n.d. http://americainclass.org/sources/becomingmodern/index.htm.

"American Civil War." American Civil War | United States Military Academy West Point.
    https://www.westpoint.edu/academics/academic-departments/history/american-civil-war.

"American Indian History and Heritage." NEH. https://edsitement.neh.gov/teachers-
    guides/american-indian-history-and-heritage.

"The American Revolution, 1763 - 1783 : U.S. History Primary Source Timeline : Classroom
    Materials at the Library of Congress : Library of Congress." The Library of Congress.
    https://www.loc.gov/classroom-materials/united-states-history-primary-source-
    timeline/american-revolution-1763-1783/.

"Ancient History ." Internet history sourcebooks project: Ancient history.
    https://sourcebooks.fordham.edu/ancient/asbook.asp.

"The Ancient World." Eyewitness to the ancient world.
    http://www.eyewitnesstohistory.com/awfrm.htm.

"Answers with Authority." Oxford Reference, January 1, 1970.
    https://www.oxfordreference.com/.

Archivera: Portal. http://7006.sydneyplus.com/Archive/Portal/Default.aspx?lang=en-US.

"Arctic Studies Center." Smithsonian National Museum of Natural History.
    https://naturalhistory.si.edu/research/anthropology/programs/arctic-studies-center.

Artlessonsforkids. "Cave Art Comes Alive!" ART LESSONS FOR KIDS, August 25, 2019.
    https://artlessonsforkids.me/2009/03/15/cave-art-comes-alive/.

Asia for Educators, Columbia University. "Primary Source Database." Primary Sources with
    DBQs | Asia for Educators | Columbia University.
    http://afe.easia.columbia.edu/main_pop/ps/ps_china.htm.

Atlas Map: World War II on the Home Front: War Industry and relocation, n.d.
    https://wps.pearsoncustom.com/wps/media/objects/2428/2487068/atlas/atl_ah5_m007.html
    .

Author: William Anderson (Schoolworkhelper Editorial Team) https://schoolworkhelper.net/
    Tutor and Freelance Writer. Science Teacher and Lover of Essays. Article last reviewed:
    2020 | St. Rosemary Institution © 2010-2022 | Creative Commons 4.0, Author: and Tutor

and Freelance Writer. Science Teacher and Lover of Essays. Article last reviewed: 2020 | St. Rosemary Institution © 2010-2022 | Creative Commons 4.0. "Reasons for the Downfall of the Middle Ages." Schoolwork Helper. https://schoolworkhelper.net/reasons-for-the-downfall-of-the-middle-ages/.

Avalon Project - 17th century documents : 1600 - 1699. https://avalon.law.yale.edu/subject_menus/17th.asp.

Avalon Project - 18th century documents : 1700 - 1799. https://avalon.law.yale.edu/subject_menus/18th.asp.

"The Baby Boom (Article)." Khan Academy. Khan Academy, n.d. https://www.khanacademy.org/humanities/us-history/postwarera/postwar-era/a/the-baby-boom.

Balaji. "Difference between Renaissance and Enlightenment." BYJU'S Exam Prep, February 17, 2023. https://byjusexamprep.com/upsc-exam/difference-between-renaissance-and-enlightenment.

"Bill of Rights in Action." Constitutional Rights Foundation. https://www.crf-usa.org/bill-of-rights-in-action.

"Black Lives Matter (BLM)." The Library of Congress, n.d. https://www.loc.gov/item/lcwaN0016241/.

Boatner, Kay. "The First Olympics." History. National Geographic Kids, July 23, 2021. https://kids.nationalgeographic.com/history/article/first-olympics.

Bodleian Library Broadside Ballads. https://chnm.gmu.edu/worldhistorysources/r/64/whm.html.

"Bog Bodies." Education. https://education.nationalgeographic.org/resource/bog-bodies/.

Brooks, Christopher. "Chapter 1: The High Middle Ages." Western Civilization A Concise History. NSCC, January 6, 2020. https://pressbooks.nscc.ca/worldhistory/chapter/chapter-1-the-high-middle-ages/.

Brooks, Christopher. "Chapter 3: The Bronze Age and the Iron Age." Western Civilization A Concise History. NSCC, January 6, 2020. https://pressbooks.nscc.ca/worldhistory/chapter/chapter-3-the-bronze-age-and-the-iron-age/.

Bureau, US Census. Census.gov, March 31, 2023. https://www.census.gov/.

"BYU Harold B. Lee Library." Europe: Religious Reformation – EuroDocs. https://eudocs.lib.byu.edu/index.php/Europe:_Religious_Reformation.

Caraballo, Written by Michael, and Written by Jeanne Willoz-Egnor. "The Mariner's Museum and Park." The Mariners' Museum and Park, March 13, 2023. https://www.marinersmuseum.org/.

Chandler, By: Daniel Ross. "The Modernist-Fundamentalist Controversy and Its Impact on Liberal Religion." UU Humanist Association, August 10, 2012. https://www.huumanists.org/publications/journal/modernist-fundamentalist-controversy-and-its-impact-liberal-religion.

Christian Classics Ethereal Library. https://ccel.org/.

Church, Saint John. "7 Differences between Orthodoxy and Catholicism." Saint John the Evangelist Orthodox Church, August 30, 2022. https://www.saintjohnchurch.org/differences-between-orthodox-and-catholic/.

"Civil War Glass Negatives and Related Prints - about This Collection." Library of Congress, January 1, 1861. https://www.loc.gov/pictures/collection/cwp/.

Claire. "Feudalism in the Middle Ages." Angelic Scalliwags Homeschool, October 25, 2022. https://angelicscalliwagshomeschool.com/feudalism-in-the-middle-ages/.

"Classical Antiquity Primary Source Collection." Perseus collections/texts. https://www.perseus.tufts.edu/hopper/collections.

Cohen, Susan, Jeniferbazzit@yahoo.com, Kristen, Denise McFall, Dawn, and Jennifer. "Teaching the Lost Colony of Roanoke." Thrive in Grade Five, October 17, 2021. https://thriveingradefive.com/teaching-the-lost-colony-of-roanoke/.

"The Collected Works of Abraham Lincoln." Collected Works of Abraham Lincoln. https://quod.lib.umich.edu/l/lincoln/.

"Collins Online Dictionary: Definitions, Thesaurus and Translations." Collins Online Dictionary | Definitions, Thesaurus and Translations. https://www.collinsdictionary.com/.

Collyer, Chris. "Grimspound." Grimspound - south of Hookney Tor, Dartmoor, Devon. http://www.stone-circles.org.uk/stone/grimspound.htm.

"Colonial Settlement." The Library of Congress. https://www.loc.gov/classroom-materials/united-states-history-primary-source-timeline/?loclr=blogtea.

"The Cornell University Witchcraft Collection." The Cornell University Witchcraft Collection: Home | Cornell University. https://rmc.library.cornell.edu/witchcraftcoll/.

CosmoLearning. "Topics: Europe - Europe 1300-1453: Late Middle Ages." CosmoLearning. https://cosmolearning.org/topics/europe-1300-1453-late-middle-ages/.

"Council of Trent and Catholic Reformation." Primary sources. https://college.cengage.com/history/world/resources/students/primary/trent.htm.

"Covid-19," n.d. https://www.who.int/health-topics/coronavirus/coronavirus.

"Danube Transnational Programme Homepage." Danube Transnational Programme. Accessed https://www.interreg-danube.eu/#!

"The Defining Moments and Historic Places of the Civil War." https://www.doi.gov/blog/defining-moments-and-historic-places-civil-war.

Deha, Mustafa, JIm from Cupertino, and Mary Brumley. "Five Events That Began the Renaissance (or Ended the Middle Ages)." Well, January 21, 2022. https://welltrainedmind.com/a/five-events-began-renaissance-ended-middle-ages/.

Den, Liesl - Homeschool. "Plague Lapbook." Homeschool Den, March 24, 2022. https://homeschoolden.com/2016/01/25/middle-ages-in-the-1300s-black-plague-simulation-worksheets-on-the-crusades-hundred-years-war/.

"Dictionary by Merriam-Webster: America's Most-Trusted Online Dictionary." Merriam-Webster. Merriam-Webster. Accessed April 4, 2023. https://www.merriam-webster.com/.

Disasters and the Politics of Memory | AP US History Study Guide from The Gilder Lehrman Institute of American History, September 12, 2014. https://ap.gilderlehrman.org/history-by-era/facing-new-millennium/essays/disasters-and-politics-memory?period=9.

"Diversity in Colonial Times - Sage Publications Inc." https://www.sagepub.com/sites/default/files/upm-binaries/23122_Chapter_3.pdf.

Documenting the American south homepage. https://docsouth.unc.edu/index.html/.

"Early Americas Digital Archive." Home. https://mith.umd.edu/research/eada/.

"Early Church History." Early church history. https://earlychurchhistory.org/daily-life/.

"The Effects of the Little Ice Age (c. 1300-1850)." Climate in Arts and History, June 30, 2021. https://www.science.smith.edu/climatelit/the-effects-of-the-little-ice-age/.

Encyclopædia Britannica. Encyclopædia Britannica, inc. Accessed April 4, 2023. https://www.britannica.com/.

"Enlightenment and Revolution - Harvard University." https://hwpi.harvard.edu/files/pluralism/files/enlightenment_and_revolution_0.pdf.

"European Union." Central Intelligence Agency. Central Intelligence Agency, n.d. https://www.cia.gov/the-world-factbook/countries/european-union/.

"Exploring the Western Frontier with the Records of Congress." National Archives and Records Administration. National Archives and Records Administration. https://www.archives.gov/legislative/resources/education/frontier.

Eyewitness to the 17th century. http://www.eyewitnesstohistory.com/17frm.htm.

"FDR's Fireside Chat ." National Archives and Records Administration. National Archives and Records Administration, n.d. https://www.archives.gov/education/lessons/fdr-fireside.

"Federalists & Anti-Federalists." iCivics. https://www.icivics.org/teachers/lesson-plans/federalists-anti-federalists.

Fogel, the phases of the Four great awakenings. https://press.uchicago.edu/Misc/Chicago/256626.html.

Foster, John, Matthew Taylor, David Boecklin, Mathias Tanner, and J. Luyken. "Religion and the Founding of the American Republic America as a Religious Refuge: The Seventeenth Century, Part 1." Library of Congress, June 4, 1998. https://www.loc.gov/exhibits/religion/rel01.html.

"Founders Online: Home." National Archives and Records Administration. National Archives and Records Administration. https://www.founders.archives.gov/.

"Free Art Lesson from Book 1." FREE art lesson from Draw and Write Through History, Book 1-DOWNLOAD. http://www.drawandwrite.com/FreeArtLesson.html.

"Free Rise of Dictators Pop up Lesson Plan." Students of History Teaching Resources, n.d. https://www.studentsofhistory.com/rise-of-dictators.

"Fun Facts and Social Studies." History for kids, July 24, 2019. https://www.historyforkids.net/.

"Fun Facts for Kids on Animals, Earth, History and More!" DK Find Out! https://www.dkfindout.com/us/history/iron-age/hill-forts/#!

George Washington's Mount Vernon. https://www.mountvernon.org/.

"The Gilded Age (1865-1898) | US History." Khan Academy. Khan Academy.. https://www.khanacademy.org/humanities/us-history/the-gilded-age.

GotQuestions.org. "Who Were the Early Church Fathers?" GotQuestions.org, May 17, 2009. https://www.gotquestions.org/early-church-fathers.html.

"The Great Depression (Article)." Khan Academy. Khan Academy, n.d. https://www.khanacademy.org/humanities/us-history/rise-to-world-power/great-depression/a/the-great-depression.

"Great Depression Primary Sources & Teaching Activities." National Archives and Records Administration. National Archives and Records Administration, n.d. https://education.blogs.archives.gov/2021/02/18/great-depression-2/.

"The Great Depression," n.d. https://www.stlouisfed.org/-/media/project/frbstl/stlouisfed/files/pdfs/great-depression/the-great-depression-wheelock-overview.pdf.

"The Great Famine of 1315" https://geoalliance.asu.edu/sites/default/files/LessonFiles/Godfrey/Famine/GodfreyFamineS.pdf.

"The Great Migration (1910-1970)." National Archives and Records Administration. National Archives and Records Administration. https://www.archives.gov/research/african-americans/migrations/great-migration.

"The Greater United States | Library of Congress." https://www.loc.gov/resource/g3701sm.gct00483/?sp=39.

"Greenback." Museum of American Finance. https://www.moaf.org/exhibits/checks_balances/abraham-lincoln/greenback.

"Guide to WWI." World War I - Guide to Online Primary Sources - LibGuides at University of California San Diego. https://ucsd.libguides.com/primarysources/ww1.

"Guides: American Military & War Primary Source Collections: First World War." First World War - American Military & War Primary Source Collections - Guides at Oklahoma State University-Stillwater. https://info.library.okstate.edu/warprimarysources/wwi.

"Guides: Primary Sources (U.S. History): Introduction." Introduction - Primary Sources (U.S. History) - Guides at Lone Star College-Kingwood. https://kwlibguides.lonestar.edu/PrimarySources-History.

"Guides: Primary Sources (U.S. History): Introduction." Introduction - Primary Sources (U.S. History) - Guides at Lone Star College-Kingwood. https://kwlibguides.lonestar.edu/PrimarySources-History.

"Guides: Primary Sources (U.S. History): Introduction." Introduction - Primary Sources (U.S. History) - Guides at Lone Star College-Kingwood. https://kwlibguides.lonestar.edu/PrimarySources-History.

"Guides: Primary Sources (U.S. History): Introduction." Introduction - Primary Sources (U.S. History) - Guides at Lone Star College-Kingwood. https://kwlibguides.lonestar.edu/PrimarySources-History.

"Guides: WWI Primary and Secondary Sources." Primary Sources - WWI Primary and Secondary Sources: Print and Online - Guides at Penn Libraries. https://guides.library.upenn.edu/WorldWarI.

Harlem Renaissance, n.d. https://www.nga.gov/learn/teachers/lessons-activities/uncovering-america/harlem-renaissance.html.

Herodotus, Simon Hornblower, and Pelling C B R. *Histories*. Cambridge: Cambridge University Press, 2017.

Higgs, Robert. "How War Amplified Federal Power in the Twentieth Century." FEE Freeman Article. Foundation for Economic Education, July 1, 1999. https://fee.org/articles/how-war-amplified-federal-power-in-the-twentieth-century/.

"High Middle Ages." Humanities: Prehistory to the 15th Century || Course Hero. https://www.coursehero.com/study-guides/atd-fscj-earlyhumanities/high-middle-ages/.

"Highest Death Toll from Wars." Guinness World Records, n.d. https://www.guinnessworldrecords.com/world-records/highest-death-toll-from-wars/.

"Highhill Homeschool: Make Your Own Medieval Village." Pinterest, September 22, 2022. https://www.pinterest.com/pin/highhill-homeschool-make-your-own-medieval-village--552324341812523057/.

"Highlighting History: How 'Tet' Began the End of Vietnam." U.S. Department of Defense, n.d. https://www.defense.gov/News/Feature-Stories/Story/Article/3291950/highlighting-history-how-tet-began-the-end-of-vietnam/.

Hirschman, Charles, and Elizabeth Mogford. "Immigration and the American Industrial Revolution from 1880 to 1920." Social science research. U.S. National Library of Medicine, December 2009. https://www.ncbi.nlm.nih.gov/pmc/articles/PMC2760060/.

"Historic Cornwall." https://www.historic-cornwall.org.uk/.

"Historical Archives: AHA." Historical Archives | AHA. https://www.historians.org/about-aha-and-membership/aha-history-and-archives/historical-archives/why-study-history-.

"Historical Maps 2: Islamic Expansion from 622 to 750." https://math.ucr.edu/~res/math153-2019/historical-maps2.pdf.

"History - Brown v. Board of Education Re-Enactment." United States Courts, n.d. https://www.uscourts.gov/educational-resources/educational-activities/history-brown-v-board-education-re-enactment.

"History for Kids." Ducksters. https://www.ducksters.com/history/.

"History of Stonehenge." English Heritage. https://www.english-heritage.org.uk/visit/places/stonehenge/history-and-stories/history.

Holly. "Survey of World History." TPT. https://www.teacherspayteachers.com/Product/Survey-of-World-History-9045888.

"Holocaust Timeline: The Rise of the Nazi Party," n.d. https://fcit.coedu.usf.edu/holocaust/timeline/nazirise.htm.

"The Home of Language Data." Oxford Languages. https://languages.oup.com/.

"Home." Cambridge University Press & Assessment, March 31, 2023. https://www.cambridge.org/.

"How to Spot 16 Types of Media Bias." AllSides, December 16, 2022. https://www.allsides.com/media-bias/how-to-spot-types-of-media-bias.

Imagining History. "Make a Stone Age Axe - Craft Activity for Kids." Imagining History. Imagining History, February 1, 2023. https://www.imagininghistory.co.uk/post/stone-age-axe-craft.

"Immigration and Americanization, 1880-1930." Immigration and Americanization, 1880-1930 | DPLA. https://dp.la/primary-source-sets/immigration-and-americanization-1880-1930.

Important examples of progressive reforms. http://www-personal.umd.umich.edu/~ppennock/Progressive%20Reforms.htm.

"Index." Icelandic Saga Database. https://www.sagadb.org/.

"The Industrial Revolution in the United States: Classroom Materials at the Library of Congress : Library of Congress." The Library of Congress. https://www.loc.gov/classroom-materials/industrial-revolution-in-the-united-states/.

"The Internet Classics Archive: 441 Searchable Works of Classical Literature." http://classics.mit.edu/index.html.

Internet History Sourcebooks: Medieval Sourcebook. https://legacy.fordham.edu/Halsall/sbook2.asp.

"An Introduction to Early Medieval England." English Heritage. https://www.english-heritage.org.uk/learn/story-of-england/early-medieval/.

Investopedia. Investopedia, n.d. https://www.investopedia.com/.

"Ireland's Famine Children 'Born at Sea.'" National Archives and Records Administration. National Archives and Records Administration. https://www.archives.gov/publications/prologue/2017/winter/irish-births.

"The Iron Age." https://www.northdowns.surrey.sch.uk/attachments/download.asp?file=5770&type=pdf.

"Iron Age Recipes." Teachit, January 19, 2022. https://www.teachit.co.uk/resources/primary/iron-age-recipes.

"Iron Trade in Western Roman Empire." National Center for Biotechnology Information. U.S. National Library of Medicine. https://www.ncbi.nlm.nih.gov/pmc/.

"Japanese-American Incarceration during World War II." National Archives and Records Administration. National Archives and Records Administration, n.d. https://www.archives.gov/education/lessons/japanese-relocation.

"JCB Archive of Early American Images - Luna Imaging, Inc." https://jcb.lunaimaging.com/luna/servlet/JCB~1~1.

"John Brown's Harpers Ferry Raid." American Battlefield Trust. https://www.battlefields.org/learn/topics/john-browns-harpers-ferry-raid.

"King Henry VIII." British Library. https://www.bl.uk/sacred-texts/articles/henry-viii-and-the-reformation.

"Korea War Lesson Plans - Free Resources." Korean War Legacy, February 20, 2023. https://koreanwarlegacy.org/teaching-tools/korean-war-legacy/.

"The Ku Klux Klan in the 1920s." Bill of Rights Institute. https://billofrightsinstitute.org/essays/the-ku-klux-klan-in-the-1920s.

"Landmark Legislation: The Pacific Railway Act of 1862." U.S. Senate: Landmark Legislation: The Pacific Railway Act of 1862, January 12, 2017. https://www.senate.gov/artandhistory/history/common/generic/PacificRailwayActof1862.htm.

"Landmark Legislation: The Pacific Railway Act of 1862." U.S. Senate: Landmark Legislation: The Pacific Railway Act of 1862, January 12, 2017. https://www.senate.gov/artandhistory/history/common/generic/PacificRailwayActof1862.htm.

"Late Middle Ages." The Late Middle Ages. http://facstaff.bloomu.edu/mhickey/late_middle_ages.htm.

"Late Middle Ages." The Late Middle Ages.
    http://facstaff.bloomu.edu/mhickey/late_middle_ages.htm.

Layers of Learning. "Map of the Viking World and a Viking People Craft." Layers of Learning,
    January 3, 2023. https://layers-of-learning.com/viking-people/.

"The League of Nations." UN GENEVA. https://www.ungeneva.org/en/library-archives/league-
    of-nations.

Learning, Lumen. "Urbanization and Its Challenges." Urbanization and Its Challenges | US
    History II (OS Collection). https://courses.lumenlearning.com/suny-
    ushistory2os2xmaster/chapter/urbanization-and-its-challenges/.

Learning, Lumen. "US History I (Ay Collection)." The Consequences of the American
    Revolution | US History I (AY Collection). https://courses.lumenlearning.com/suny-
    ushistory1ay/chapter/the-consequences-of-the-american-revolution/.

"Lend-Lease Program." U.S. Department of State. U.S. Department of State, n.d.
    https://history.state.gov/milestones/1937-1945/lend-lease.

"Lesson Plan: Cast Your Vote-1812! - National Park Service."
    https://www.nps.gov/fomc/castyourvote/CastYourVote-curriculum46.pdf.

"Lessons: 1870-1900." National Archives and Records Administration. National Archives and
    Records Administration. https://www.archives.gov/education/lessons/industrial-us.html.

"Lessons: 1945 to Early 1970s." National Archives and Records Administration. National
    Archives and Records Administration, n.d.
    https://www.archives.gov/education/lessons/postwar-us.html.

"Libguides: American History 1--Hist 2111 (OER): Chapter 8: The Market Revolution." Chapter
    8: The Market Revolution - American History 1--HIST 2111 (OER) - LibGuides at
    Georgia Highlands College.
    https://getlibraryhelp.highlands.edu/c.php?g=677685&p=4779061.

"Libguides: American History 2--Hist 2112 (OER): Chapter 17: Conquering the West." Chapter
    17: Conquering the West - American History 2--HIST 2112 (OER) - LibGuides at Georgia
    Highlands College. https://getlibraryhelp.highlands.edu/c.php?g=768076&p=5508089.

"Libguides: American History: The Revolutionary War: Aftermath." Aftermath - American
    History: The Revolutionary War - LibGuides at John Jay College of Criminal Justice,
    CUNY. https://guides.lib.jjay.cuny.edu/c.php?g=288395&p=1922311.

"Libguides: American History: The Revolutionary War: Key Personalities." Key Personalities -
    American History: The Revolutionary War - LibGuides at John Jay College of Criminal
    Justice, CUNY. https://guides.lib.jjay.cuny.edu/c.php?g=288395&p=1922291.

"Libguides: Guide to Online Primary Sources: Native Americans." Native Americans - Guide to Online Primary Sources - LibGuides at University of California San Diego. https://ucsd.libguides.com/primarysources/nativeamericans.

"Libguides: Hist 674- Seminar Recent U.S. History: Cold War Primary Sources." Cold War Primary Sources - HIST 674- Seminar Recent U.S. History - LibGuides at California State University, Northridge, n.d. https://libguides.csun.edu/hist674/coldwarsources.

"Libguides: HST 330: Frontier & the American West: Primary Documents Sites." Home - LibGuides at Furman University. https://libguides.furman.edu/frontier/primary.

"Libguides: Primary Sources: Ancient History: Persian Empire." Persian Empire - Primary Sources: Ancient History - LibGuides at Christopher Newport University. https://cnu.libguides.com/primaryancient/persianempire.

"Libguides: Primary Sources: Energy: Edison, Thomas." Edison, Thomas - Primary Sources: Energy - LibGuides at Christopher Newport University. https://cnu.libguides.com/psenergy/thomasedison.

"Libguides: Primary Sources: Medieval and Renaissance Periods: Women." Women - Primary Sources: Medieval and Renaissance Periods - LibGuides at Christopher Newport University. https://cnu.libguides.com/c.php?g=23214&p=136623.

"Libguides: Primary Sources: The American West: General Sources." General Sources - Primary Sources: The American West - LibGuides at Christopher Newport University. https://cnu.libguides.com/c.php?g=23306&p=136967.

"Libguides: Primary Sources: The Great Depression and the 1930s." Contents - Primary Sources: The Great Depression and the 1930s - LibGuides at Christopher Newport University, n.d. https://cnu.libguides.com/psthegreatdepression.

"Libguides: Primary Sources: U.S. Presidents: Adams, J.Q." Adams, J.Q. - Primary Sources: U.S. Presidents - LibGuides at Christopher Newport University. https://cnu.libguides.com/primarypresidents/johnquincyadams.

"Libguides: Primary Sources: U.S. Presidents: Adams, J." Adams, J. - Primary Sources: U.S. Presidents - LibGuides at Christopher Newport University. https://cnu.libguides.com/primarypresidents/johnadams.

"Libguides: Primary Sources: U.S. Presidents: Harrison, W.H." Harrison, W.H. - Primary Sources: U.S. Presidents - LibGuides at Christopher Newport Universityhttps://cnu.libguides.com/primarypresidents/williamhenryharrison.

"Libguides: Primary Sources: U.S. Presidents: Jackson." Jackson - Primary Sources: U.S. Presidents - LibGuides at Christopher Newport University. https://cnu.libguides.com/primarypresidents/andrewjackson.

"Libguides: Primary Sources: U.S. Presidents: Monroe." Monroe - Primary Sources: U.S. Presidents - LibGuides at Christopher Newport University.. https://cnu.libguides.com/primarypresidents/jamesmonroe.

"Libguides: Primary Sources: U.S. Presidents: Van Buren." Van Buren - Primary Sources: U.S. Presidents - LibGuides at Christopher Newport University. https://cnu.libguides.com/primarypresidents/martinvanburen.

"Libguides: Primary Sources: U.S. Presidents: Washington." Washington - Primary Sources: U.S. Presidents - LibGuides at Christopher Newport University. https://cnu.libguides.com/primarypresidents/georgewashington.

"Libguides: Primary Sources: Wars & Conflicts: French and Indian War." French and Indian War - Primary Sources: Wars & Conflicts - LibGuides at Christopher Newport University. https://cnu.libguides.com/primarywars/frenchandindian.

"Libguides: U.S. History, 1945-1960 ." Primary Sources - U.S. History, 1945-1960 -- Post-War America -- History 430 - LibGuides at Phillips Exeter Academy, n.d. https://libguides.exeter.edu/c.php?g=465071&p=3179188.

"Libguides: United States History (1970s) Research Guide: Primary Sources." Primary Sources - United States History (1970s) Research Guide - LibGuides at Elon University, n.d. https://elon.libguides.com/US_history_1970s/Primary_Sources.

"Library Guides: History : Ancient: Primary Sources." Primary Sources - History : Ancient - Library Guides at University of Washington Libraries. https://guides.lib.uw.edu/research/ancient/primary.

"Library Guides: History : Military: Primary Sources -- WWII." Primary Sources, n.d. https://guides.lib.uw.edu/research/history-military/wwii.

"Library Guides: Irish Studies: Primary Sources." Primary Sources - Irish Studies - Library Guides at University of Notre Dame. https://libguides.library.nd.edu/irish-studies/primary-sources.

"Life of John F. Kennedy." Life of John F. Kennedy | JFK Library, n.d. https://www.jfklibrary.org/learn/about-jfk/life-of-john-f-kennedy.

"Loc.gov/Rr/Program/Bib/Ourdocs/Newnation.html." A century of lawmaking for a new nation: U.S. congressional documents and debates, 1774-1873. https://memory.loc.gov/ammem/amlaw/lawhome.html.

Lopez, Albert. "History Lesson 1: History of Immigration through the 1850s." History Lesson 1: History of Immigration Through the 1850s. http://crfimmigrationed.org/index.php/lessons-for-teachers/71-immigrant-article-1.

"Loyalists and Patriots - American Experience." https://americanexperience.si.edu/wp-content/uploads/2014/07/Loyalists-and-Patriots.pdf.

"Lutheran Electronic Archive: Texts by and about Martin Luther and Other Lutherans." Project Wittenberg - Electronic Texts by and About Martin Luther and Lutherans. https://www.projectwittenberg.org/etext/.

"Map of Europe, 979 CE: Early Medieval History." TimeMaps, September 23, 2022. https://timemaps.com/history/europe-979ad/.

"Map of Federally Recognized Tribes." https://www.bia.gov/sites/default/files/dup/assets/bia/ots/bia/pdf/idc1-029628.pdf.

"Map of Routes." National Parks Service. U.S. Department of the Interior. Accessed April 5, 2023. https://www.nps.gov/nr/travel/underground/routes.htm.

Map of the United States - early Native American tribes. http://emersonkent.com/map_archive/united_states_indian_tribes.htm.

"Maps of Immigrants in the United States." migrationpolicy.org, May 18, 2021. https://www.migrationpolicy.org/programs/data-hub/maps-foreign-born-united-states.

Marcy. "Make Your Own Quadrant (Astrolabe) Used for Early Navigation." Uplifting Mayhem, August 31, 2020. https://www.upliftingmayhem.com/quadrant-used-for-early-navigation/.

McLean, Assistant Professor John. "Western Civilization." Lumen. https://courses.lumenlearning.com/atd-herkimer-westerncivilization/chapter/the-rise-of-charlemagne/.

Medieval Illuminated Manuscripts. https://chnm.gmu.edu/worldhistorysources/r/21/whm.html.

"Medieval Law." Medieval Legal History. http://www.legalhistorysources.com/.

"Medieval Sourcebook." De Re Militari. https://deremilitari.org/primary-sources/.

Medievalists.net. "The 50 Most Important Events of the Middle Ages." Medievalists.net, October 28, 2022. https://www.medievalists.net/2018/04/most-important-events-middle-ages/.

Medievalists.net. "Vocabulary Terms." Medievalists.net, September 16, 2022. https://www.medievalists.net/2021/09/everyday-magic-middle-ages/.

"Memorable Days: The Emilie Davis Diaries." Experience the U.S. Civil War in real time. https://davisdiaries.villanova.edu/.

Mesoweb. https://www.mesoweb.com/.

Middle East Wars - U.S. Military History - Henry Buhl Library at Grove City College, n.d. https://hbl.gcc.libguides.com/c.php?g=339608&p=2285680.

"Missouri Compromise (1820)." National Archives and Records Administration. National Archives and Records Administration. https://www.archives.gov/milestone-documents/missouri-compromise.

"Missouri Compromise (1820)." National Archives and Records Administration. National Archives and Records Administration. //www.archives.gov/milestone-documents/missouri-compromise.

"Modern Day Abolition." National Underground Railroad Freedom Center. https://freedomcenter.org/learn/modern-day-abolition/.

A More Perfect Union? Barack Obama and the Politics of Unity | AP US History Study Guide from The Gilder Lehrman Institute of American History, June 4, 2013. https://ap.gilderlehrman.org/history-by-era/facing-new-millennium/essays/more-perfect-union-barack-obama-and-politics-unity?period=9.

"National Constitution Center – Constitutioncenter.org." https://constitutioncenter.org/media/files/CK130001_CivicsKids-2013-PAGES-FNL-Lesson3.pdf.

"Native American History Primary Sources, Articles & Other Resources - Gale." Accessed April 5, 2023. https://www.gale.com/native-american-history.

"Native American History." National Archives and Records Administration. National Archives and Records Administration. https://www.archives.gov/news/topics/native-american-heritage-month.

Occupy Wall Street - Case - Faculty & Research - Harvard Business School, n.d. https://www.hbs.edu/faculty/Pages/item.aspx?num=43632.

"Online Textbook." The classical age (500-336 BC). https://www.penfield.edu/webpages/jgiotto/onlinetextbook.cfm?subpage=1647293.

Overview of the 1920s, n.d. https://www.digitalhistory.uh.edu/era.cfm?eraid=13&smtid=1.

"Overview : The New Nation, 1783 - 1815 : U.S. History Primary Source Timeline : Classroom Materials at the Library of Congress : Library of Congress." The Library of Congress. https://www.loc.gov/classroom-materials/united-states-history-primary-source-timeline/new-nation-1783-1815/overview/.

"Overview : the Post War United States, 1945-1968 : U.S. History Primary Source Timeline ." The Library of Congress, n.d. https://www.loc.gov/classroom-materials/united-states-history-primary-source-timeline/post-war-united-states-1945-1968/overview/.

"Overview : the Post War United States, 1945-1968 : U.S. History Primary Source Timeline ." The Library of Congress, n.d. https://www.loc.gov/classroom-materials/united-states-history-primary-source-timeline/post-war-united-states-1945-1968/overview/.

"Oxford Bibliographies ." Oxford Bibliographies. https://www.oxfordbibliographies.com/.

"The Peasants' Revolt - the Peasants' Revolt - KS3 History - Homework Help for Year 7, 8 and 9. - BBC Bitesize." BBC News. BBC, February 25, 2022. https://www.bbc.co.uk/bitesize/topics/z93txbk/articles/zyb77yc.

"Period 6: 1865-1898." The Gilder Lehrman Institute of American History AP US History Study Guide Period 6: 1865-1898. https://ap.gilderlehrman.org/period/6.

"Perseus Collection Renaissance Materials." Renaissance Materials. https://www.perseus.tufts.edu/hopper/collection?collection=Perseus%3Acollection%3ARenaissance.

Phillip S. Greenwalt Phill Greenwalt is co-founder of Emerging Revolutionary War and is also a full-time contributor to Emerging Civil War. Phill graduated from George Mason University with a M.A. in American History and als. "British Perspective American Revolution." American Battlefield Trust, March 25, 2021. https://www.battlefields.org/learn/articles/british-perspective-american-revolution.

"Plymouth Colony Archive Project." The Plymouth Colony Archive Project. http://www.histarch.illinois.edu/plymouth/.

"Popular Culture and Mass Media in the 1950s (Article)." Khan Academy. Khan Academy, n.d. https://www.khanacademy.org/humanities/us-history/postwarera/1950s-america/a/popular-culture-and-mass-media-cnx.

"Post War United States (1945-1970s)." The American Experience in the Classroom, n.d. https://americanexperience.si.edu/historical-eras/post-war-united-states/.

"The Postwar Era (1945-1980) | US History." Khan Academy. Khan Academy, n.d. https://www.khanacademy.org/humanities/us-history/postwarera.

"Prehistoric Period until 1050." National Museum of Denmark. https://en.natmus.dk/historical-knowledge/denmark/prehistoric-period-until-1050-ad/the-viking-age/.

"Primary Documents in American History." American Revolution and The New Nation, 1763-1815: Primary Documents of American History (Virtual Programs & Services, Library of Congress). https://www.loc.gov/rr/program/bib/ourdocs/newnation.html.

"Primary Documents in American History." Gilded Age and Progressive Era, 1878-1920: Primary Documents in American History (Virtual Programs & Services, Library of Congress). https://www.loc.gov/rr/program/bib//ourdocs/gilded.html.

"Primary Documents in American History." Pacific Railway Act: Primary Documents of American History (Virtual Programs & Services, Library of Congress). Accessed April 5, 2023. https://www.loc.gov/rr/program/bib//ourdocs/pacificrail.html.

"Primary Source Sets." Primary Source Sets | DPLA. https://dp.la/primary-source-sets/.

"Primary Sources (U.S. History)." Introduction - Primary Sources (U.S. History) - Guides at Lone Star College-Kingwood, n.d. https://kwlibguides.lonestar.edu/PrimarySources-History.

"The Progressive Era" Khan Academy. Khan Academy. https://www.khanacademy.org/humanities/us-history/rise-to-world-power/age-of-empire/a/the-progressive-era.

"The Progressive Era." Khan Academy. Khan Academy. https://www.khanacademy.org/humanities/us-history/rise-to-world-power/age-of-empire/a/the-progressive-era.

"The Progressive Era." Khan Academy. Khan Academy. https://www.khanacademy.org/humanities/us-history/rise-to-world-power/age-of-empire/a/the-progressive-era.

"Progressive Era." Miller Center, August 17, 2020. https://millercenter.org/the-presidency/teacher-resources/primary-resources/progressive-era.

"The Progressives." Constitutional Rights Foundation. https://www.crf-usa.org/election-central/the-progressives.html.

"Prohibition: Primary Sources." Primary Sources- "Roaring Twenties" - HST: Prohibition - Everett Library at Everett Library, n.d. https://library.queens.edu/prohibition/resources.

"The Protestant Reformation." Education. https://education.nationalgeographic.org/resource/protestant-reformation/.

"Published Primary Sources Relating to American Indians." National Archives and Records Administration. National Archives and Records Administration. https://www.archives.gov/research/native-americans/published-resources.html.

"Reformation Europe." Internet history sourcebooks: Modern history. https://sourcebooks.fordham.edu/mod/modsbook02.asp.

"Renaissance Facts for Kids." Renaissance Facts for Kids. https://kids.kiddle.co/Renaissance.

"The Renaissance Inventors." Nomad Press, April 5, 2023. https://nomadpress.net/nomadpress-books/renaissance-inventors/.

"Research Guides: American History to 1865: Colonial Period." Colonial Period - American History to 1865 - Research Guides at Baruch College. https://guides.newman.baruch.cuny.edu/c.php?g=188261&p=1243339.

"Research Guides: Gilded Age & Progressive Era - Archive Sources: Progressive Era & the Gilded Age." Progressive Era & the Gilded Age - Gilded Age & Progressive Era - Archive Sources - Research Guides at Washington University in St. Louis. https://libguides.wustl.edu/gilded-progressive.

"Research Guides: Primary Sources - Advanced Methods: Primary Sources - Options." Primary Sources - Options - Primary Sources - Advanced Methods - Research Guides at University of Northern Iowa, n.d. https://guides.lib.uni.edu/primary-sources-advanced-methods.

"Research Guides: U.S. History: Primary Source Collections Online: Native Americans." Native Americans - U.S. History: Primary Source Collections Online - Research Guides at Sam Houston State University. https://shsulibraryguides.org/c.php?g=86715&p=558322.

"Researchguides: Early Christianity: Primary Sources and Translations." Primary Sources and Translations - Early Christianity - ResearchGuides at Southeastern Baptist Theological Seminary. https://library.sebts.edu/c.php?g=264648&p=1775511.

"The Roaring 1920s." Miller Center, August 17, 2020. https://millercenter.org/the-presidency/teacher-resources/primary-resources/roaring-1920s.

The Roaring Twenties | AP US History Study Guide from The Gilder Lehrman Institute of American History, March 6, 2012. https://ap.gilderlehrman.org/essays/roaring-twenties.

Robb S. Harvey (with special thanks to Mark DeVries and Stuart Gordon). "Protestant Reformation." Protestant Reformation. https://mtsu.edu/first-amendment/article/1064/protestant-reformation.

Robinson, Selena. "Middle Ages History: Make a Codex Activity." Tina's Dynamic Homeschool Plus, April 30, 2022. https://tinasdynamichomeschoolplus.com/how-to-make-a-codex/.

Rose O'Neal Greenhow Papers at duke. https://library.duke.edu/rubenstein/scriptorium/greenhow/.

"The Rush of Immigrants by USHistory.org." CommonLit. https://www.commonlit.org/en/texts/the-rush-of-immigrants.

Salem Witch Trials Documentary Archive. https://salem.lib.virginia.edu/home.html.

Sarah Thompson Papers - Duke University Special Collections Library. https://library.duke.edu/rubenstein/scriptorium/thompson/.

"SCSU Hilton C. Buley Library: United States History - Primary Resources: Immigration."
Immigration - United States History - Primary Resources - SCSU Hilton C. Buley Library
at Southern Connecticut State University.
https://libguides.southernct.edu/ushistoryprimary/immigration.

"Sectionalism - Essential Civil War Curriculum."
https://www.essentialcivilwarcurriculum.com/sectionalism.html.

"Sectionalism in the Civil War." StudySmarter US.
https://www.studysmarter.us/explanations/history/us-history/sectionalism-in-the-civil-war/.

"Selected Sources: The Crusades." Internet history sourcebooks: Medieval sourcebook.
https://sourcebooks.fordham.edu/sbook1d.asp.

"Silk Road Worksheet."
https://www.cloverleaflocal.org/Downloads/Silk%20Road%20Worksheet.pdf.

"The Silk Road." International dunhuang project.
https://chnm.gmu.edu/worldhistorysources/r/99/whm.html.

Sites community portal. https://www.sites.si.edu/s/topic/0TO36000000acs4GAA/world-war-i-
lessons-and-legacies.

Smiley, Gene, Related Content, Jeffrey Rogers Hummel, Arnold Kling, Steven Horwitz, and E.
Roy Weintraub. "Great Depression." Econlib, n.d.
https://www.econlib.org/library/Enc/GreatDepression.html.

Society, SEC Historical. 2000s | Timeline | Virtual Museum and Archive of the History of
Financial Regulation, n.d. https://www.sechistorical.org/museum/timeline/2000-
timeline.php.

A Spotlight on a Primary Source by Ulysses S. Grant. "The Gilder Lehrman Institute of
American History." Statue of Liberty, 1884 | Gilder Lehrman Institute of American
History. https://www.gilderlehrman.org/history-resources/spotlight-primary-source/statue-
liberty-1884.

"Stone Age Bread Activity." ResearchParent.com, March 19, 2022.
https://researchparent.com/stone-age-bread-activity/.

"Story of the Battle." National Parks Service. U.S. Department of the Interior.
https://www.nps.gov/libi/learn/historyculture/battle-story.htm.

StudentSavvy. "Early Medieval Europe - Stem Challenges!" Student Savvy, July 17, 2018.
https://www.teachstudentsavvy.com/2018/07/early-medieval-europe-stem-challenges.html.

"Take Online Courses. Earn College Credit. Research Schools, Degrees & Careers." Study.com | https://study.com/.

"A Timeline of Church History - St. Sophia Greek Orthodox Church ..." https://www.saintsophias.org/uploads/1/8/6/1/18612444/a_timeline_of_church_history_ex panded_version.pdf.

"Timeline of Greek Antiquity." Timeline of Greek & Roman antiquity. https://people.umass.edu/dfleming/english704-timeline.html.

"Timeline of the Revolution." National Parks Service. U.S. Department of the Interior. Accessed https://www.nps.gov/subjects/americanrevolution/timeline.htm.

"Tribes - Native Voices." U.S. National Library of Medicine. National Institutes of Health. https://www.nlm.nih.gov/nativevoices/timeline/index.html.

"Trigger Events of the Civil War." American Battlefield Trust, August 24, 2021. https://www.battlefields.org/learn/articles/trigger-events-civil-war.

Tripp, Karyn. "Learning about Vikings." Teach Beside Me, July 26, 2017. https://teachbesideme.com/learning-about-vikings/.

U.S. Department of State. U.S. Department of State, n.d. https://2001-2009.state.gov/r/pa/ho/time/index.htm.

"U.S. History Primary Source Timeline ." The Library of Congress. https://www.loc.gov/classroom-materials/united-states-history-primary-source-timeline/.

"U.S. History Primary Source Timeline ." The Library of Congress. https://www.loc.gov/classroom-materials/united-states-history-primary-source-timeline/.

"U.S. History Primary Source Timeline : Classroom Materials at the Library of Congress ." The Library of Congress, n.d. https://www.loc.gov/classroom-materials/united-states-history-primary-source-timeline/great-.

"U.S. History Primary Source Timeline : Classroom Materials at the Library of Congress : Library of Congress." The Library of Congress. https://www.loc.gov/classroom-materials/united-states-history-primary-source-timeline/.

"U.S. History Primary Source Timeline : Classroom Materials at the Library of Congress : Library of Congress." The Library of Congress. https://www.loc.gov/classroom-materials/united-states-history-primary-source-timeline/.

"U.S. History Primary Source Timeline : Classroom Materials at the Library of Congress : Library of Congress." The Library of Congress.. https://www.loc.gov/classroom-materials/united-states-history-primary-source-timeline/.

"U.S. History Primary Source Timeline." The Library of Congress, n.d. https://www.loc.gov/classroom-materials/united-states-history-primary-source-timeline/great-.

"UH - Digital History." https://www.digitalhistory.uh.edu/teachers/lesson_plans/pdfs/unit1_3.pdf.

"Underground Railroad 19th Century - NYPL Digital Collections." https://digitalcollections.nypl.org/items/863f0211-4262-2898-e040-e00a18060f45.

"Underground Railroad 19th Century." NYPL Digital Collections. https://digitalcollections.nypl.org/items/863f0211-4262-2898-e040-e00a18060f45.

"United Nations, Main Body, Main Organs, General Assembly." United Nations. United Nations, n.d. https://www.un.org/en/ga/.

"United States Army Center of Military History." https://history.army.mil/html/books/075/75-7/cmhPub_75-7.pdf.

University, Stanford. "The Fall of Rome Was Europe's Lucky Break." Stanford News, April 30, 2020. https://news.stanford.edu/2019/10/23/fall-rome-europes-lucky-break/.

"UTEP Library Research Guides: Ancient Egypt and Mesopotamia: Primary Sources." Primary Sources - Ancient Egypt and Mesopotamia - UTEP Library Research Guides at University of Texas El Paso. https://libguides.utep.edu/c.php?g=429735&p=2931027.

Wang, Hansi Lo. "The Map of Native American Tribes You've Never Seen Before." NPR. NPR, May 5, 2021. https://www.npr.org/sections/codeswitch/2014/06/24/323665644/the-map-of-native-american-tribes-youve-never-seen-before.

"War in Galicia." The National Archives, March 26, 1915. https://www.nationalarchives.gov.uk/pathways/firstworldwar/document_packs/eastern.htm.

"Western Civilizations: His 101." Western Civilization. https://blogs.nvcc.edu/westernciv/history-of-western-civilization/western-civilizations-his-101/.

"Western Frontier Life in America." Western frontier life. https://faculty.chass.ncsu.edu/slatta/cowboys/essays/front_life2.htm.

"What Is Archaeology - Surreycc.gov.uk." https://www.surreycc.gov.uk/__data/assets/pdf_file/0019/225262/Downloadable-Resource-1-What-is-Archaeology_compressed.pdf.

"What Is Brexit?" La Moncloa., n.d. https://www.lamoncloa.gob.es/lang/en/brexit/AboutBrexit/Paginas/index.aspx.

"What Was Life like in the Bronze Age?" BBC Bitesize. BBC, June 24, 2022. https://www.bbc.co.uk/bitesize/topics/z82hsbk/articles/z874kqt.

Why did FDR's Bank Holiday succeed?, n.d. https://www.newyorkfed.org/research/epr/09v15n1/0907silb.html.

Wisser, Nancy. "Garden Stonehenge." CLONEHENGE. https://clonehenge.com/tag/garden-stonehenge/.

"A World at War : Articles and Essays : Stars and Stripes: The American Soldiers' Newspaper of World War I, 1918-1919 ." The Library of Congress. https://www.loc.gov/collections/stars-and-stripes/articles-and-essays/a-world-at-war/.

"World History Encyclopedia." World History Encyclopedia RSS. https://www.worldhistory.org#organization. https://www.worldhistory.org/.

"World War I: Building the American Military." www.army.mil, n.d. https://www.army.mil/article/185229/world_war_i_building_the_american_military.

"World War II Timeline Experience ." seal of the American Battle Monuments Commission., n.d. https://api.abmc.gov/sites/default/files/interactive/interactive_files/WW2/index.html.

"World War II." DocsTeach, n.d. https://www.docsteach.org/topics/wwii.

"Would You Have Been a Federalist or an Anti-Federalist?" Bill of Rights Institute. Accessed April 5, 2023. https://billofrightsinstitute.org/would-you-have-been-a-federalist-or-an-anti-federalist.

"Wright Brothers National Memorial (U.S. National Park Service)." National Parks Service. U.S. Department of the Interior. Accessed April 5, 2023. https://www.nps.gov/wrbr/index.htm.

"WWII: A Resource Guide." Library of Congress Resources - World War II: A Resource Guide - Research Guides at Library of Congress, n.d. https://guides.loc.gov/ww2/library-of-congress-resources.

"Y2K." U.S. Department of State. U.S. Department of State, n.d. https://history.state.gov/milestones/1989-1992/gulf-war.

Yalepress. "The High Middle Ages." Yale University Press, April 13, 2022. https://yalebooks.yale.edu/2020/08/18/the-high-middle-ages/.

Yalepress. "The High Middle Ages." Yale University Press, April 13, 2022. https://yalebooks.yale.edu/2020/08/18/the-high-middle-ages/.

Resources

K-6th Lesson Plans

Year: _____ - _____   Student: _____ Grade: _____

WEEK_____ DATE _____ TRACK _____
LESSON TITLE _____

Book(s):

Enrichment Activity:

Video(s):

Website(s):

WEEK_____ DATE _____ TRACK _____
LESSON TITLE _____

Book(s):

Enrichment Activity:

Video(s):

Website(s):

Library Book List

Date Needed	Date Requested	Date Due	Title(s)

Letters from the Past

Academic Year: _____

Name: _____

Book of Eras

Academic Year: _____

Name: _____

Book of Bios

Academic Year: _____

*Name:*_____

Book of Bios

Name:_____

Born: _____   Died:_____

Title/occupation: _____

What he/she is known for:

_____

Famous quote:

_____

How this person changed history:

A Taste of History

Academic Year: _____

Name: _____

Travel Thru History

Academic Year: _____

Name: _____

Fashion Through the Ages

Academic Year: _____

Name: _____

Timeline

Stone Age to Modern Era: A Journey to USA History

Ancient Period

Stone Age (?-3300 BC)

8000 BC: end of the last ice age

Archaic Period

7500: food production and animal domestication begins in China

7000: pigs first domesticated in Greece

6500: Jericho in the Jordan valley

6000: food production begins in Europe

5500:

- Pastoralism (cattle, sheep, goats) in the Sahara
- Potters' wheels in Mesopotamia.
- agricultural developments in Japan
- Niles' flood cycles began to be used by settlers

4000:

- first iron object found in Egypt
- horse domesticated in the Ukraine

3500:

- first earthen pyramids made in Peru
- Sumerian Period in Mesopotamia(?): city states: Kish, Uruk, Ur, Lagash. Gilgamesh, cuneiform, ziggurat.

Bronze Age (3300-1200 BC)

3300:

- writing developed in Sumerian
- first known board game, senet, played in Egypt
- The Bronze Age begins in Greece: the Minoans and Mycenaeans
- Stongehenge building begins
- papyrus used in Egypt

3200:

- Egyptian hieroglyphics used
- Upper Kingdom of Egypt and Lower are merged to create a single Egypt (Old Kingdom)

3000

- first known board game, senet, played in Egypt
- The Bronze Age begins in Greece: the Minoans and Mycenaeans
- Native American Archaic Period ends; Woodland Period begins

2800: Minoan culture on island of Crete in Aegean Sea

2500:

- First Great Pyramid of Giza built
- mammoths extinct

2430: first slaves recorded in Mesopotamia

2348: estimated date of the Great Flood (from the Young Earth Creation perspective.[148]

2100: Stone Henge begins its final stage

2000: irrigation system in Egypt

1950: Sumer falls to the Babylonians

---

[148] answersingenesis.org/bible-timeline/timeline-for-the-flood

1920: Abraham in Ur

1900-1100: Mycenaean civilization

1875: Xia Dynasty begins in China (1st permanent civilization in the Far East)

1800:

- Mayans first appear in small settlements (will become a true civilization in 250 AD)
- Sodom and Gomorrah destroyed
- Alphabetic writing begins; Epic of Gilgamesh written
- first Chinese dynasty formed

1782 VC: Hammurabi's code

1700: Jacobs family migrates for Goshen

1600-1500: Hittite kingdom begins, Shang Dynasty in China

1500: Mayan empire rises; Babylon is sacked

1400: oldest known hymn is written (Hurian)

1350: Jerichos walls fall down

1250: Israelite Exodus from Egypt (?) under Moses and Aaron

1200:

- Bronze Age Collapse
- Olmecs appear in Mesoamerica (the first Pre-Columbian civilization of that area)

Iron Age (1200-550 BC)

1184: Fall of Troy

1046 Zhou dynasty crushes Shang

1010-931: Israelite Kingdom: kings Saul, David and Solomon reign over United 12 Hebrew Tribes (Kingdom)

1000: **Adena Culture in North America begins**

890: Iliad and the Odyssey

814: Carthage founded by Phoenicians

800:

- Greek city-states
- Homer's Iliad and Odyssey

785: Kingdom of Kush

776: Olympic Games in Greece

750-300: Etruscan civilization

740: Israelite prophet Isaiah receives his vocation in the Temple and begins to prophesy.

Classical Antiquity (700 BC -500 AD)

753: founding of Rome

612: Ninevah, followed by Assyria, falls

605: Nebuchadnezzar king of Babylon (Chaldean Empire)

604: Nebuchadnezzar (or 605-562?); builds "Hanging Gardens"

600: Indisputably independent invention of writing, by people in modern Mexico (Mexican Amerindians)

563: Siddhartha Gautama (Buddha)

551: Confucius

550: Cyrus the Great

539: Cyrus, king of the Persians, enters Babylon (538 The Edict of Cyrus is proclaimed, allowing the Jewish exiles to return to the Promised Land)

521: 485 Darius I

508: Athenian democracy at Athens

499: Greco-Persian wars

475: Warring States Era in China

470: birth of Socrates

460-430: The Golden Age of Pericles in Athens (map). Pericles builds up Athens and strengthens democracy. Athens becomes increasingly antagonistic to Sparta.

447-432: Parthenon built

431: Peloponnesian War (until 404)

427: Plato born

384: Birth of Aristotle

331: Alexander the Great conquers Persia

323: the Hellenistic Age begins (until 146 BC

321: Seleucid Empire established

221: China unified under Qin dynasty

206: Han Dynasty: Silk Road begins

200: paper invented in China

197: Roman Empire begins

167: Maccabean revolt

146: Rome conquers Greece

140: Hipparchus of Nicaea (190-125 BC), makes important astronomical discoveries and invents trigonometry.

103: Spartacus born

63: Romans conquer Judea

44: Julius Caesar murdered by Marcus Brutus; end of Roman republic

37: Herod the Great king of Roman Judea

30: Cleopatra dies

27: Roman Empire begins

27: Roman Senate gives Octavian the title of (Caesar) Augustus

23: first sumo wrestler, Sukune, wins first contest of the sport

6 BC: Jesus Christ birth date

4 BC; death of King Herod

AD/CE BEGINS

5: Apostle Paul born in Tarsus

26: Pontius Pilate Prefect of Judea

27: Jesus' ministry begins

30: Jesus crucified

37: Death of Tiberius

37-41: Caligula emperor, assassinated before he can see fulfilled his order to erect his statue in the Temple of Jerusalem

41-54: Claudius emperor; expels the Jews from Rome

44: Herod Agrippa imprisons Peter in Jerusalem

45-49: Paul's first missions

c48: "Council" of Jerusalem declares gentile Christians exempt from the Law of Moses

49-52: Paul's missions to Galatia, Macedonia, Athens, Corinth

c50: First letters of Paul, the first Christian theologian

54-68: Nero emperor

57-58: Paul writes letters to Corinthians, Galatians, Romans

61-63: Paul in Rome, under military guard, writes letters to Colossians, Ephesians, and Philippians

64: Great Fire of Rome; allows rebuilding and improvement of the City

64-67: Martyrdoms of Peter and Paul at Rome. Gospel of Mark is thought to have been written

75: Josephus, Jewish historian living in Roman Empire, writes history

c80: Gospels of Matthew and Luke and Acts of the Apostles are written < p>81-96 | Domitian emperor

c85: Gospel of John written by the only apostle not to be martyred

c95: Final text of the Revelation; soon thereafter, final text of John's Gospel and the three letters of John the Elder

105: Invention by Cai Lun (China 66-125) of paper as we know it today.

Early church fathers:

- Clement (1): 65-100?
- Ignatius, Bishop of Antioch: 85-115, or 105-140 (student of the Apostle John)
- Polycarp: 100-155/165: bishop of Smyrna and student of John
- 120-Ptolemy creates the first flat map of the world.
- Justin Martyr: 150-165: most important Christian thinker between Paul and Origen
- Melito: 150-180: first to call it the "Old Testament"
- Irenaeus: 150-200, knew Polycarp as a boy; wrote "Against the Heretics" (excellent source of early church history)
- Tatian: 160-185, Assyrian who wrote the Diatessaron (one "single, coherent narrative)—later replaced by the 4 separate gospels
- Clement of Alexandria (180-215): First great intellectual and theologian of Christianity. Transitional figure to the more sophisticated authors of later centuries. Founded the first Christian academy at Alexandria.
- Origen: 200-250: first Christian Bible scholar
- Tertullian: 200-240
- Cyprian of Carthage: 245-260

- 250: Diophantus of Alexandria (200-284) writes the first book on what is now conceived as algebra.
- 310-Eusebius (310-340): Bishop of the old Roman capital of Judea, Caesarea Maritima. Important Church historian. His works are often the sole source we have for earlier church fathers.

271: Compass first used in China

313: Edict of Toleration (Christianity is legalized)

325 | Council of Nicaea; oldest known Bibles (as in the collection of books which form the Christian Bible to this day)

330

- Byzantium becomes the capital of the Roman world; named New Rome or Constantinople
- 330: Athanasius: Controversial Patriarch of Alexandria. First to define the canon of New Testament exactly as we have it.

350: First celebration of December 25 as Christmas

375-395: Ambrose: Bishop of Milan. Major influence on church-state relations through the Middle Ages.

380: Edict of Thessalonica: Christianity made the state religion

380: Jerome: Compiler of the Latin Vulgate (405), a translation of the Bible into Latin; correspondent of Augustine

390-430; Augustine: Bishop of Hippo. Most influential theologian of all the Fathers in the West.

390-407: John Chrysostom: Patriarch of Constantinople. Greatest preacher of the Fathers.

410: Rome sacked by the Visigoths (decline in Western Roman Empire)

455: Rome sacked by the Vandals

476: Odoacer deposes Roman Emperor Romulus Augustulus (end of Roman Empire: beginning of the Middle Ages)

Middle Ages

Early Middle Ages (500-1050)

??500: Battle of Mons Badonicus (King Arthur?)

500: Clovis conquers France and Belgium, converting the territory to Catholicism

507: Franks defeat Visogoths

525: Dionysius Exiguus: initiated Anno Domini

527: Justinian 1-Eastern Roman Empire (Code of Civil Law)

541: Plague of Justinian (25 million dead)

550; chess invented in India

563: Saint Columba founds mission in Iona (Christianity comes to Scotland)

570: Muhammad is born

590: St Gregory the Great is Pope (strengthens the papacy, spreads Christianity)

597: Augustine arrives in Kent (Christianization of England begins)

610: Heraclius becomes Emperor in Constantinople: the beginning of the Byzantine Empire

618: Tang Dynasty

622: Islam invented

627: Persia is conquered by Byzantine forces. The Jerusalem cross is retrieved from the Persians, who stole the relic in 614. Heraclius reigns until his death in 641.

632: all Arabia under Islam

638: Jerusalem captured by Arab army

639: Arabian Empire arises. Muslim armies take control of Syria, Egypt, Jordan and the Holy Land

648: Muslims conquer Persia

674: First Arab siege Constantinople

691: Buddhism becomes state religion in China

700: Christianization of England (began by St Gregory the Great) is complete

717: Siege of Constantinople by the Muslims

740: The Iconoclastic movement is initiated by Byzantine Emperor Leo the Isaurian, but the movement flourishes under the reign of his son Constantine V who rules until 775. The Iconoclasts advocate doing away with paganistic icon worship (images of Christ or saints). For them, Christ cannot be manifested or conceived of through human art. The Iconoclast controversy ends in the ninth century when a new Byzantine spirituality recognizes that the contemplation of icons may help someone assend from the material to the immaterial.

750:

- The first great English epic poem, Beowulf, is written in Old English. The work is anonymous and untitled until 1805. It is a Christian poem that exemplifies early medieval society in England and shows roots in Old Testament Law.
- Irish monks establish early-medieval art. The greatest surviving product of these monks is the Book of Kells, a Gospel book of decorative art.

751: St. Boniface anoints Pepin a divinely sanctioned king, and the Frankish monarchy is fused into the papal order. The western European empire, based on the alliance between the Frankish monarchy and the Latin Church, provides the image of Western cultural unity for Europeans, though it does not last long.

768: Beginning of Charlemagne's reign: Pepin's son, Carolus Magnus (Charlemagne), succeeds his father and is one of the most important rulers of medieval history. In time, his empire, known as the Carolingian dynasty, includes the greater section of central Europe, northern Italy and central Italy in addition to realms already conquered by Frankish rule. Charlemagne's system of government divides the vast realm into different regions, ruled by local "counts" who are overseen by representatives of Charlemagne's own court. In addition, to aid expansion and administration of the kingdom, Charlemagne promotes, what is called later, the "Carolingian Renaissance." Prior to this revival of learning, practically the entire realm (with the exception of Benedictine England) is illiterate due to the decay of the Roman Empire. The director of the "renaissance" is Anglo-Saxon Benedictine Alcuin, who receives his learning from a student of Bede. Alcuin sets up schools, sees to the copying of classical Latin texts and develops a new handwriting.

793: Vikings raid Lindisfarne (beginning of Viking attacks in Europe)

800: Charlemagne crowned Holy Roman Emperor by Pope Leo III (first person to have this title): Charlemagne establishes schools in all bishoprics and monasteries under his control.

800: Gunpowder invented in China

800: Inca city of Machu Picchu in Peru founded? (rediscovered, 1911

800: 800-1200, the Medieval Warm Period

814: Charlemagne dies without leaving competent successors to continue the glory of the Carolingian dynasty. His sole surviving son, Louis the Pious, divides his inheritance between his own three sons, who engage in civil war. Charlemagne's united realm is invaded by Scandinavian Vikings, Hungarians and Muslims during these civil wars. The Carolingian Empire falls apart.

820: birth of famous Viking Ragnar Lodbrok

843: Treaty of Verdun creates France and Germany

850: The Arabian goatherder Kaldi credited with the discovery of coffee

871: Alfred the Great assumes the throne: King Alfred the Great of England constructs a system of government and education which allows for the unification of smaller Anglo-Saxon states in the ninth and tenth centuries. Alfred is responsible for the codification of English law, public interest in local government and the reorganization of the army. He founds schools and promotes Anglo-Saxon literacy and the establishment of a national culture. Alfred dies in 899. His innovations are continued by his successors.

874: Iceland settled by Norsemen

911: Rollo (the Viking) settles in Normandy

927: King Aethelstan the Glorious unites the Anglo-Saxon territories of Wessex, Sussex, Essex, Kent, East Anglia, Mercia, and North Umbria: the Kingdom of England is founded

936: Otto the Great is crowned king of Germany: makes several decisions which unify and strengthen Germany (named emperor in Rome in 962): establishes a pattern of resistance to political fragmentation and a close alliance with the Church.

955: Catholic Church declines in moral value under John XII

969: Cairo is founded (becomes capital of Egypt)

982: Norse Chieftian, Eric the Red discovers Greenland and in c.986 establishes colony of 500 there

1000: Leif Ericson, son of Eric the Red, is the first from the Old World to "discover" America (Nova Scotia)

1054: Eastern Schism: separation of Christendom into two halves, the western Roman Catholic Church and the Eastern Orthodox Church

High Middle Ages (1050-1300)

1050:

- Agricultural Revolution in Europe
- Westminster Abbey is built

1066: Anglo-Saxon rule ends in Britain, and Norman rule begins, when the Duke of Normandy (William the Conqueror) invades England (Battle of Hastings) and becomes king: The Norman Conquest fuses French and English cultures because William is both the King of England and the Duke of Normandy
The Battle of Hastings and the defeat of Harold Godwinson
The Building of Norman castles in England including the Tower of London in 1073

1077: Building of the Tower of London begins

1086 - Compilation of the Doomsday book

1087-1100: The reign of King William Rufus (son of William): William invades Wales and builds castles on the borders

1095: Pope Urban issues the first of 9 Crusades to capture the Holy Lands

1099: First Crusade. Jerusalem is re-taken from the Muslims on the urging of Pope Urban II

1100:
- The reign of King Henry I begins
- Mary the Mother of Jesus is pronounced a Saint

c. 1100-1200 – Cahokia, Illinois, near modern-day St. Louis, Missouri, reaches its peak population.

1135-1154: The reign of King Stephen

1118: The Knights Templar founded to protect Jerusalem and European pilgrims on their journey to the city

1139: The Second Lateran Council declares clerical marriages invalid (Catholic priests can no longer be married)

1147: Second Crusade

1154-1189: The reign of King Henry II (grandson of Henry I)

1156: Kremlin built in Moscow

1163: The building begins on Notre Dame in Paris

1164: Henry II constructs the Constitutions of Clarendon in an attempt to regain power for the civil courts, which have been losing authority to ecclesiastical ones. The archbishop of Canterbury, Thomas Becket, strongly resists the decision of Henry and a quarrel breaks out. Becket is murdered in Canterbury Cathedral. He is quickly made a martyr by the English public and is revered as the greatest saint of English history. The political result is the abandonment of Henry's court program. Aside from this event, Henry II is considered one of England's greatest kings due to his judicial reforms and legal innovations.

1165: The noble code of chivalry is accompanied with the improvement of noble life and the status of noblewomen as a result of the French book "Arthurian Romances".

1184: The first of many Inquisitions begins

1170: Thomas a Becket is murdered in Canterbury Cathedral

1189-1199: The reign of King Richard I (third son of Henry II) 1189: Richard the Lionhearted, son of Henry II, assumes the English crown. He rules for ten years and is only present in the country a total of six months. His rule exemplifes the strength of the governmental foundations set up by Henry II. During Richard's absence, ministers take care of administration and help to raise taxes for the support of the crusades.

1190: Third Crusade. Saladin manages to unite the Muslim world and recapture Jerusalem, sparking the Third Crusade

1193: first merchant guild developed

1198: -1198: Innocent III, the founder of the Papal State, is thirty-seven when he is elected pope. He is trained in canon law and theology. His primary concern of administration is the unification of all Christendom under the papal monarchy, including the right to interfere with the rule of kings. He is the organizer of the Fourth Crusade, ordered to recapture Jerusalem from Islam.

1199-1216: The reign of King John (fifth son of Henry II)

1200:
- Fourth Crusade embarks. Eventually sacks Constantinople
- Intellectual "Renaissance" begins in Europe as men enter schools without the intention to become priests: literacy increased, universities grew, and books were translated into European languages other than Latin.

1206:
- Genghis Khan elected: Mongol Empire established
- St. Francis of Assisi, at the age of twently-five begins his twenty year allegiance to Christ Jesus until his death in 1226. He is the founder of the Franciscan order which seeks to imitate the life of Jesus by embracing poverty. St. Francis wins the support of Pope Innocent III.

1209: St Francis of Assisi founds the Franciscan Order in the Catholic Church

1212: Children's Crusade

1214:
- Barons revolt
- Roger Bacon predicts the technological advancement of automobiles and airplanes and extends Grosseteste's observations in optics

1215: Magna Carta is signed by King John of England

1216-1272: The reign of King Henry III (son of John)

1225: Thomas Aquinas, the most influential Scholastic theologian, is teaching at the University of Paris: His philosophy emphasizes human reasoning, life in the material order and the individual's participation in personal salvation.

1244: Jerusalem is lost by the West and is not recaptured again until 1917.

1258: Provisions of Oxford forced upon Henry III of England, establishing a new form of government limited regal authority

1266: Marco Polo's first visit to Court of Kublia Khan in China

1267: Florentine Giotto, the most important painter of the later Middle Ages, begins the modern tradition in painting. He is a naturalist whose paintings include depictions of Christ's entrance into Jerusalem and the death of St. Francis.

1272-1307: The reign of King Edward I (son of Henry III)

1273: Rudolph I of Germany is elected Holy Roman Emperor

1274: Thomas Aquinas' work, Summa Theologiae is published

1280: eyeglasses are invented

1295: Marco Polo publishes his tales of China

1297: William Wallace emerges as the leader of the Scottish resistance to England

1298: Marco Polo publishes his tales of China

1299: Ottoman Empire founded (Islamic empire lasting 600 years)

Late Middle Ages (1300-1500)/ Renaissance (1300-1600):

1300-1500: "Little Ice Age" cools the North Atlantic

1305: William Wallance executed for treason

1308 - Dante writes his epic poem the Divine Comedy.

1307:
- The reign of King Edward II begins (son of Edward I)
- The Knights Templar are rounded up and murdered by Philip the Fair of France, with the backing of the Pope

1312: Mansa Musa became ruler of Mali and one of the richest men to live

1314: Robert the Bruce restores Scotland as an independent kingdom (national hero)

1315-1317: The Great Famine: Bad weather and crop failure result in famine across northwestern Europe. Unsanitary conditions and malnutrition increase the death rate.

1325: Renaissance begins in Italy.

1327:
  • Aztec Empire arises in Central America
  • The reign of King Edward III (son of Edward II)

1330
  • Oxford theologian John Wyclif is born
  • The use of heavy cannons in warfare begins.

1337: The Hundred Years War begins. England and France struggle for dominance of Western Europe

1341 - The first great humanist, Petrarch, is named the poet laureate of Rome.

1347: The Black Death ravages Europe for the first time (50% of Europe dies)

1377-1399: The reign of King Richard II (grandson of Edward III, son of the Black Prince)

1380: Chaucer begins to write The Canterbury Tales

1381: Peasants Revolt in England

1382: The Bible is translated into English by John Wycliffe.

1386: Donatello is born

1399-1413: The reign of King Henry IV (grandson of Edward III, son of John of Gaunt)

1400: Early Modern Age 1400-1700

1400:

- Czech students of John Wyclif bring Wyclifism to the Bohemian capital of Prague. Preacher John Hus (1373-1415) adopts Wyclif's theories to support his own claims against ecclesiastical extravagance.
- Little Ice Age freezes Europe in the 1400s and kills off Viking settlements in Greenland.

1413-1422: The reign of King Henry V (son of Henry IV)

1415: Battle of Agincourt

1419 - Architect Brunelleschi designs the dome for the Florence Cathedral.

1422-1461: The reign of King Henry VI (son of Henry V)

1428: Aztec empire is founded

1429: Joan of Arc lifts the siege of Orleans for the Dauphin of France, enabling him to eventually be crowned at Reims

1430:
- Prince Henry of Portugal (1394-1460) active in supporting development of navigational skills and reconnaissance of West African coast
- Capture, trial, and execution of Joan of Arc

1434 - The Medici family becomes the head of the city-state of Florence.

1438: Incan empire is founded

1439: Gutenberg invents the printing press

1444:

- first European slave market in Lagos, Portugal
- Botticelli is born.

1448: Portuguese establish first trading post in Africa

1450: slaves brought to Cape Verde islands

1450 - Johannes Gutenberg invents the printing press.

1452: Leonardo da Vinci is born

1453 - The Ottoman Empire captures the city of Constantinople, signaling an end to the Byzantine Empire; The Hundred Years War ends; Calais is the only English possession on Continental Europe

1455: Johann Gutenberg prints the first of his Bibles on his new printing press; The Wars of the Roses begins in England

1469:
- Lorenzo de Medici becomes head of the city-state of Florence. He is one of the great patrons of the arts.
- Ferdinand of Aragon marries Isabella of Castile, and the two Spanish kingdoms end their conflicts but remain separate powers.
- Machiavelli is born

1473: Copernicus born

1475: Michelangelo born

1483: Raphael is born

1485 - Henry VII becomes king of England beginning the reign of the House of Tudor.

1486 - Botticelli completes the painting The Birth of Venus.

1492:
- Reconquista ends: Muslims are expelled and Spain is unified under Ferdinand and Isabella
- Explorer Christopher Columbus discovers the Americas.
- Western Europeans come into direct contact with peoples of the Americas for the first time. Native Americans killed mostly (up to 99%) by epidemics for which they have no immunity. Decreased immunity due to lack of domestication of large mammals, since their ancestors drove them to extinction 13,000 years ago.

1493: pope divides South America between Spain and Portuguese

1495 - Leonardo da Vinci paints the Last Supper.

1497:
- Copernicus makes first recorded European astronomical observations
- John Cabot discovers Newfoundland

1498 - Vasco da Gama arrives in India after sailing around the southern tip of Africa from Portugal.

1500-1700: Scientific Revolution begins with Nicolaus Copernicus and his assertion of the sun-centered cosmos.

1501 - Michelangelo begins his work on the sculpture David.

1502: Spanish begin importing African slaves into New Spain

1503 - Leonardo da Vinci paints the Mona Lisa.

1508 - Michelangelo begins his painting on the ceiling of the Sistine Chapel.

1509 - Henry VIII becomes king of England; Humanist author Erasmus writes Praise of Folly.

1510: first African slaves brought to the new world (Haiti)

1511- Raphael paints his masterpiece The School of Athens.

1512: Michelangelo completes the Sistine Chapel

1513: balboa reaches Pacific Ocean, and Ponce de Leon reaches Florida

1515: coffee from Arabia appears in Europe

1516:
- Sir Thomas More publishes his work Utopia on political philosophy.
- Erasmus publishes Novum Instrumentum, first Greek New Testament

1517:
- Martin Luther posts his 95 theses on the door of the Church of Wittenberg, beginning the Reformation.
- Hernando Cortes reaches Aztec capital Tenochtitlan (Mexico City)

1519: Ferdinand Magellan begins his voyage around the world.

1520: chocolate brought from Mexico to Spain; 1520: Montezuma II dies (last Aztec ruler)

1521:

- Spanish conquistidor Hernando Cortez besieges Tenochtitlan (Mexico City) with the last recorded use of a "trebuchet" siege engine and subjugates Aztec Empire in Central Mexico, which is soon ravaged by European intrusion and disease
- Hernando Cortes conquers Mexico

1522:

- Luther finished writing the New Testament from Latin to German
- Magellan's ship, the Victoria, completes circumnavigation of globe, September 6
- Ulrich Zwingli begins Reformation in Zurich

1525:

- William Tyndale visits Luther in Wittenberg; influenced by Luther's translation, Tyndale's English translation of the New Testament is printed in Worms; over 18,000 copies eventually smuggled into England
- 1525: George Blaurock is rebaptized by Conrad Grebel; marks formal beginning of Anabaptist movement

1527 - Rome is sacked by the troops of Holy Roman Emperor Charles V.

1532: Conquest of Inca empire by Spain

1533:

- Ivan IV ("the Terrible") becomes Russian czar at age 3
- English King Henry VIII excommunicated, July 11

1534 - Henry VIII separates the Church of England from the Catholic Church of Rome so that he can divorce Catherine of Aragon and marry Anne Boleyn.

1536: King Henry VIII allows English Bibles in England.

1536: John Calvin publishes first edition of Institutes of the Christian Religion

1539: Catholic Counter-Reformation begins

1541: Hernando de Soto reaches the Mississippi River

1543: Copernicus's *On the Revolution of Heavenly Bodies*, describing a sun-centered universe, published

1545: The Council of Trent begins to address issues which brought on the Protestant Reformation

1550: The work of Copernicus ushers in the modern scientific revolution(?) in Europe: the systematic, collaborative study of nature.

1553: Mary Tudor begins her reign, attempts to return England to Catholicism ("Bloody Mary")

1558 - Elizabeth I becomes Queen of England; the Spanish Armada is defeated by the English navy.

1558: English Uniformity Act legally requires Anglican Church attendance (under Elizabeth)

1561: Francis Bacon (Father of experimental philosophy)

1564: Galileo is born

1564: William Shakespeare is born

1577: Francis Drake begins circumnavigating globe

1582: Russia, a small Slavic state centered on Moscow, begins its expansion beyond the Ural Mountains, swallowing up dozens of non-Slavic peoples

1586: Colony of Roanoke in Virginia

1588: British Empire rises

1596: René Descartes, a key leader of the Enlightenment, born, March 31

1598: French King Henry IV grants religious freedom to Protestants via Edict of Nantes, April 13

1599 - William Shakespeare builds the Globe theatre.

1610 - Galileo discovers the moons of Jupiter.

1611-Publication of the King James Version of the Bible.

1618:
- The Thirty Years War begins.
- The Synod of Dort: Five-point Calvinism is affirmed to opposition to Arminianism.

1618-48-Protestant/Catholic conflict in Germany (The Thirty Years War).

1685-Revocation of the edict of Nantes by Louis XIV. Exodus of Protestants from France.

Age of Exploration/Age of Discovery (1492-1602):[149]

870   Swedish Viking Garðar Svavarsson circumnavigates Iceland.

870   Náttfari becomes the first permanent resident of Iceland.

874   Ingólfur Arnarson builds his homestead in present-day Reykjavík.

982   Eric the Red discovers Greenland.

1002   Leif Ericson discovers North America.

1271   Marco Polo goes to China.

1418   João Gonçalves Zarco and Tristão Vaz Teixeira discover Porto Santo.

1419   Gonçalves and Vaz discover Madeira.

1427   Diogo de Silves discovers the Azores.

1434   Gil Eanes passes Cabo de Não and rounds Cape Bojador.

1443   Nuno Tristão passes Cape Blanco.

1444   Dinis Dias reaches the mouth of the Senegal River.

1446   The Portuguese reach Cape Verde and the Gambia River.

1450   Prince Henry the Navigator builds school for sailors.

---

[149] Source for these dates: https://www.explorationmuseum.com/timeline/

1453 Turkish Empire cuts off the land route for spices from Asia to Europe. Search for sea route begins.

1456 Alvise Cadamosto and Diogo Gomes explored the Cape Verde Islands.

1460 Pêro de Sintra reaches Sierra Leone.

1470 Cape Palmas is passed.

1472 Fernão do Pó discovers Bioko.

1473 Lopo Gonçalves is the first to cross the equator.

1474 Ruy de Sequeira discovers São Tomé and Príncipe.

1482 Diogo Cão reaches the Congo River, where he erects a "padrão" (pillar of stone).

1485 Cão reaches Cape Cross, where he erects his last padrão.

1487 Bartholomeu Dias discovers the southern tip of Africa.

1492 Columbus sails to the New World.

1497 John Cabot discovers Newfoundland while he searches for the Northwest Passage.

1497 Vasco da Gama sails to India and back.

1502 Amerigo Vespucci returns from his explorations of the New World. American continents named after him by German mapmaker.

1513 Vasco Nunez de Balboa discovers the eastern shore of the Pacific Ocean.

1519 Ferdinand Magellan and his crew sail around the world from 1519-1522.

America: The Europeans Arrive in North America (1585)[150]

1585 - The Roanoke Colony is founded. It will disappear and become known as the "Lost Colony."

1605: Cervantes writes Don Quixote de la Mancha, the first modern novel.

1607 - The Jamestown Settlement is established.

1608: Lippershey invents telescope; Galileo Galilei makes astronomical observations.

1609 - Only 60 out of 500 settlers in Jamestown survive the winter of 1609-1610. It is called the "Starving Time."

1609 - Henry Hudson explores the northeast coast and the Hudson River.

1611: Authorized King James Version of the Bible produced under reign of King James of England

1614:
- Jamestown settler John Rolfe marries Pocahontas, the daughter of the Powhatan Indian chief.
- The Dutch colony of New Netherland is established.

1619 - The first African slaves arrive in Jamestown. The first representative government, the Virginia House of Burgesses, meets at Jamestown.

1620: Pilgrims land at Plymouth (MA) (Gov. William Bradford writes, "Of Plymouth Plantation.")

1625: Puritans actively persecuted in England under Archibald Laud

1626:
- Salem, MA founded
- New York colony founded
- The Dutch purchase Manhattan Island from the local Native Americans.

1629 -A royal charter is issued for the Massachusetts Bay Colony.

---

[150] Source: https://www.ducksters.com/history/colonial_america/timeline.php

1630:

- Puritans found the city of Boston.
- Massachusetts Bay Colony founded (700 Puritans) (John Winthrop writes, "A Model of Christian Charity")

1632:

- Lord Calvert, the first Baron of Baltimore, is granted a charter for the Colony of Maryland.
- Williamsburg, VA
- John Locke born (father of liberalism)

1633: Maryland colony founded

1636:

- Roger Williams begins the colony of Providence Plantation after being expelled from Massachusetts.
- Thomas Hooker moves to Connecticut and establishes what will become the Connecticut Colony.
- Harvard founded; 1636: Rhode Island colony founded

1637 - The Pequot War occurs in New England. The Pequot peoples are nearly wiped out.

1638 - New Sweden is founded along the Delaware River.

1639 - The Fundamental Orders of Connecticut describe the government of Connecticut. It is considered the first written Constitution of the Americas.

1643: Roger Williams argues for the importance of and purpose for learning the language of Native Americans in "A Key to the Language of America," a book in which he lays out everything he has learned about speaking Native American languages.

1644: Roger Williams writes "The Bloody Tenet of Persecution," he argues for the principle of separation of church and state and against government persecution of anyone for their religious belief or unbelief.

1654: North Carolina colony founded

1655 - The Dutch take control of New Sweden.

1656 - The Quakers arrive in New England.

1663 - The Province of Carolina is created; -1663: South Carolina colony founded

1664 - England captures the New Netherlands and names it the Province of New York. The city of New Amsterdam is renamed New York.

1670 - The city of Charlestown, South Carolina is founded.

1672: Louis Joliet and Jacque Marquette explore Illinois territory

1675 - King Philip's War begins between the colonists in New England and a group of Native American tribes including the Wampanoag people.

1676 - Bacon's Rebellion occurs. Settlers led by Nathanial Bacon rebel against Virginia Governor William Berkeley.

1681 - William Penn is granted the charter for the Province of Pennsylvania.

1682:
- The city of Philadelphia is founded.
- Pennsylvania colony founded

1690:
- Spain begins to colonize the land of Texas.
- First newspaper in the United States is published in Boston

1692 - The Salem witch trials begin in Massachusetts. Twenty people are executed for witchcraft.

1699 - The capital of Virginia moves from Jamestown to Williamsburg.

Late Modern Period 1700-1900
(Begins with Industrial Revolution in 1750 in England and the American Revolution in 1770s; ends with Industrial Revolution in US)

1700: Scientific Revolution ended with Isaac Newton, who proposed universal laws and a mechanical universe.

1701 - Delaware separates from Pennsylvania becoming a new colony.

1702:
- The Colony of New Jersey is formed by the merging of East and West Jersey.
- Queen Anne's War begins.

1706: Benjamin Franklin born

1709: first piano invented by Bartolomeo Cristifori

1711: David Hume (Scottish philosopher who wrote A Treatise of Human Nature)

1712:
- The Province of Carolina separates into North Carolina and South Carolina.
- Jean-Jacques Rousseau born

1718 - The city of New Orleans is founded by the French.

1724: Immanuel Kant born

1730-1760: First Great Awakening

1732 - The Province of Georgia is formed by James Oglethorpe.

1733 - The first settlers arrive in Georgia.

1741: Sinners in the Hands of an Angry God (Jonathan Edwards: First Great Awakening 1730s-1740s)

1742: Benjamin Franklin develops the Franklin stove

American Colonial Period: After Colonies are established and leading to the American Revolution (1730-1775)

1746 - The College of New Jersey is founded. It will later become Princeton University.

1748: Baron de Montesquieu's "Spirit of the Laws" (foundational document on modern political theory)

1752: Ben Franklin invents the lightning Rod

1752 - The Liberty Bell is cracked when it is first rung in testing. It was fixed by 1753.

1753: Phyllis Wheatley born (first black poet)

1754 - The French and Indian War begins between the British colonists and the French: most Algonquian tribes allied with the French; the Iroquois with the British.

1763 - The British win the French and Indian War and gain a significant amount of territory in North America including Florida.

1765 - The British government passes the Stamp Act taxing the colonies. The Quartering Act is also passed allowing British troops to be housed in private homes.

1765: James Watt invents the improved steam engine

1770 - The Boston Massacre occurs.

1773 - Bostonian colonists protest the Tea Act with the Boston Tea Party 1773: Boston Tea Party: protests "taxation without representation"1775: Lexington and Concord; Battle of Bunker Hill (first battles in Revolutionary War)

1774 - The First Continental Congress meets in Philadelphia, Pennsylvania.

1775 - The Revolutionary War begins.

1775:
- March 23 - Patrick Henry's "Liberty or Death" speech, Richmond, VA
- April 18 - Revere and Dawes Ride
- April 19 - Battles of Lexington and Concord, MA
- May 10 - Ethan Allen and Green Mountain Boys seize Fort Ticonderoga, Second Continental Congress meets
- June 15 - George Washington appointed commander-in-chief
- June 17 - Battle of Bunker Hill
- July 3 - George Washington assumes command of the Army outside Boston
- July 5 - Congress approves the Olive Branch Petition, a final attempt to avoid war with Britain
- October 13 - The U.S. Navy is established
- November 19-21 - First Siege of Ninety Six, SC
- November 13 - Americans take Montreal

- December 9 - Battle of Great Bridge, VA
- December 22 - Battle of Great Canebreak, SC
- December 23-30 - Snow Campaign, SC
- December 30-Jan 1 - Battle of Quebec

1776:

- January 10 - Thomas Paine publishes Common Sense
- February 27 - Battle of Moore's Creek, NC
- March 3 - Continental Navy captures New Providence Island, Bahamas
- March 17 - British evacuate Boston
- April 12 - Halifax Resolves, NC—First colony to authorize its delegates to vote for independence
- June 7 - Lee Resolution: Richard Henry Lee proposes independence to the Second Continental Congress
- June 28 - Battle of Sullivan's Island, SC
- July 1 - Cherokee attack the southern frontier
- July 4 - Congress adopts the Declaration of Independence
- August 27 - Battle of Brooklyn, NY
- September 15 - British occupy Manhattan
- September 16 - Battle of Harlem Heights, NY
- September 22 - British execute Nathan Hale, a soldier in the Continental Army
- October 11 - Battle of Valcour Island, Lake Champlain
- October 28 - Battle of White Plains, NY
- November 16 - Battle of Fort Washington, NY
- November 20 - British capture Fort Lee, NJ
- December 23 - Thomas Paine publishes The American Crisis
- December 26 - Battle of Trenton, NJ

1777:

- January 3 - Battle of Princeton, NJ
- January 6 - May 28 - Continental Army winters at Morristown, NJ
- April 27 - Battle at Ridgefield, CT
- June 14 - Flag Resolution- Congress declared "That the flag of the thirteen United States be thirteen stripes, alternate red and white; that the union be thirteen stars, white in a blue field"
- July 5 - British capture Fort Ticonderoga
- August 6 - Battle of Oriskany, NY
- August 16 - Battle of Bennington, VT (Walloomsac, NY)
- September 11 - Battle of Brandywine, PA
- September 19 - Battle of Saratoga, NY (Freeman's Farm)

- September 20-21 - Battle of Paoli, PA
- September 26 - British take Philadelphia
- October 4 - Battle of Germantown, PA
- October 7 - Battle of Saratoga, NY (Bemis Heights)
- October 17 - British surrender at Saratoga, NY
- October 22 - Battle of Fort Mercer, NJ
- November 16 - British capture Fort Mifflin, PA
- December 5–7 - Battle of White Marsh, PA
- December 19 - Washington and his army winter in Valley Forge

1778:
- February 6 - The United States and France become allies
- February 7 - British General William Howe replaced by Henry Clinton
- May 20 - Battle of Barren Hill, PA
- June 18 - British abandon Philadelphia, Continental Army marches out of Valley Forge
- June 28 - Battle of Monmouth, NJ
- July 4 - George Rogers Clark captures Kaskaskia, in modern Illinois
- July 29–August 31 - French and American forces besiege Newport, RI
- December 29 - British capture Savannah, GA

1779:
- February 3 - Battle of Port Royal Island, SC
- February 14 - Battle of Kettle Creek, GA
- February 23–24 - George Rogers Clark captures Vincennes, in modern Indiana
- March 3 - Battle of Brier Creek, GA
- June 18 - Sullivan expedition attacks Indian villages in NY
- June 20 - Battle of Stono River, SC
- June 21 - Spain declares war on Great Britain
- July 7 - British burn Fairfield, CT
- July 11 - British burn Norwalk, CT
- July 16 - Americans capture Stony Point, NY
- July 24 - August 14 - Penobscot Expedition (Castine, ME)
- July 28 - Battle of Fort Freeland, PA
- August 19 - Battle of Paulus Hook, NJ
- August 29 - Battle of Newtown, NY
- September 16 - October 19 - American/French effort to retake Savannah fails
- September 23 - John Paul Jones and the USS Bonhomme Richard capture HMS Serapis near English coast
- November - Washington's Main Army begins camping at Morristown, NJ

1780:

- January 28 - Fort Nashborough established (now Nashville, TN)
- March 14 - Spanish capture Mobile
- May 12 - British capture Charleston, SC
- May 25 - Mutiny of Connecticut regiments at Morristown, NJ
- May 26 - Battle at St. Louis, now in Missouri
- May 29 - Battle of Waxhaws, SC
- June 20 - Battle of Ramseur's Mill, NC
- June 23 - Washington's Main Army leaves their winter camps at Morristown, NJ
- July 11 - French troops arrive at Newport, RI
- August 6 - Battle of Hanging Rock, SC
- August 16 - Battle of Camden, SC
- August 19 - Battle of Musgrove Mill, SC
- September 23 - British officer John Andre arrested for spying
- October 7 - Battle of Kings Mountain, SC
- October 14 - Gen. Nathanael Greene named commander of the southern Continental Army
- October 18 - British occupy Wilmington, NC

1781:

- January 17 - Battle of Cowpens, SC
- February 1 - Battle of Cowan's Ford, NC
- February 12 - Spanish forces take Fort St. Joseph, now Miles, MI
- March 2 - Articles of Confederation adopted; Battle of Clapp's Mill, NC
- March 6 - Battle of Weitzel's Mill, NC
- March 15 - Battle of Guilford Courthouse, NC
- April 25 - Battle of Hobkirk's Hill, SC
- May 9 - Spanish capture Pensacola
- May 15 - Battle of Fort Granby, SC
- May 22–June 18 - Siege of Ninety Six, SC
- June 6 - Americans retake Augusta, GA
- July 6 - Battle at Green Spring, VA
- August 28 - Battle of Elizabethtown, NC
- September 5 - Battle of the Capes, Chesapeake Bay
- September 8 - Battle of Eutaw Springs, SC
- September 28 - October 19 - Siege of Yorktown, VA
- October 19 - General Cornwallis officially surrenders at Yorktown, VA

1782

- 1782: French-American farmer, J. Hector St. John de Crevecouer writes "Letters from an American Farmer" which describe the culture of the US during this era.
- March 8—9 - Indians attacked by militia at Gnadenhutten, in modern OH
- March 20 - Lord North resigns as Prime Minister of Great Britain
- April 19 - Netherlands recognizes American independence
- May 8 - American and Spanish forces capture Nassau, Bahamas
- July 11 - British evacuate Savannah, GA
- July 13 - British/Indian raid on Hannahstown, PA
- August 7 - Washington establishes the Badge of Military Merit, now known as the Purple Heart
- August 19 - Battle of Blue Licks, KY
- November 4 - Encounter at John's Ferry, SC
- November 10 - George Rogers Clark raids Chillicothe, modern OH
- November 30 - British and Americans sign preliminary Articles of Peace
- December 14 - British evacuate Charleston, SC

1783

- 1783: Claude de Jouffroy builds the first steamboat/ Joseph-Ralf and Jacques-Etienne Montgolfier invent the first manned hot air balloon
- 1783: Treaty of Paris recognizes American independence
- March 15 - Washington addresses the Newburgh Conspiracy and discontent in the Continental Army, Newburgh, NY
- April 19 - April: John Adams, Benjamin Franklin, John Jay, and Henry Laurens travel to Paris to negotiate a preliminary peace treaty with the British, which Congress then ratifies.
- September 3 - US and Great Britain sign the Treaty of Paris: Spain recognizes American Independence, followed quickly by Sweden and Denmark. Russia will also recognize America's independence before the year is out.
- November 23: George Washington officially issues a "Farewell Address to the Army" in November and formally discharges the Army. He later resigns as Commander in Chief.
- November 25 - British evacuate New York City
- December 4 - Washington bids farewell to his officers in New York City
- December 23 - Washington resigns as commander in Annapolis, MD

1784

- 1784: Immanuel Kant writes "An Answer to the Question: What is the Enlightenment?

- October 22: In the Treaty of Fort Stanwix, the Six Nations of the Iroquois give up all claims to territory west of the Niagara River. The Creeks also sign a treaty giving up their land and expanding Georgia's territory.

1785:

- January 21: In the Treaty of Fort McIntosh, the Chippewa, Delaware, Ottawa, and Wyandot Indigenous nations sign a treaty where they give America all their land in present-day Ohio.
- June: James Madison (1751–1836) publishes Memorial and Remonstrance Against Religious Assessments advocating the separation of church and state.

- July 13: The Land Ordinance of 1785 is passed providing for the division of the northwestern territories into townships with lots to be sold for $640 each.

1786: January 16: Virginia adopts Thomas Jefferson's Ordinance of Religious Freedom, which guarantees freedom of religion.

1787:

- The Federalist Papers (written by Alexander Hamilton, John Jay, and James Madison)
- French Revolution begins

1788:

- U. S. Constitution ratified1789: Bill of Rights adopted
- May 25–September 17: The Constitutional Convention meets and results in the creation of the U.S. Constitution. It needs to be ratified by nine states before it goes into effect.

- July 13: The Northwest Ordinance of 1787 was enacted by Congress, including policies for creating new states, accelerated westward expansion, and fundamental rights of citizens. Arthur St. Clair (1737–1818) is made the first governor of the Northwest Territory.

- October 27: The first of 77 essays called collectively The Federalist Papers is published in New York's The Independent Journal. These articles are written to persuade individuals in the state to ratify the new Constitution.

1789:

- April 30: George Washington is inaugurated in New York as the first President. He is sworn in by Robert Livingston and then delivers his inaugural address to Congress. A week later, the first inaugural ball is held.

- July 14: The French Revolution begins when revolutionaries stormed the Bastille Prison, events witnessed by the American minister Thomas Jefferson.

- July 27: The Department of State (called the Department of Foreign Affairs at first) is established with Thomas Jefferson as his head.

- August 7: The War Department is also established with Henry Knox as its head.

- September 2: The new Treasury Department is headed by Alexander Hamilton. Samuel Osgood is named the first Postmaster General under the new constitution.

- September 24: The Federal Judiciary Act creates a six-man Supreme Court. John Jay is named the Chief Justice.

- September 29: Congress establishes the U.S. Army before adjourning.

- November 26: The first national Thanksgiving Day is proclaimed by George Washington at the request of Congress.

1790:

- Thomas Saint creates the first sewing machine
- Second Great Awakening (began in New England. This movement is typically regarded as less emotionally charged than the First Great Awakening. It led to the founding of several colleges, seminaries and mission societies.)
- February 12–15: Benjamin Franklin sends an anti-slavery petition to Congress on behalf of the Quakers asking for the abolition of slavery.

- March 26: The Naturalization Act passes and requires a two-year residency for new citizens and their children but limiting it to free White people.

- August 4: The Coast Guard is created

1791

- January 27: The Whiskey Act is signed putting a tax on whiskey. This is opposed by farmers and many states pass laws protesting the tax, eventually leading to the Whiskey Rebellion.

- February 25: The First Bank of the United States is officially chartered after President Washington signs it into law.

- March: President Washington chooses the site for the District of Columbia on the Potomac River. Benjamin Banneker (1731–1806), a Black mathematician and scientist, is named one of three individuals appointed to survey the site for the federal capital.

- Fall: Violence repeatedly breaks in the Northwest Territory with repeated conflicts between Indigenous peoples and the U.S. Army on settlements along the Ohio frontier, culminating in the Battle of the Wabash in November.

- December 15: The first 10 amendments are added to the U.S. Constitution as the Bill of Rights.

1792:

- April 2: The national mint is established in Philadelphia.
- December 5: George Washington is reelected as president in the second presidential election.

1793:

- Over the year, France's revolutionary movement loses a lot of American support upon the execution of Louis XVI (January 21) and Marie Antoinette (October 16) along with the declaration of war against Great Britain, Spain, and the Netherlands.

- February 12: A Fugitive Slave Act is passed, allowing enslavers to recapture self-liberated enslaved people.

1794:

- March 22: The Slave Trade Act is passed, banning the trade of enslaved people with foreign nations.

- August 20: The Battle of Fallen Timbers occurs in northwest Ohio where General Anthony Wayne (1745–1796) defeated Indigenous peoples in the region.

1795: August 3: The Treaty of Greenville is signed with the 12 Ohio Indigenous tribes who had been defeated at the Battle of Fallen Timbers. They give large amounts of land to America.

1797: French-American unofficial naval war caused by the "XYZ Affair"
August 19: The U.S.S. Constitution (Old Ironsides) is launched.

1798:
- Edward Jenner develops the smallpox vaccine
- Summer: The Alien and Sedition Acts are passed to silence political opposition and signed into law by President Adams. In response, the Kentucky and Virginia Resolutions are passed at Thomas Jefferson's and James Madison's behest.
- July 13: George Washington is named Commander-in-Chief of the U.S. Army.

1799:

- November 11: Napoleon Bonaparte (1769–1821) becomes the first consul of France.
- December 14: George Washington dies suddenly of a throat infection. He is mourned in the United States, given honors in England, and a week of mourning begins in France.

1800:

- Industrial Revolution begins in Britain
- April 24: The Library of Congress is created, with a beginning budget of $5,000 for books for the use of Congress.
- Fall: Johnny Appleseed (John Chapman, 1774–1845) begins distributing apple trees and seeds to new settlers in Ohio.

1803
- Jefferson buys Louisiana from France, doubling the size of the country.
- Ralph Waldo Emerson born

1804:

- U.S. explorers Lewis and Clark head west on their two-year, 8,000-mile expedition to explore the new Louisiana Purchase territory.
- Richard Trevithick invents the steam locomotive.[343]
- U.S. founding fathers Aaron Burr and Alexander Hamilton fight a duel; Hamilton is killed and Burr is ruined.

1807: François Isaac de Rivaz designs the first automobile powered by an internal combustion engine fuelled by hydrogen.

1809: Writer Washington Irving (1783–1859) publishes "A History of New York by Diedrich Knickerbocker," defining American literature.

1811:

- The first contracts for The National Road are signed and the first 10 miles are constructed westward from Cumberland, Maryland, which will make westward migration possible.
- Friedrich Koenig invents the first powered printing press, which was also the first to use a cylinder.
- At the Battle of Tippecanoe, Indigenous peoples led by Tecumseh fight and lose a major battle opposing White settlement.

1812: Congress declares war on Britain (War of 1812)

1814:

- August 24, 1814: The British burn the White House and the Capitol, but first lady Dolley Madison saves the Gilbert Stuart portrait of George Washington.
- George Stephenson designs the first steam locomotive.
- December 23, 1814–January 8, 1815: Andrew Jackson becomes an American hero at the Battle of New Orleans.

1815: Napoleon Bonaparte surrenders after a devastating loss at the Battle of Waterloo, ending the Napoleonic Wars in Europe.

1820: The Missouri Compromise, precariously balancing the practice of enslavement, holds the Union together, at least temporarily.

1824: The U.S. election that made John Quincy Adams president is bitterly contested and must be resolved by the House of Representatives.

1825: The Erie Canal opens, making New York the Empire State.

1826: *The Last of the Mohicans* written by James Fenimore Cooper

1828: The election of Andrew Jackson is no less bitter than the previous one, and Jackson's inaugural party nearly wrecks the White House.

1830:
- Indian Removal Act: leads to forced removal of several tribes from their homes in the southern states and territories to Oklahoma ("Trail of Tears")
- Edwin Budding invents the lawn mower.
- Emily Dickinson born

1835: Pioneer scientist Charles Darwin visits the Galapagos Islands.

1836: A tragic siege at the Alamo becomes a legendary battle in the Texas War for Independence.

1837: Samuel Morse invents Morse code.

1839: baseball invented

1840: The song "Tippecanoe and Tyler Too" helps usher in a presidential election win for William Henry Harrison, who dies of pneumonia a month later.

1841:
- Spring: A free Black New Yorker, Solomon Northup, was lured to Washington, D.C., drugged, kidnapped, and enslaved. He would tell his story in the powerful memoir "Twelve Years a Slave."
- November 9: Edward VII of England, son of Queen Victoria and Prince Albert, was born.

1843: Mass migration to Oregon ("Oregon Fever")

1845:
- January 23: The U.S. Congress established a uniform date for federal elections, naming the first Tuesday after the first Monday in November as Election Day.
- Edgar Allen Poe writes *The Raven*
- Frederick Douglass writes his autobiography, *Narrative of the Life of Frederick Douglass, An American Slave*

- Ireland is ravaged by the Great Famine, spurring one of the great migrations of people to the U.S.-1848: First Women's Rights convention in Seneca Falls, NY-1849: California Gold Rush-

1846: May 13: The U.S. Congress declared war against Mexico.

1848:

- January 24: James Marshall, a mechanic at John Sutter's sawmill in northern California, recognized some unusual nuggets. His discovery would set off the California Gold Rush.
- July 12-19: A conference at Seneca Falls, New York, organized by Lucretia Mott and Elizbeth Cady Stanton, took up the issue of Women's Rights and planted the seeds of the suffrage movement in the U.S.

1850:

- Fugitive Slave Act: Declares that runaway slaves must be returned to masters, even from Northern States
- The ominous Compromise of 1850 over enslavement delays the Civil War.

1851: Herman Melville writes *Moby Dick*

1852: Harriet Beecher Stowe writes *Uncle Toms Cabin*

1854:

- Henry D. Thoreau writes *Walden, or Life in the Woods*
- The Kansas-Nebraska Act breaks the previous compromises over enslavement.

1857: Dred Scott Case—Supreme Court ruled that no slave or descendent of slave could be a U.S. citizen

1858: Stephen Douglas debates (with Abe Lincoln)

1859: Abolitionist John Brown (1800–1859) leads a raid on Harper's Ferry, Virginia, hoping to initiate a revolt of enslaved people that would put America back on the path to war.

1860:

- Pony Express begins
- South Carolina secedes
- Henry Wadsworth Longfellow writes "Paul Revere's Ride"

1861:
- Abraham Lincoln becomes President
- Confederate States of America (the Confederacy) established under President Jefferson Davis
- American Civil War begins at Fort Sumter
- Kansas admitted to the Union as a free state
- First Battle of Bull Run

1862
- Homestead Act
- Pacific Railway Act
- Battle of Antietam
- Lincoln issues Emancipation Proclamation

1863
- National Banking Act of 1863
- Battle of Gettysburg
- Pro-Union counties become sovereign state of West Virginia
- New York City draft riots

1864
- National Banking Act of 1864
- Sand Creek Massacre
- Nevada becomes a state
- Louis Pasteur invents the pasteurization process

1865
- Abraham Lincoln assassinated
- Andrew Johnson becomes President
- United States Civil War ends
- 13th Amendment
- Freedman's Bureau
- Cornell University founded under the 1862 Morrill Act

1866
- Civil Rights Act of 1866
- Ku Klux Klan founded

1867
- Reconstruction Acts
- Alaska Purchase from Russia

- Nebraska becomes a state
- Louisa May Alcott writes *Little Women*
- Alfred Nobel invents dynamite, the first safely manageable explosive stronger than black powder.
- Lucien B. Smith invents barbed wire, which Joseph F. Glidden will modify in 1874, leading to the taming of the West and the end of the cowboys.

1868

- 14th Amendment
- University of California chartered
- Scottish naturalist John Muir (1838–1914) arrives in Yosemite Valley, California, where he would find his spiritual home.
- Carnegie Steel Company founded
- Typewriter invented
- Treaty of Fort Laramie with Lakota nation

1869

- Ulysses S. Grant becomes President
- Wyoming becomes first state to grant woman suffrage
- Golden spike nailed in, completing the First Transcontinental Railroad

1870

- 15th Amendment
- First graduate programs (at Yale and Harvard)

1871

- Great Chicago Fire
- Treaty of Washington with the British Empire regarding the Dominion of Canada
- National Rifle Association developed by Civil War veterans to promote marksmanship

1872: President Ulysses S. Grant establishes Yellowstone Park as the first National Park.

1873

- Panic of 1873
- William "Boss" Tweed (1823–1878) goes to jail, ending his corrupt New York political machine "Tammany Hall.

1875 - Civil Rights Act of 1875

1876

- National League of baseball founded
- Centennial Exposition in Philadelphia
- Colorado becomes a state
- Lt. Colonel George A. Custer meets his end in an ill-considered fight with assembled Indigenous troops at the Battle of the Little Bighorn.
- Alexander Graham Bell invents the telephone
- Mark Twain writes *The Adventures of Tom Sawyer* (*The Adventures of Huckleberry Finn,* 1885)

1877

- Federal troops removed from southern states (end of Reconstruction, less protection for rights of African Americans in southern states)
- Thomas Edison invents the first working phonograph.

1879: Joseph Swan and Thomas Edison both patent a functional incandescent light bulb.

1886: The Statue of Liberty is dedicated in New York Harbor.

1890: Massacre at Wounded Knee

1891:

- Whitcomb Judson invents the zipper.
- basketball invented

1895:

- Booker T. Washington gives Atlanta Compromise speech
- volleyball invented
- Wilhelm Conrad Röntgen invented the first radiograph (xrays).

1896: Plessy v. Ferguson Supreme Court case upholds principle of separate but equal (allowing racial segregation)

1898: Spanish-American War (USS Maine sunk, Dewey captures Philippines)

1900: US helps put down the Boxer Rebellion in China

1901

- Booker T. Washington wrote "Up From Slavery"

- McKinley dies from complications of being shot during his second inauguration, and succeeded by Theodore Roosevelt
- The first motorized cleaner using suction, a powered "vacuum cleaner", is patented independently by Hubert Cecil Booth and David T. Kenney.

1903
- WEB DuBois writes "The Souls of Black Folk"
- The Wright Brothers' fly their first aircraft in Kitty Hawk, NC
- Ford Motor Company formed
- First World Series

1905: Teddy Roosevelt second inauguration

1906: Upton Sinclair's *The Jungle* published; Pure Food and Drug Act (created the FDA); Pure Food and Drug Act and Meat Inspection Act

1908:
- Ford Model T on the market
- Bureau of Investigation created (forerunner of the FBI)

1909:
Robert Peary plants American flag at North pole
Taft inauguration
NAACP founded by WEB DuBois

1911: Supreme Court breaks up Standard Oil

1912: Titanic sinks

1913: Wilson inauguration

1914:
- Archduke Franz Ferdinand (prince to Austria-Hungary throne) is assassinated in Sarajevo, launching WWI.
- Panama Canal open

1915: First long distance phone service

1916: Robert Frost writes *The Road Less Taken*

1917

- Russian Revolution begins, led by Vladmir Lenin: Tsar Nicholas II removed
- January 19 - The British intercept the Zimmerman Telegram in which Germany tries to convince Mexico to join the war. This will result in the United States declaring war on Germany.
- November 11 - Germany agrees to an armistice and the fighting comes to an end at 11am on the 11th day of the 11th month

1918: world-wide flu epidemic kills millions (500,000 Americans die)

1919: The Treaty of Versailles is signed by Germany and World War I comes to an end.

1920: 19th Amendment

1921: Harding Inaugurated, dies from a stroke in 1923.

1923:
- Coolidge inauguration
- Yankee Stadium opens
- Teapot Dome Scandal

1924 - Indian Reorganization Act

1925
- Scopes trial (over evolution in schools)
- F. Scott's Fitzgerald writes *The Great Gatsby*

1927
- Charles Lindbergh flies solo across the Atlantic
- The Jazz Singer, the first motion picture with sound, is released

1928
- Disney's Steamboat Willie is released
- Penicillin is first observed to exude antibiotic substances by Nobel laureate Alexander Fleming.
- Philo Farnsworth demonstrates the first practical electronic television to the press.

1929: Stock Market crashes, beginning the Great Depression

1931
Empire State Building opens
Star-Spangled Banner becomes National Anthem

1932: Bonus Army marches on DC, Amelia Earhart flies across the Atlantic Ocean
1933:

- FDR becomes president and passes:
- 20th Amendment
- Agricultural Adjustment Act
- Civil Works Administration
- Civilian Conservation Corps
- Farm Credit Administration
- Home Owners Loan Corporation
- Tennessee Valley Authority
- Public Works Administration
- National (Industrial) Recovery Act

1934: Federal Housing Administration (FHA) by FDR

1935: Social Security Act, Works Progress Administration, Fair Labor Standard Act (minimum wage)

1935:

- Alcoholics Anonymous founded
- US athlete Jesse Owens set five world records and equaled a 6th in 45 minutes

1936: Spanish Civil War begins

1938:

- Orson Welles' *The War of the Worlds* broadcast
- Nuclear fission discovered in experiment by chemists Otto Hahn and Fritz Strassmann and physicists Lise Meitner and Otto Robert Frisch.

1939

- Hitler invades Czechoslovakia and Poland (starts WW II)
- Germany invades Poland, beginning WWII
- John Steinbeck writes *The Grapes of Wrath*
- US declares its neutrality in European conflict (Sept. 5, 1939).

1941:
- Roosevelt's third inauguration (Jan. 20, 1941). He is the first and only president elected to a third term.
- Japan attacks Hawaii, Guam, and the Philippines (Dec. 7, 1941).
- U.S. declares war on Japan (Dec. 8).
- Germany and Italy declare war on the United States
- U.S. reciprocates by declaring war on both countries (Dec. 11).

1942
- US enters WWII
- Allies invade North Africa (Oct.–Dec. 1942)

1943: Allies invade Italy (Sept.–Dec. 1943).

1944: Allies invade France on D-Day (June 6, 1944)

1945
- President Roosevelt, Churchill, and Stalin meet at Yalta in the USSR to discuss postwar occupation of Germany (Feb. 4–11).
- President Roosevelt dies of a
- stroke (April 12) and is succeeded by his vice president, Harry Truman. Germany surrenders unconditionally (May 7).
- First atomic bomb is detonated at Alamogordo, N.M. (July 16).
- President Truman, Churchill, and Stalin meet at Potsdam, near Berlin, Germany, to demand Japan's unconditional surrender and to discuss plans for postwar Europe (July 17–Aug. 2).
- U.S. drops atomic bomb on Hiroshima, Japan (Aug. 6).
- U.S. drops atomic bomb on Nagasaki, Japan (Aug. 9).
- Japan agrees to unconditional surrender (Aug. 14). Japanese envoys sign surrender terms aboard the USS Missouri in Tokyo harbor (Sept. 2).

1947: CIA established

1948: Russians begin the blockade of Berlin (begins the Cold War with the US)

1949
- Truman's second inauguration
- NATO established

Post-Modern Age 1950s-present
1950-1953: Korean War

1950-1975: Vietnam War

1951
- 27nd Amendment passed (2-term presidency)
- First use of nuclear power to produce electricity for households in Arco, Idaho
- First coast-to-coast, live, television broadcast by Truman

1952: Puerto Rico becomes a US commonwealth

1953: Eisenhower inauguration

1954
- Senator McCarthy accuses public officials of being Communists during public hearings
- Brown VS Board of Education (Topeka, Kansas) declares that segregation in schools is unconstitutional

1956: The hard disk drive is invented by IBM

1957
- The first personal computer used by one person and controlled by a keyboard, the IBM 610, is invented in 1957 by IBM.
- President sends federal troops to Central High School in Little Rock, Ark., to enforce integration of black students (Sept. 24).

1958: First American satellite (Explorer 1) is launched

1959: Alaska is 49th state, Hawaii is 50th

1960: The first functioning laser is invented by Theodore Maiman.

1961:
- JFK inauguration
- Bay of Pigs Cuba invasion fails
- Freedom Fighters (mixed-race group of volunteers sponsored by the Committee on Racial Equality) travels through the south to protest segregated bus facilities

1962: Lt Col. John Glenn becomes first U.S. astronaut to orbit Earth

1963
MLK "I have a Dream" speech (assassinated in 1968)
JFK assassinated, succeeded by LB Johnson

1964: Johnson signs the Civil Rights Act

1969:
- Richard Nixon inauguration
- Aldrin and Armstrong first men to walk on the moon

1970: The pocket calculator is invented.

1972:
- Nixon visits Communist China, US signs arms agreement with Russia, and members of Nixons re-election campaign are caught in the DMC headquarters in Watergate
- The first video game console, used primarily for playing video games on a TV, is the Magnavox Odyssey

1973
- Roe V Wade legalized abortion in the first trimester
- Senate begins to investigate Nixon
- Ford sworn in as Vice President
- End of US involvement in Vietnam War (officially ends 1975)

1974: Nixon resigns, pardoned by Ford

1975: End of Vietnam War

1977
- Jimmy Carter inauguration
- Dr. Walter Gilbert and Frederick Sanger invented a new DNA sequencing method for which they won the Nobel Prize.

1978
- The Global Positioning System (GPS) enters service
- Muhammad Ali becomes the first fighter to win the world heavyweight boxing title for the third time

1979: Iranian hostage crisis

1981: Reagan inauguration; Sandra Day O'Connor first woman Supreme Court Justice

1982
- Direct to home satellite television transmission
- first personal laptop created

1985
- Reagan second inauguration
- The lithium-ion battery is invented

1986: Space shuttle, Challenger, explodes just after lift-off, killing its seven crew members

1987: Reagan challenges Soviet leader Mikhail Gorbachev to —tear down this wall and open Eastern Europe to political and economic reform.

1989
George H Bush inauguration
The World Wide Web is invented by computer scientist Tim Berners-Lee

1990: Iraqi troops invade Kuwait, leading to the Persian Gulf War (i.e.. Desert Storm)

1991: Soviet Union breaks up in Russia

1992: Bush and Russian President Boris Yeltsin sign an agreement which officially ends the Cold War

1993: Bill Clinton inauguration.

1994: IBM Simon, World's first smartphone is developed by IBM.

1995
US begins diplomatic relations with Vietnam.
DVD is an optical disc storage format, invented and developed by Philips, Sony, Toshiba, and Panasonic

1997: Clinton's second inauguration

1998: Clinton impeachment (acquitted)

1999: School shooting at Columbine high school

2001: Two hijacked planes crash into the World Trade Center (and one in rural PA), killing 3,000. This launched a global War on Terror campaign (War in Afghanistan, 2001)

2003: Britain and US wage war on Iraq (ends 2011)

2005: Hurricane Katrina

2007
- Pelosi first female speaker of the House
- Obama the first black President

2021: War in Afghanistan ends (US Troops pull out)

Made in the USA
Las Vegas, NV
16 August 2023

76170324R00221